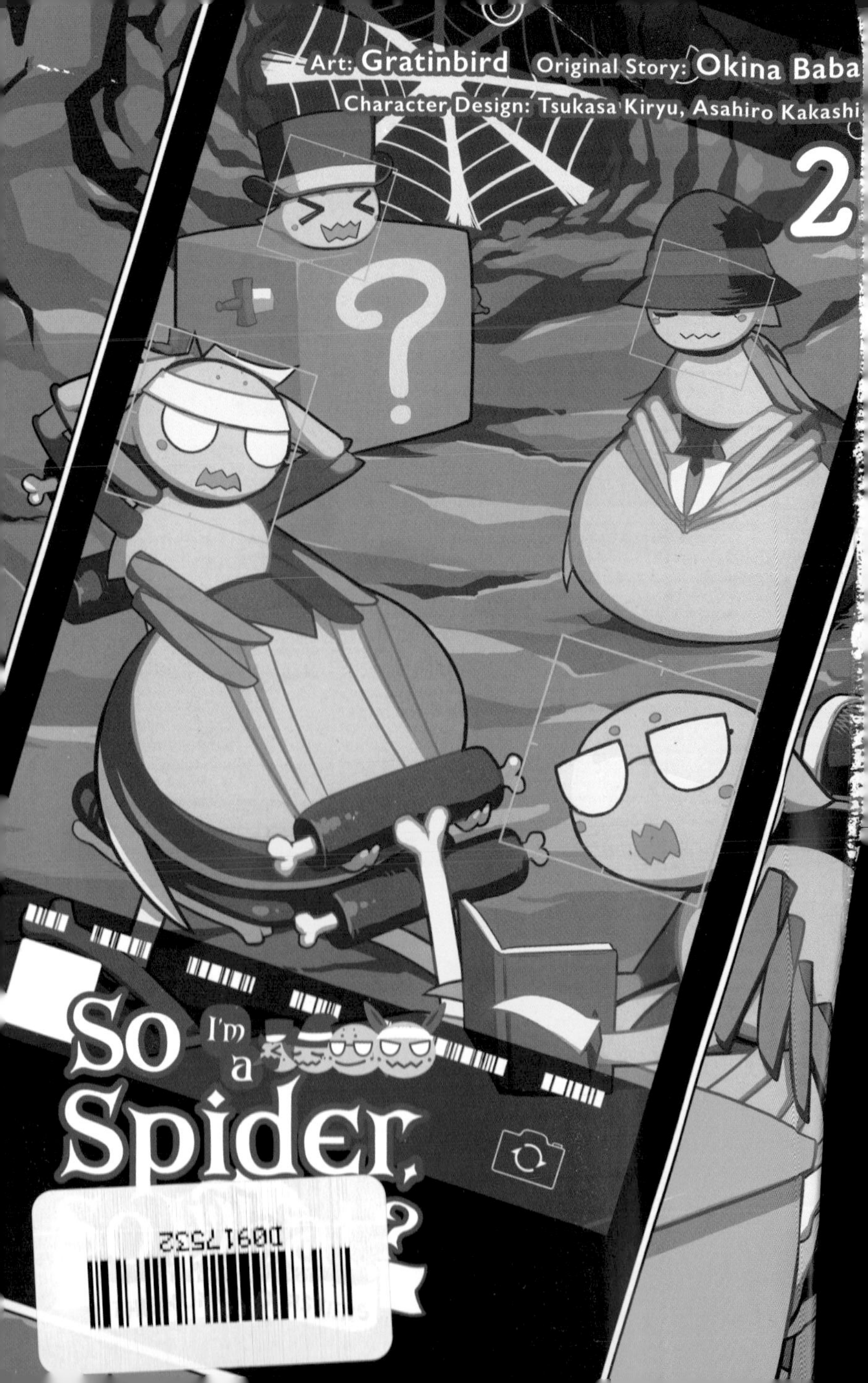

Art: Gratinbird
Original Story: Okina Baba
Character Design: Tsukasa Kiryu, Asahiro Kakashi
2
So I'm a Spider,
?

CONTENTS

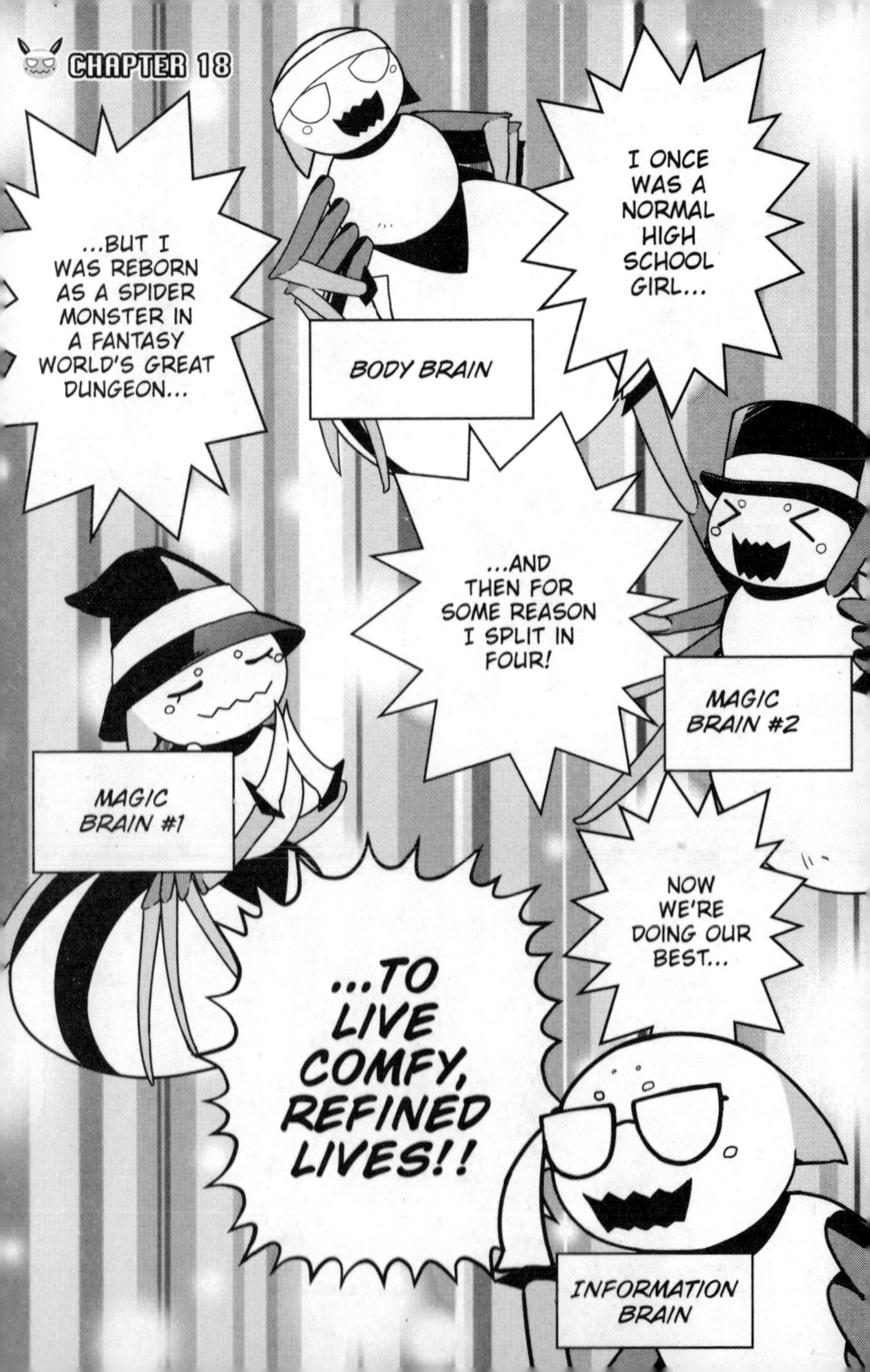
CHAPTER 18
I ONCE WAS A NORMAL HIGH SCHOOL GIRL...
BODY BRAIN
...BUT I WAS REBORN AS A SPIDER MONSTER IN A FANTASY WORLD'S GREAT DUNGEON...
...AND THEN FOR SOME REASON I SPLIT IN FOUR!
MAGIC BRAIN #2
MAGIC BRAIN #1
NOW WE'RE DOING OUR BEST...
...TO LIVE COMFY, REFINED LIVES!!
INFORMATION BRAIN

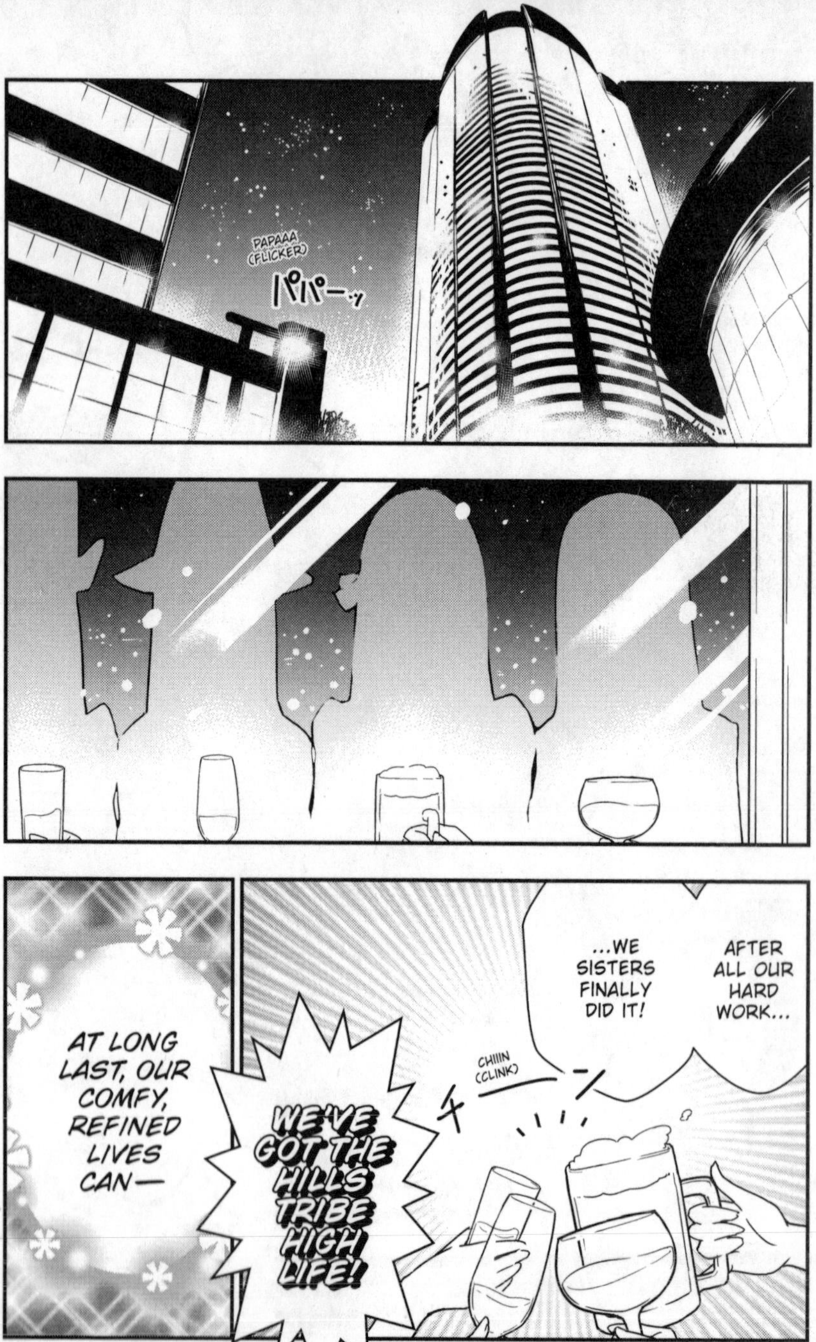
PAPAAA (FLICKER)
パパーッ
AFTER ALL OUR HARD WORK...
...WE SISTERS FINALLY DID IT!
CHIIIN (CLINK)
チーン
AT LONG LAST, OUR COMFY, REFINED LIVES CAN—
WE'VE GOT THE HILLS TRIBE HIGH LIFE!

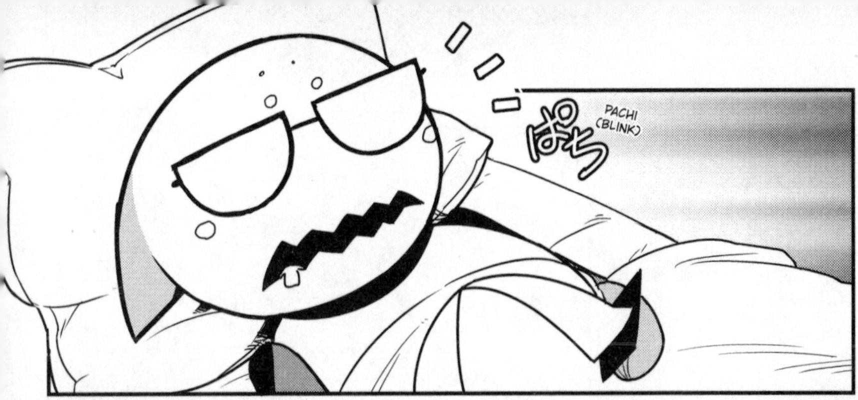
ぱち
PACHI (BLINK)
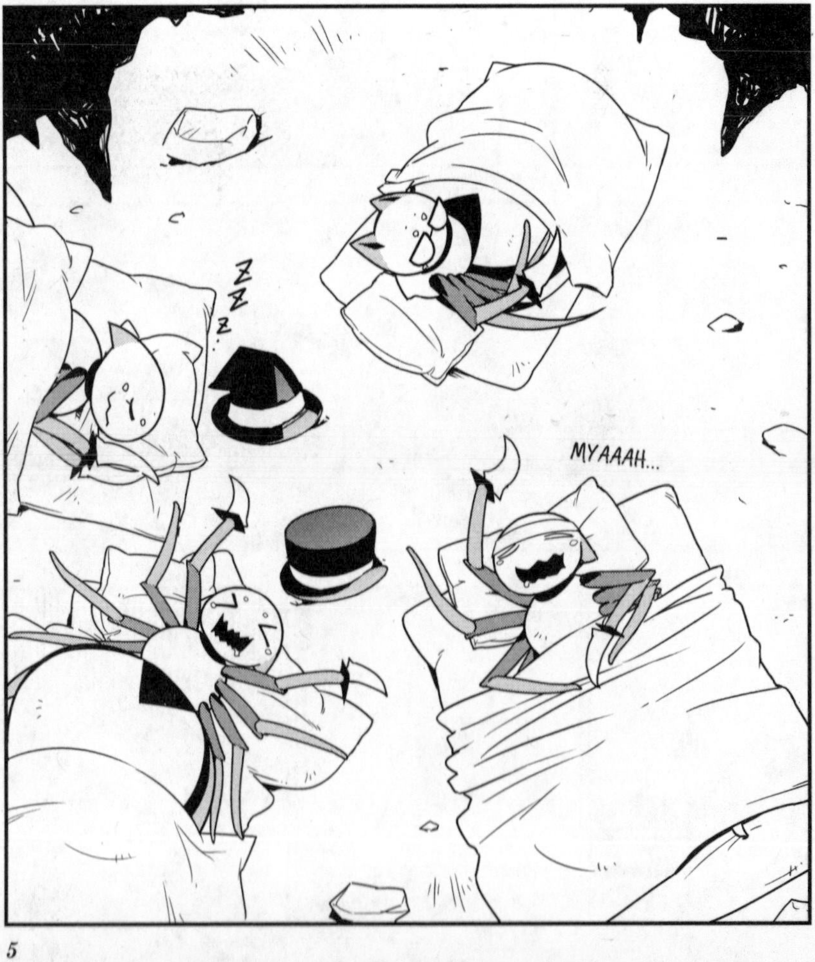
ZZZ
MYAAAH...

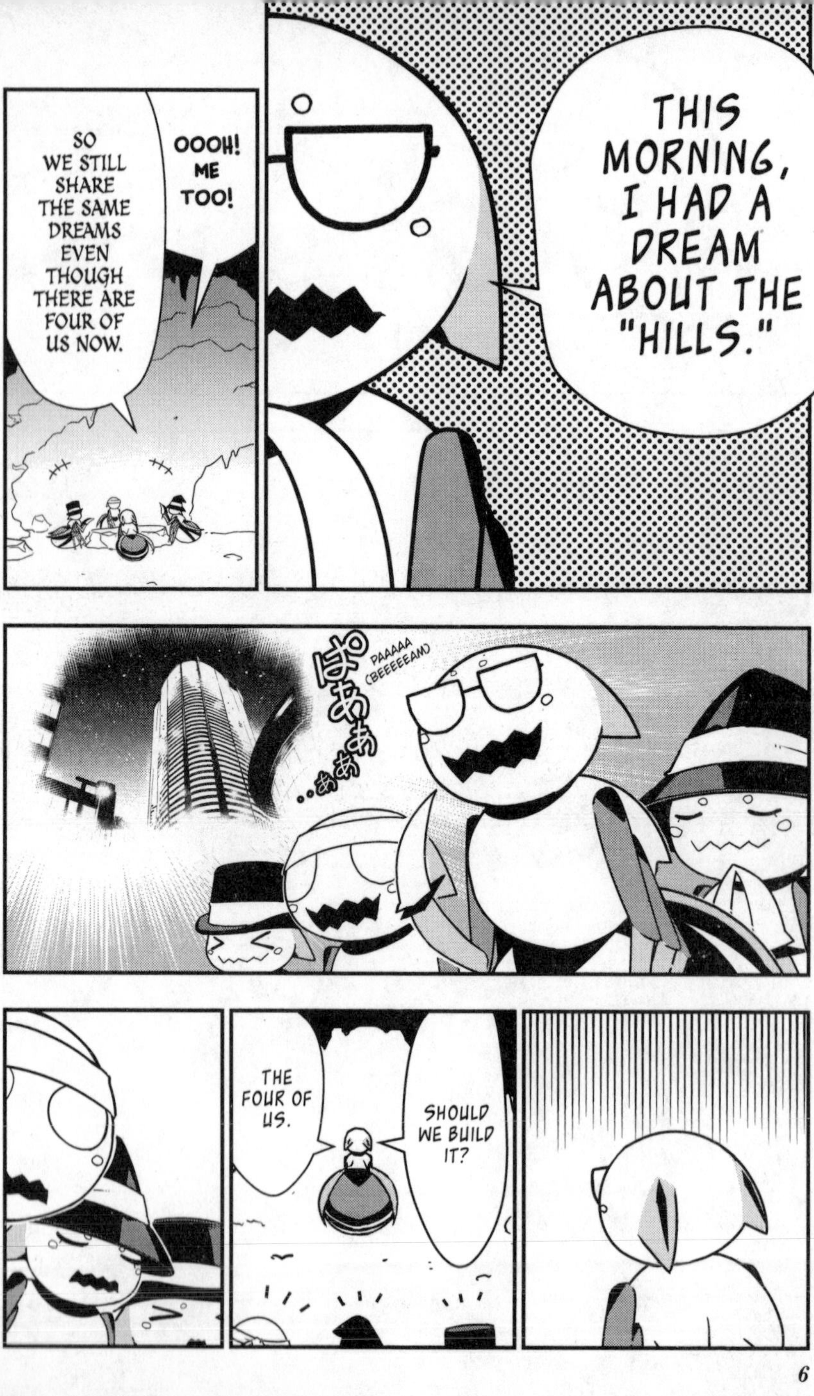
THIS MORNING, I HAD A DREAM ABOUT THE "HILLS."
OOOH! ME TOO!
SO WE STILL SHARE THE SAME DREAMS EVEN THOUGH THERE ARE FOUR OF US NOW.
ぱあああ…ああ
PAAAAA (BEEEEEAM)
SHOULD WE BUILD IT?
THE FOUR OF US.

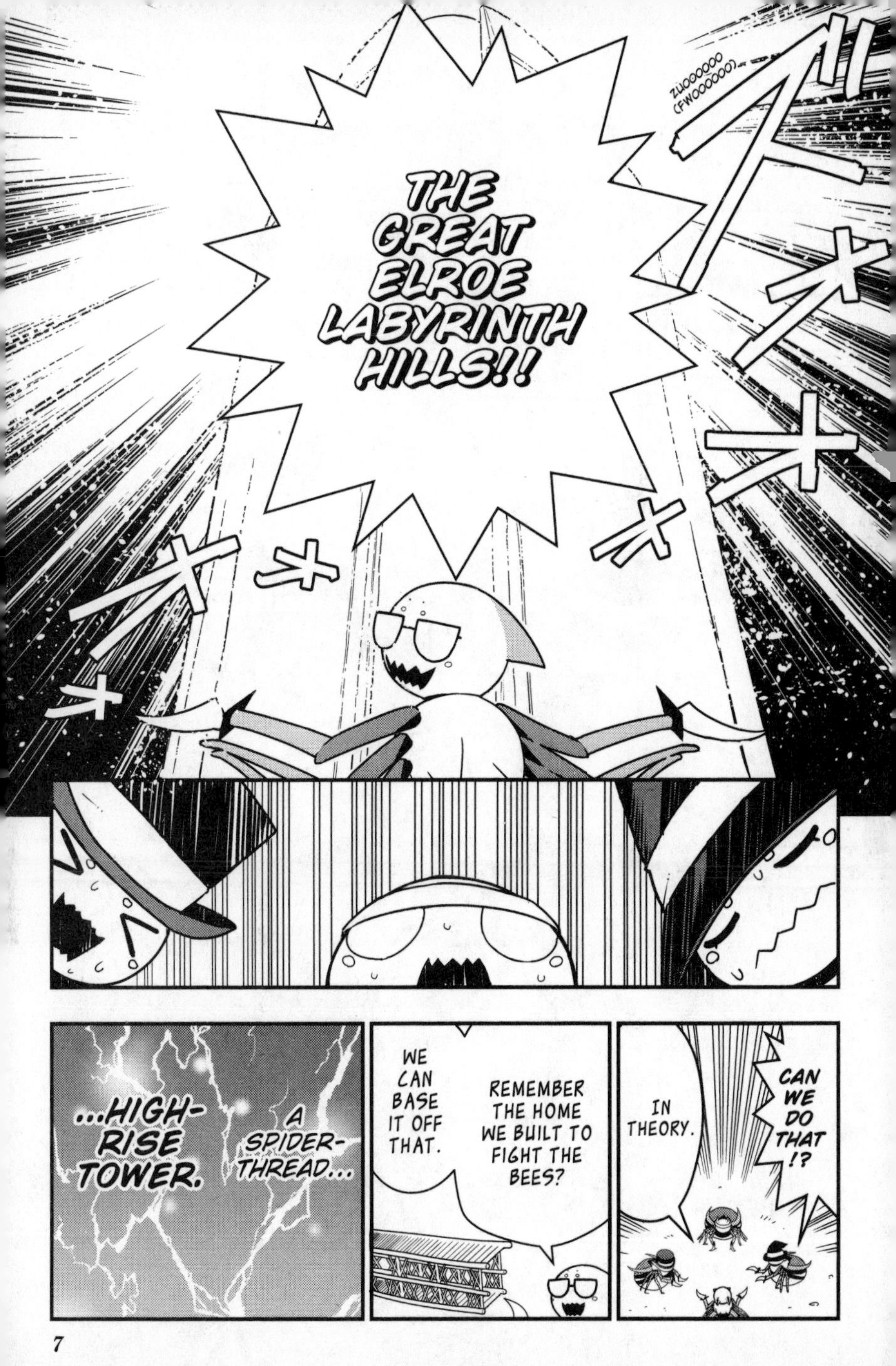
ZUOOOOOO (FWOOOOOOO)
THE GREAT ELROE LABYRINTH HILLS!!
CAN WE DO THAT!?
IN THEORY.
REMEMBER THE HOME WE BUILT TO FIGHT THE BEES?
WE CAN BASE IT OFF THAT.
A SPIDER-THREAD...
...HIGH-RISE TOWER.

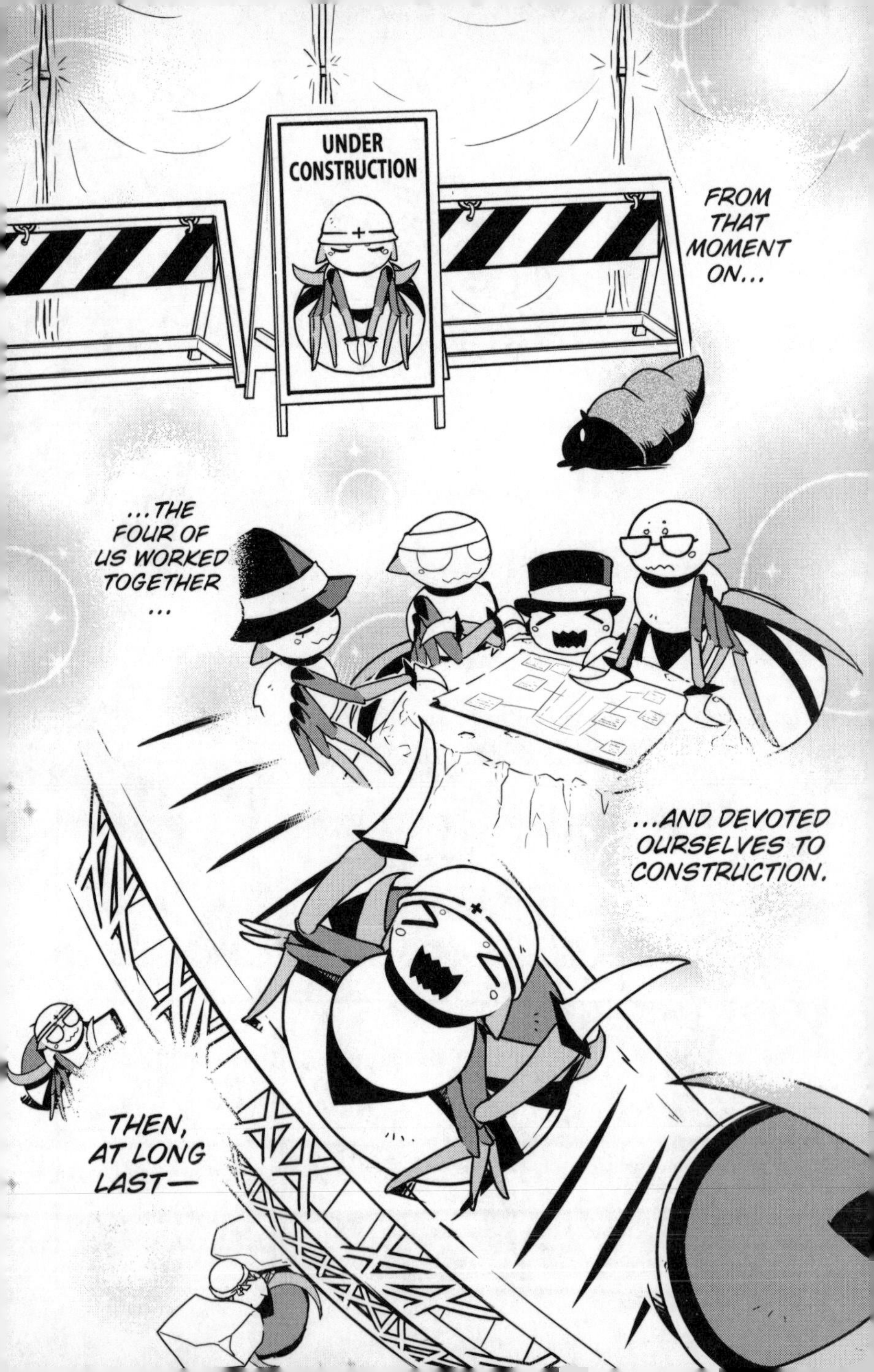
UNDER CONSTRUCTION
FROM THAT MOMENT ON...
...THE FOUR OF US WORKED TOGETHER...
...AND DEVOTED OURSELVES TO CONSTRUCTION.
THEN, AT LONG LAST—

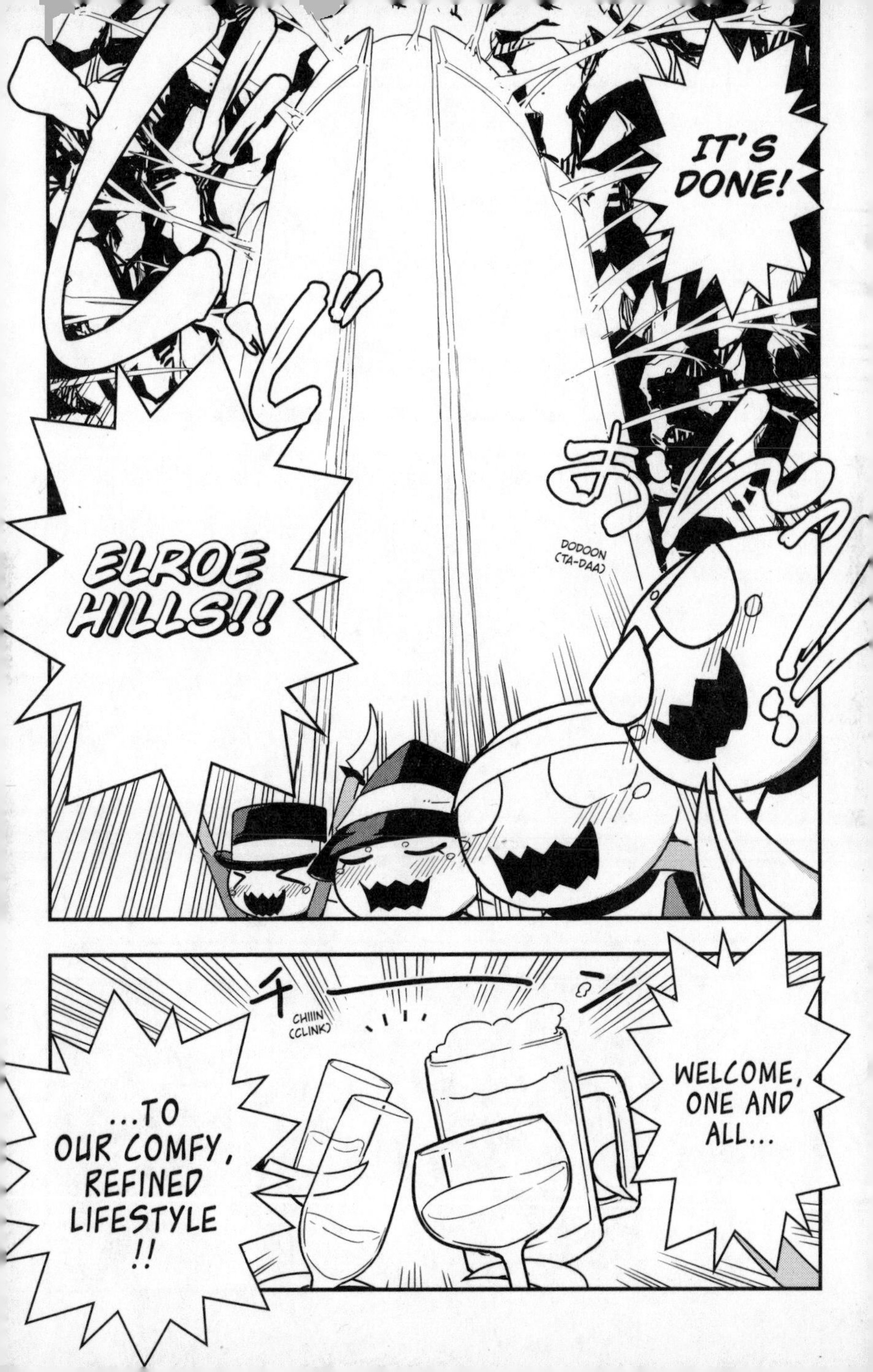
IT'S DONE!
DODOON (TA-DAA)
ELROE HILLS!!
WELCOME, ONE AND ALL...
CHIIIN (CLINK)
...TO OUR COMFY, REFINED LIFESTYLE!!

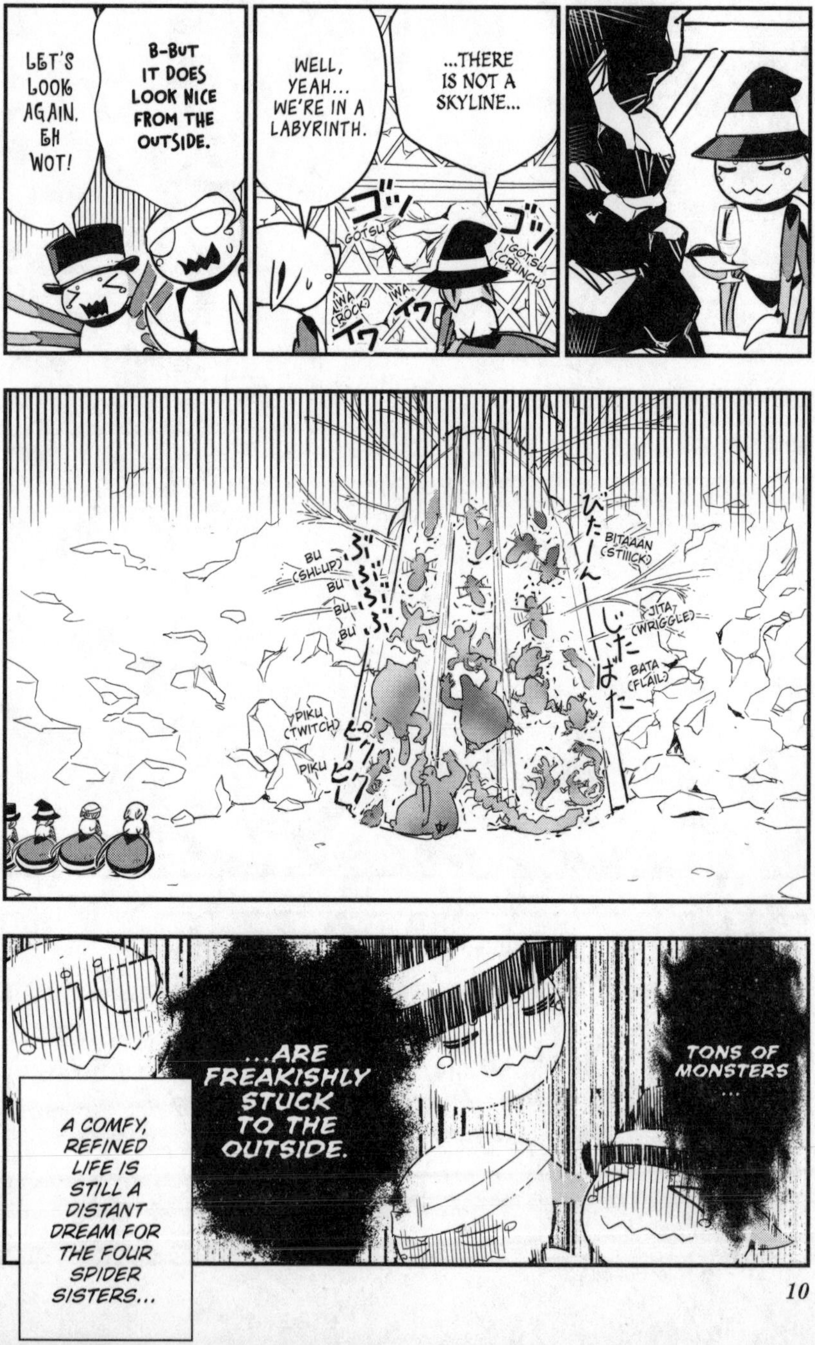
...THERE IS NOT A SKYLINE...
WELL, YEAH... WE'RE IN A LABYRINTH.
ゴツ
GOTSU (CRUNCH)
ゴツ
GOTSU
イワ
IWA
イワ
IWA (ROCK)
B-BUT IT DOES LOOK NICE FROM THE OUTSIDE.
LET'S LOOK AGAIN. EH WOT!
びたーん
BITAAAN (STIIICK)
じたばた
JITA (WRIGGLE)
BATA (FLAIL)
ぶぶぶぶ
BU (SHLUP)
BU
BU
BU
ピクピク
PIKU (TWITCH)
PIKU
TONS OF MONSTERS...
...ARE FREAKISHLY STUCK TO THE OUTSIDE.
A COMFY, REFINED LIFE IS STILL A DISTANT DREAM FOR THE FOUR SPIDER SISTERS...

So I'm a Spider, So What?

THE DAILY LIVES OF THE KUMOKO SISTERS

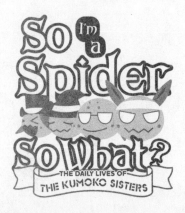

CHAPTER 19

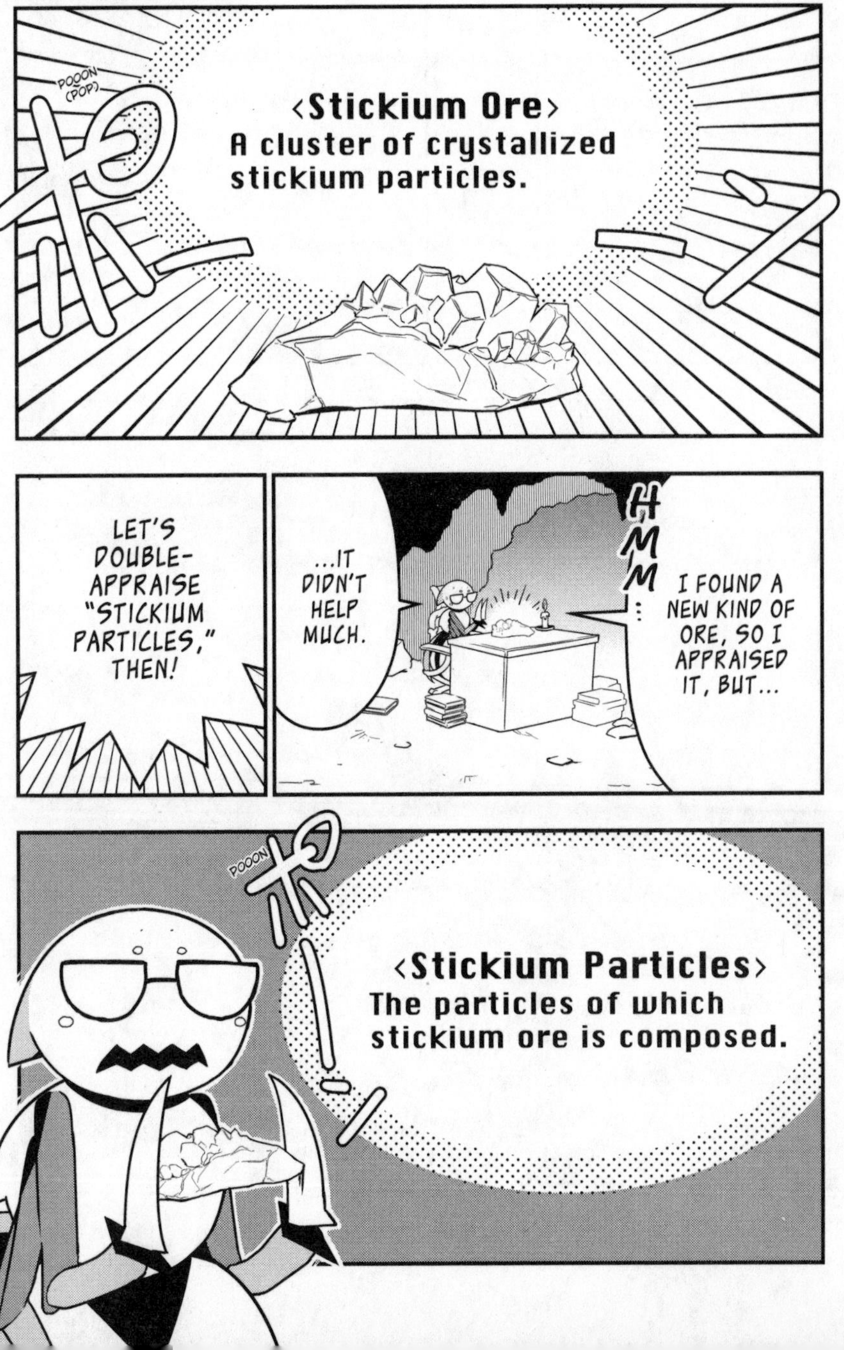
POOON (POP)
<Stickium Ore>
A cluster of crystallized stickium particles.
HMM...
I FOUND A NEW KIND OF ORE, SO I APPRAISED IT, BUT...
...IT DIDN'T HELP MUCH.
LET'S DOUBLE-APPRAISE "STICKIUM PARTICLES," THEN!
POOON
<Stickium Particles>
The particles of which stickium ore is composed.

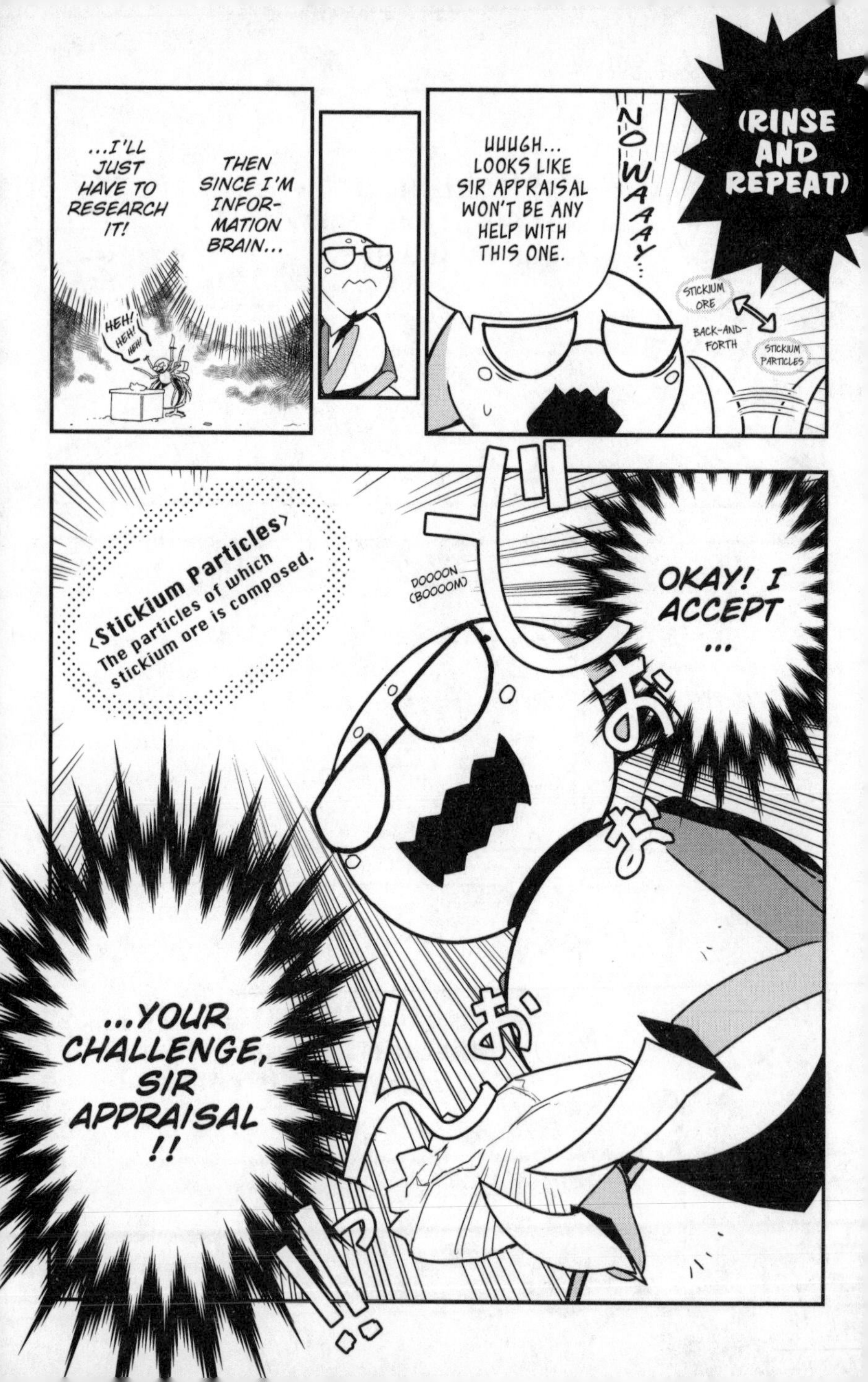
(RINSE AND REPEAT)
NO WAAAAY...
UUUGH... LOOKS LIKE SIR APPRAISAL WON'T BE ANY HELP WITH THIS ONE.
STICKIUM ORE
BACK-AND-FORTH
STICKIUM PARTICLES
THEN SINCE I'M INFORMATION BRAIN...
...I'LL JUST HAVE TO RESEARCH IT!
HEH! HEH! HEH!
OKAY! I ACCEPT ...
DOOOON (BOOOOM)
‹Stickium Particles› The particles of which stickium ore is composed.
...YOUR CHALLENGE, SIR APPRAISAL !!
どおおおんっ!!

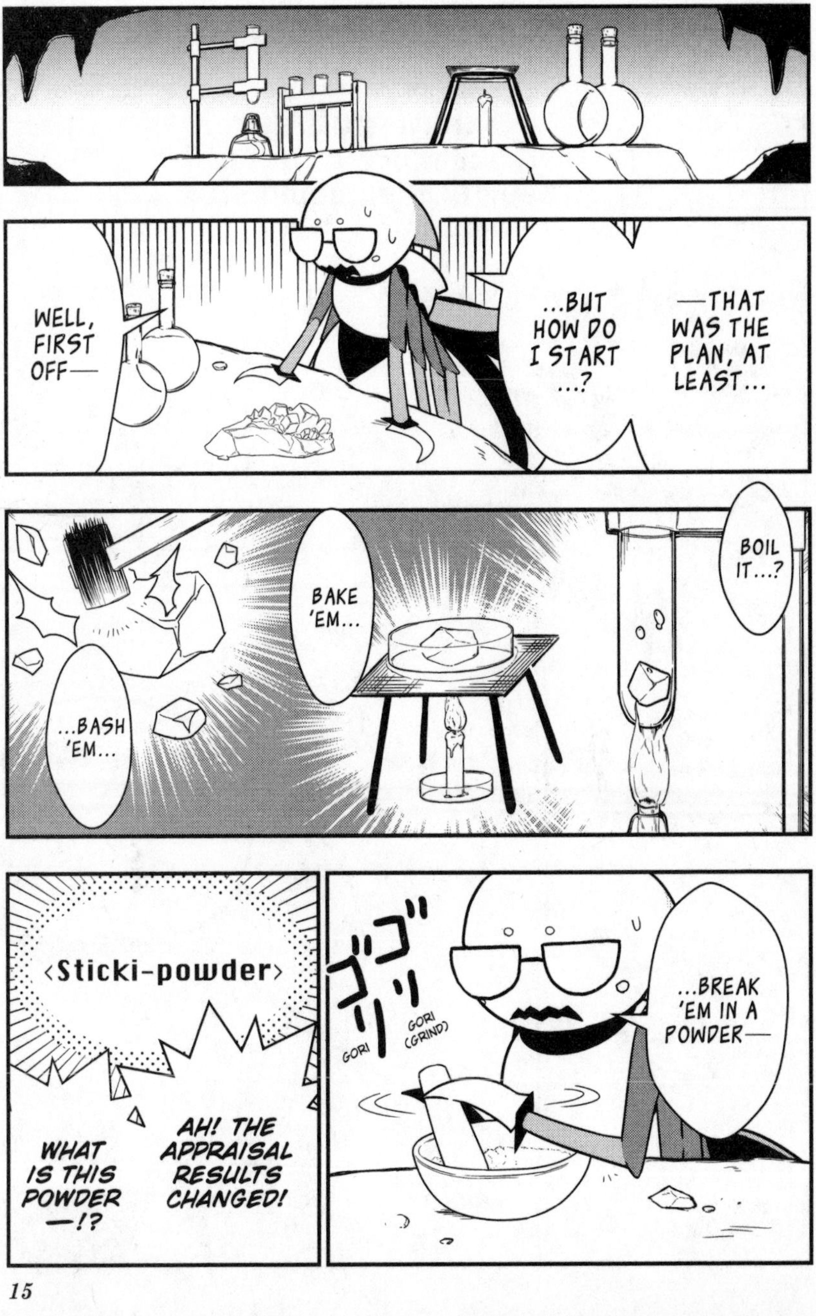
—THAT WAS THE PLAN, AT LEAST...
...BUT HOW DO I START ...?
WELL, FIRST OFF—
BOIL IT...?
BAKE 'EM...
...BASH 'EM...
ゴリゴリ
GORI GORI (GRIND)
...BREAK 'EM IN A POWDER—
‹Sticki-powder›
AH! THE APPRAISAL RESULTS CHANGED!
WHAT IS THIS POWDER—!?

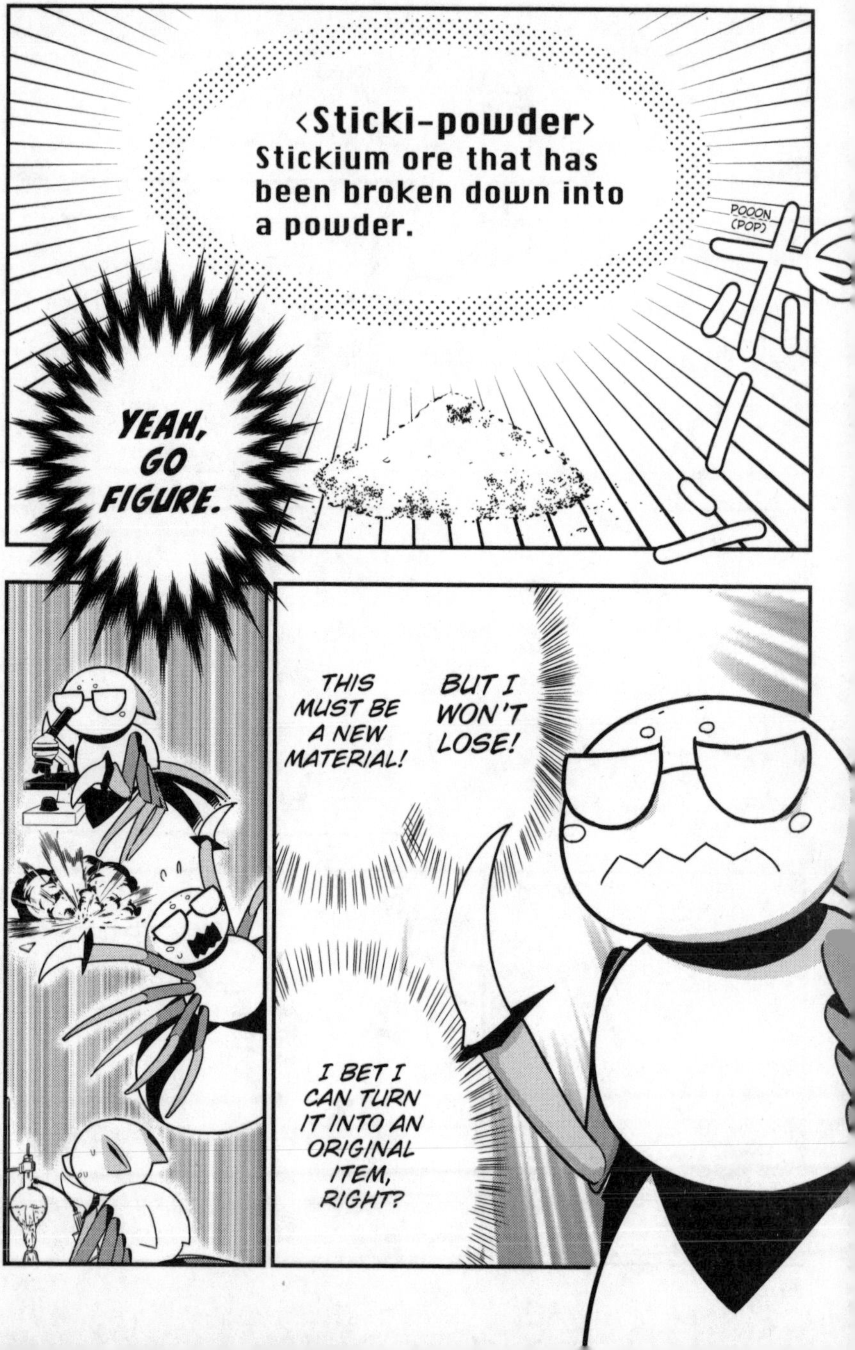
‹Sticki-powder›
Stickium ore that has been broken down into a powder.
POOON (POP)
YEAH, GO FIGURE.
BUT I WON'T LOSE!
THIS MUST BE A NEW MATERIAL!
I BET I CAN TURN IT INTO AN ORIGINAL ITEM, RIGHT?

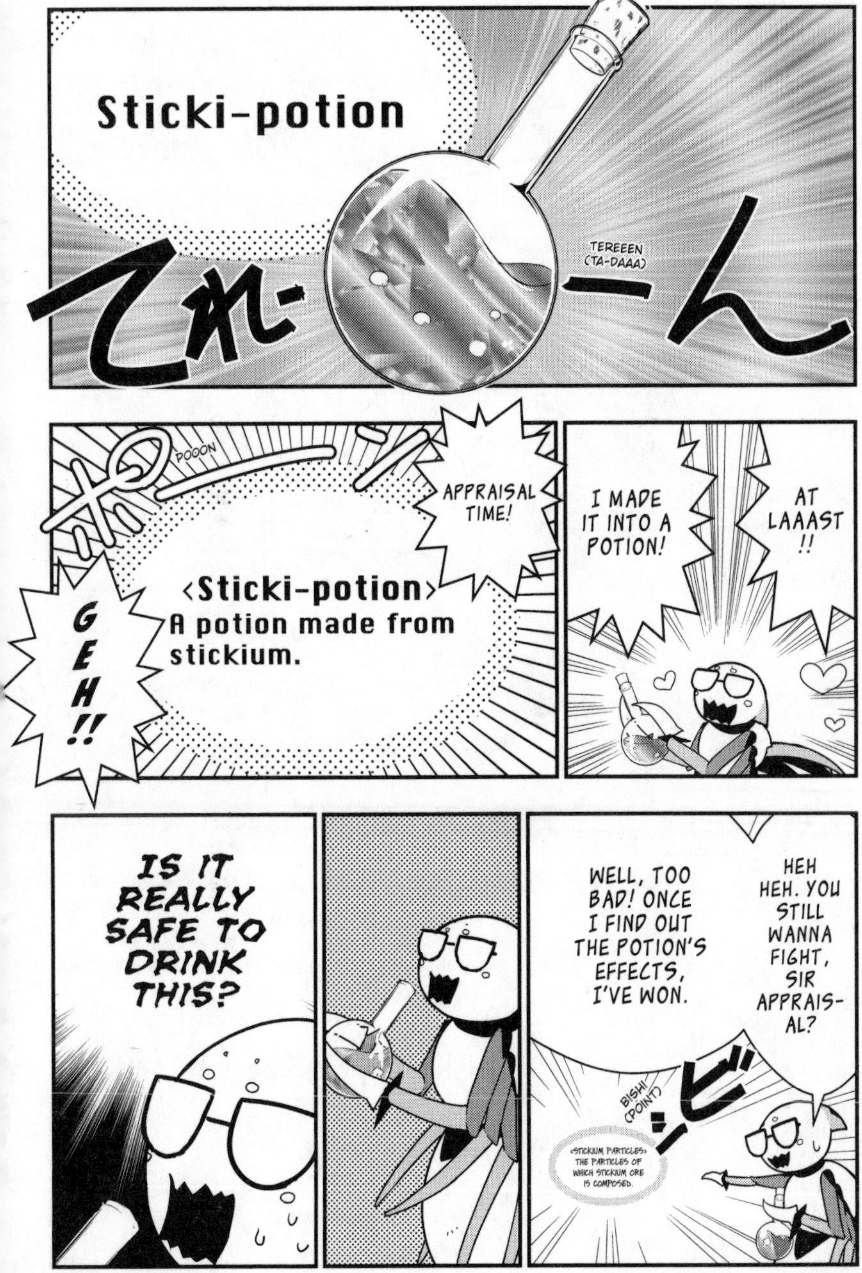
Sticki-potion
TEREEEN (TA-DAAA)
AT LAAAST !!
I MADE IT INTO A POTION!
APPRAISAL TIME!
POOON
‹Sticki-potion› A potion made from stickium.
GEH!!
HEH HEH. YOU STILL WANNA FIGHT, SIR APPRAISAL?
WELL, TOO BAD! ONCE I FIND OUT THE POTION'S EFFECTS, I'VE WON.
BISHI (POINT)
‹STICKIUM PARTICLES› THE PARTICLES OF WHICH STICKIUM ORE IS COMPOSED.
IS IT REALLY SAFE TO DRINK THIS?

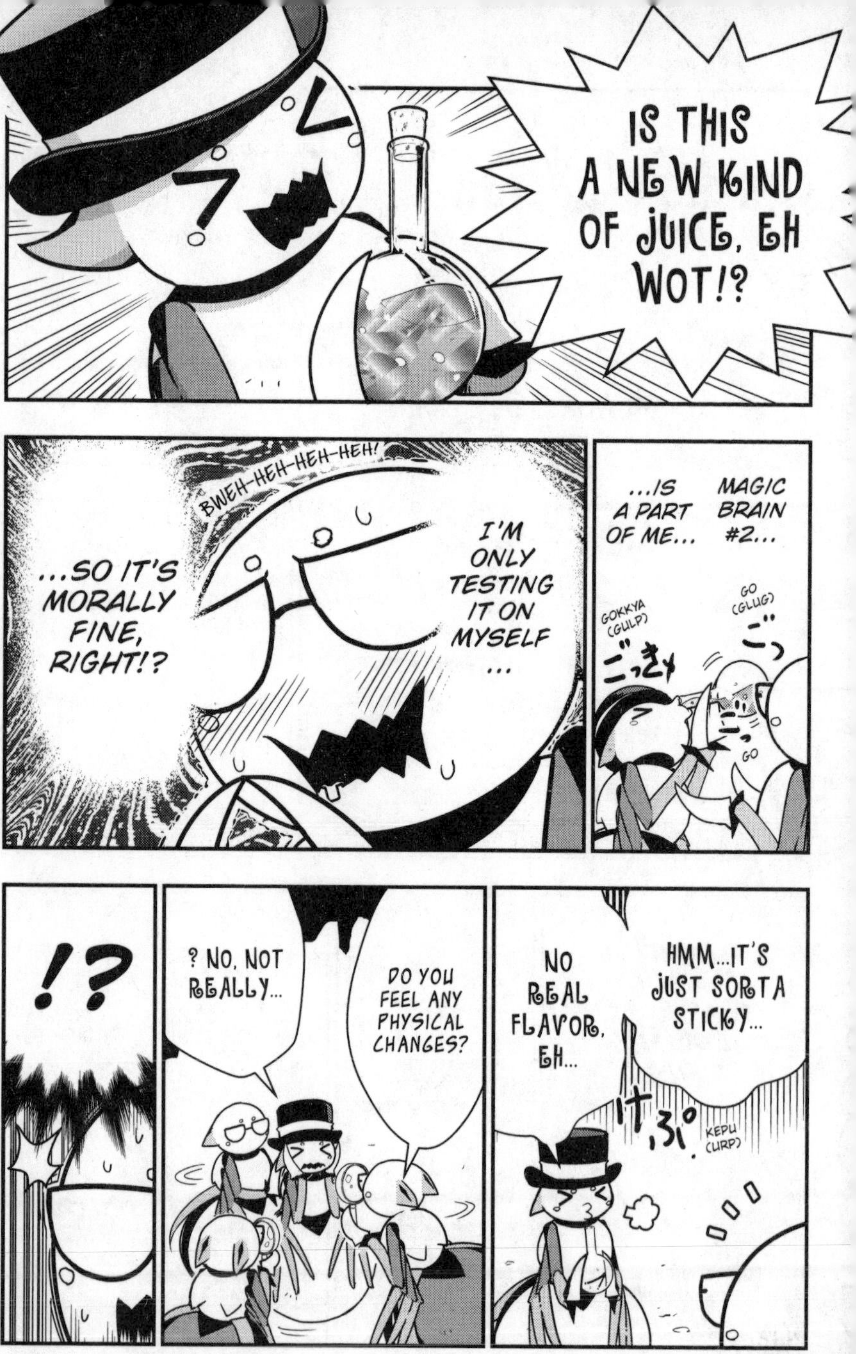
IS THIS A NEW KIND OF JUICE, EH WOT!?
MAGIC BRAIN #2...
...IS A PART OF ME...
GOKKYA (GULP)
GO (GLUG)
GO
BWEH-HEH-HEH-HEH!
I'M ONLY TESTING IT ON MYSELF...
...SO IT'S MORALLY FINE, RIGHT!?
HMM...IT'S JUST SORTA STICKY...
NO REAL FLAVOR, EH...
KEPU (URP)
DO YOU FEEL ANY PHYSICAL CHANGES?
? NO, NOT REALLY...
!?

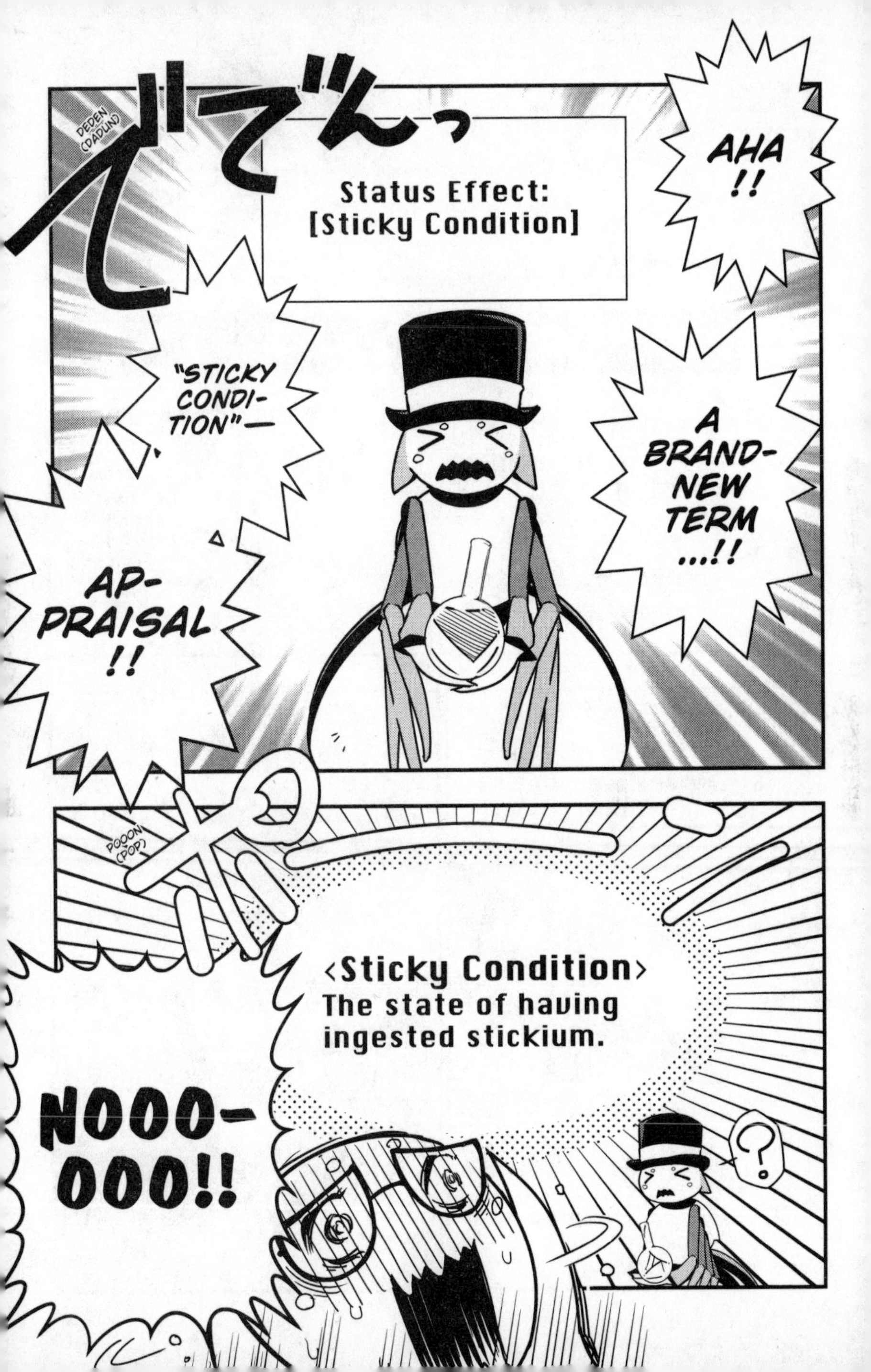
AHA!!
ででんっ
DEDEN (DADUN)
Status Effect:
[Sticky Condition]
A BRAND-NEW TERM...!!
"STICKY CONDITION"—
APPRAISAL!!
POOON (POP)
‹Sticky Condition›
The state of having ingested stickium.
?
NOOOOOO!!

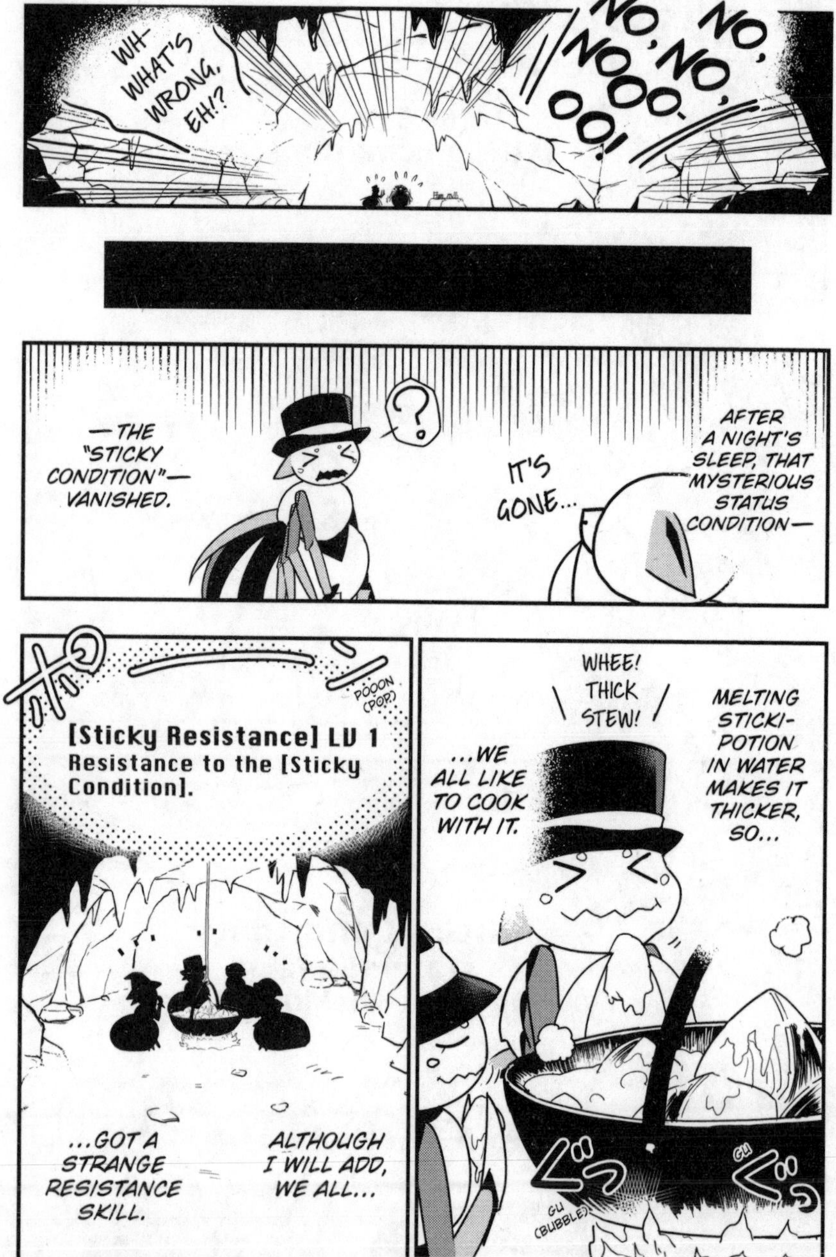
NO, NO, NO, NOOO-OO!
WH- WHAT'S WRONG, EH!?
AFTER A NIGHT'S SLEEP, THAT MYSTERIOUS STATUS CONDITION—
IT'S GONE...
—THE "STICKY CONDITION"— VANISHED.
?
MELTING STICKI-POTION IN WATER MAKES IT THICKER, SO...
WHEE! THICK STEW!
...WE ALL LIKE TO COOK WITH IT.
GU
GU (BUBBLE)
POOON (POP)
[Sticky Resistance] LV 1
Resistance to the [Sticky Condition].
ALTHOUGH I WILL ADD, WE ALL...
...GOT A STRANGE RESISTANCE SKILL.

So I'm a Spider so What?
THE DAILY LIVES OF THE KUMOKO SISTERS

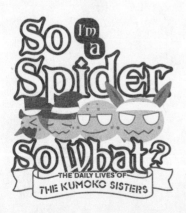

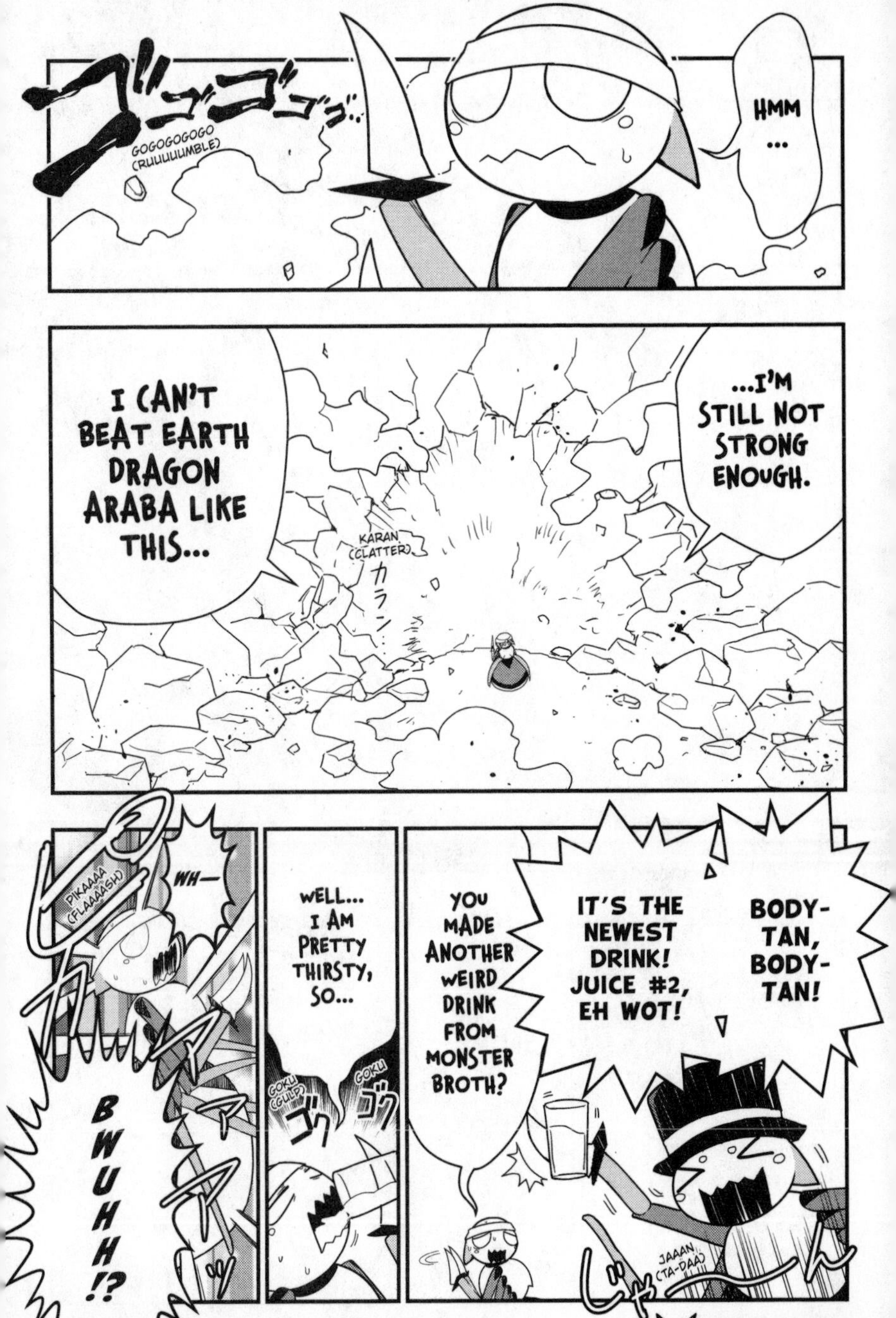
HMM ...
GOGOGOGOGO (RUUUUUMBLE)
...I'M STILL NOT STRONG ENOUGH.
I CAN'T BEAT EARTH DRAGON ARABA LIKE THIS...
KARAN (CLATTER)
BODY-TAN, BODY-TAN!
IT'S THE NEWEST DRINK! JUICE #2, EH WOT!
YOU MADE ANOTHER WEIRD DRINK FROM MONSTER BROTH?
JAAAN (TA-DAA)
WELL... I AM PRETTY THIRSTY, SO...
GOKU GOKU (GULP)
WH—
PIKAAAA (FLAAAASH)
BWUHH!?

CHAPTER 20

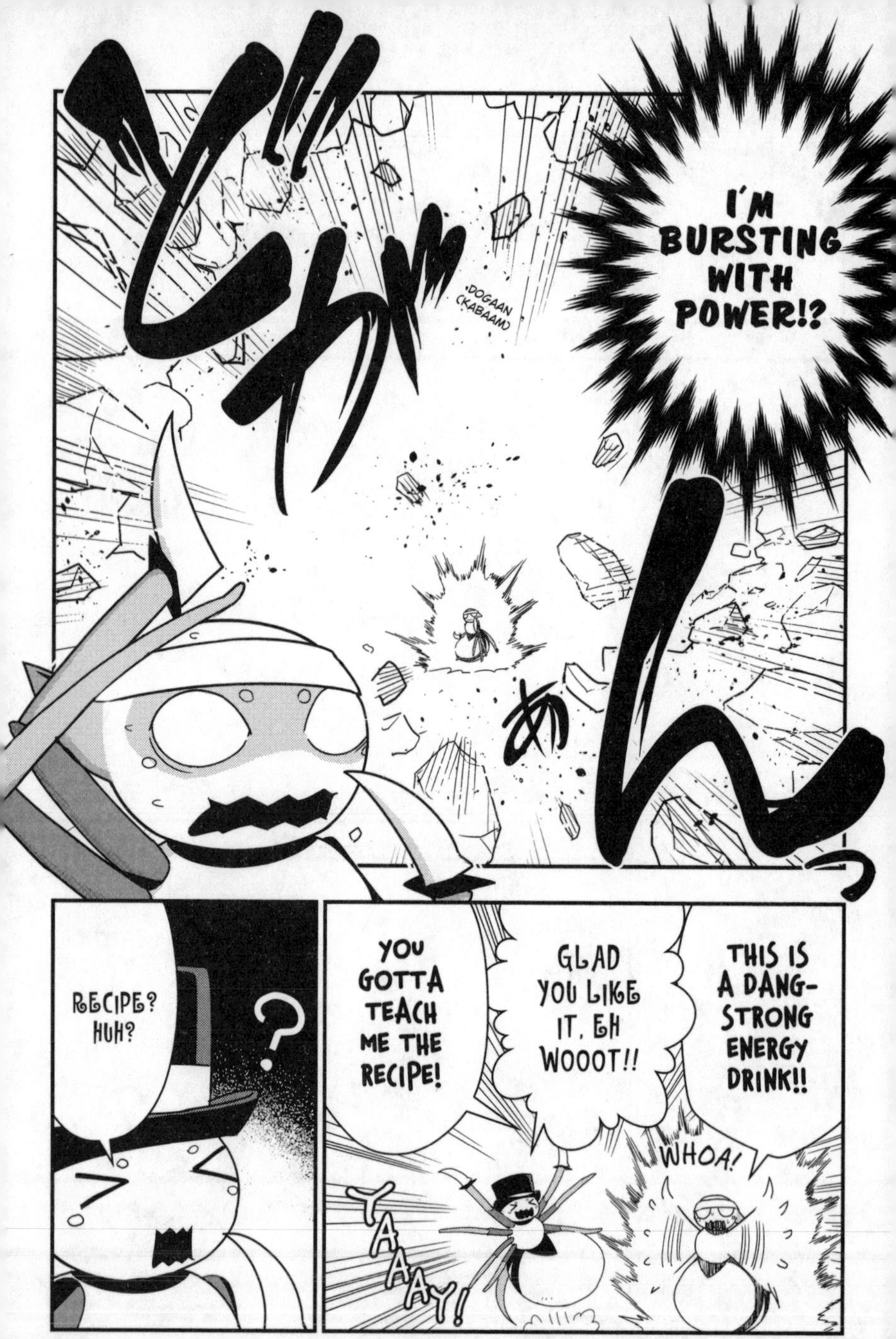
I'M BURSTING WITH POWER!?
DOGAAN (KABAAM)
THIS IS A DANG-STRONG ENERGY DRINK!!
GLAD YOU LIKE IT, EH WOOOT!!
YOU GOTTA TEACH ME THE RECIPE!
WHOA!
YAAAY!
RECIPE? HUH?

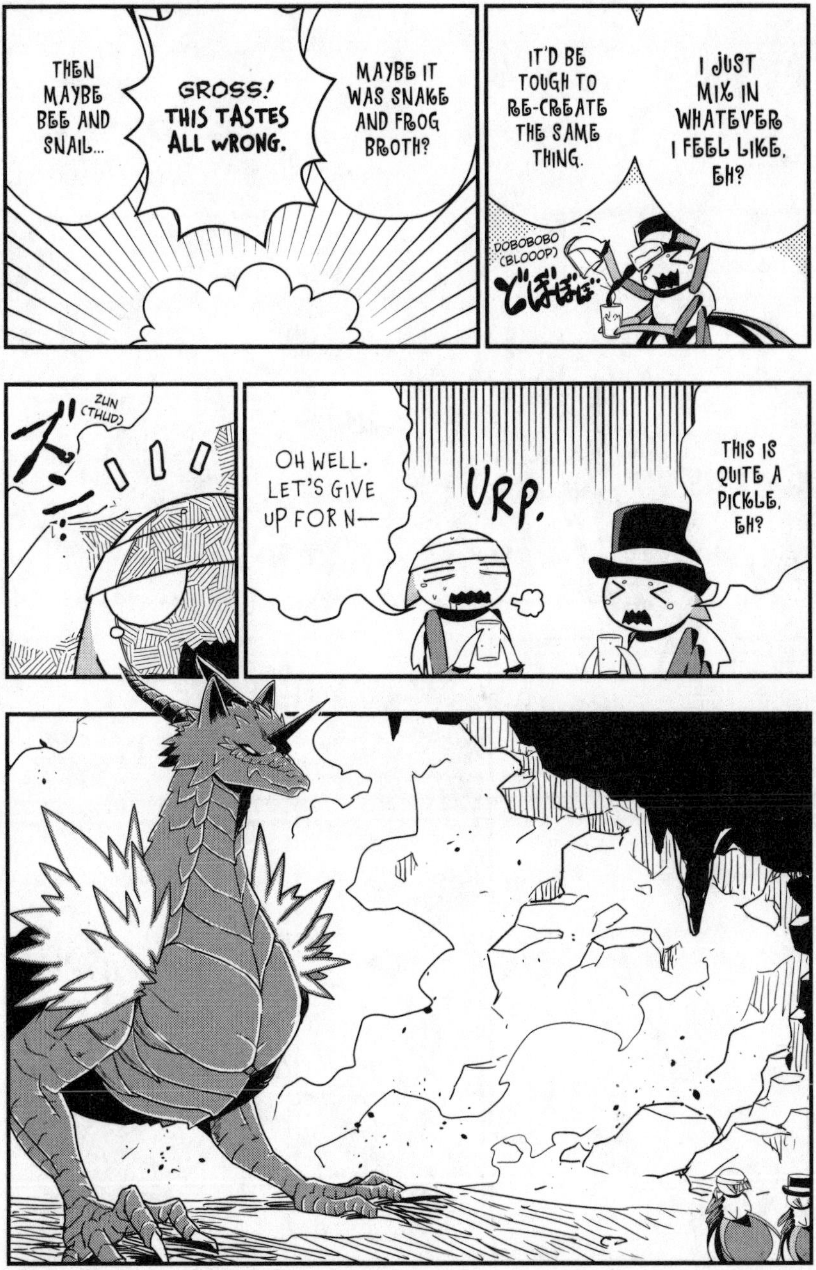
I JUST MIX IN WHATEVER I FEEL LIKE, EH?
IT'D BE TOUGH TO RE-CREATE THE SAME THING.
DOBOBOBO (BLOOOP)
どぼぼぼ
MAYBE IT WAS SNAKE AND FROG BROTH?
GROSS! THIS TASTES ALL WRONG.
THEN MAYBE BEE AND SNAIL...
THIS IS QUITE A PICKLE, EH?
URP.
OH WELL. LET'S GIVE UP FOR N—
ZUN (THUD)
ズン

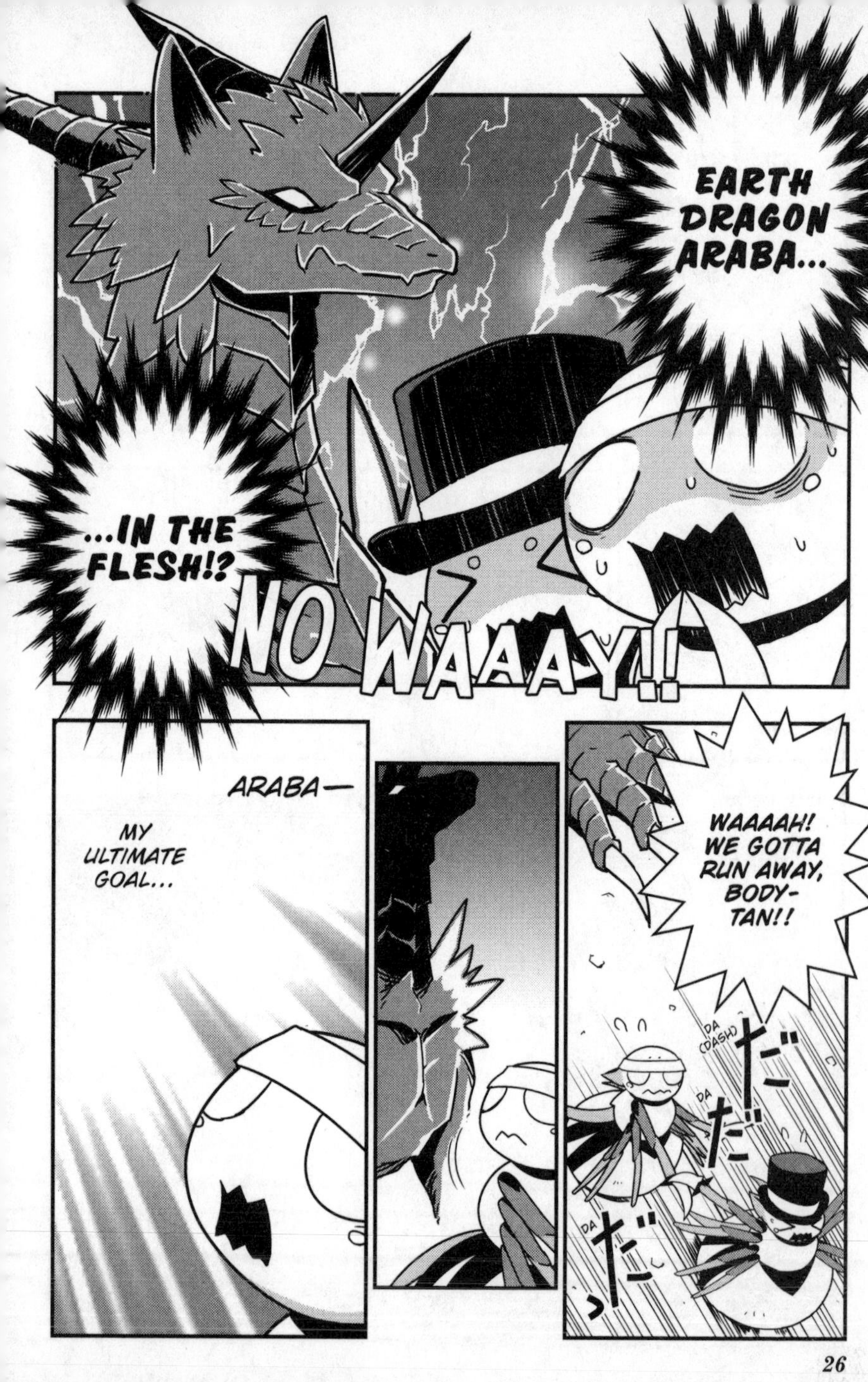
EARTH DRAGON ARABA...
...IN THE FLESH!?
NO WAAAY!!
WAAAAH! WE GOTTA RUN AWAY, BODY-TAN!!
DA (DASH)
DA
DA
ARABA—
MY ULTIMATE GOAL...

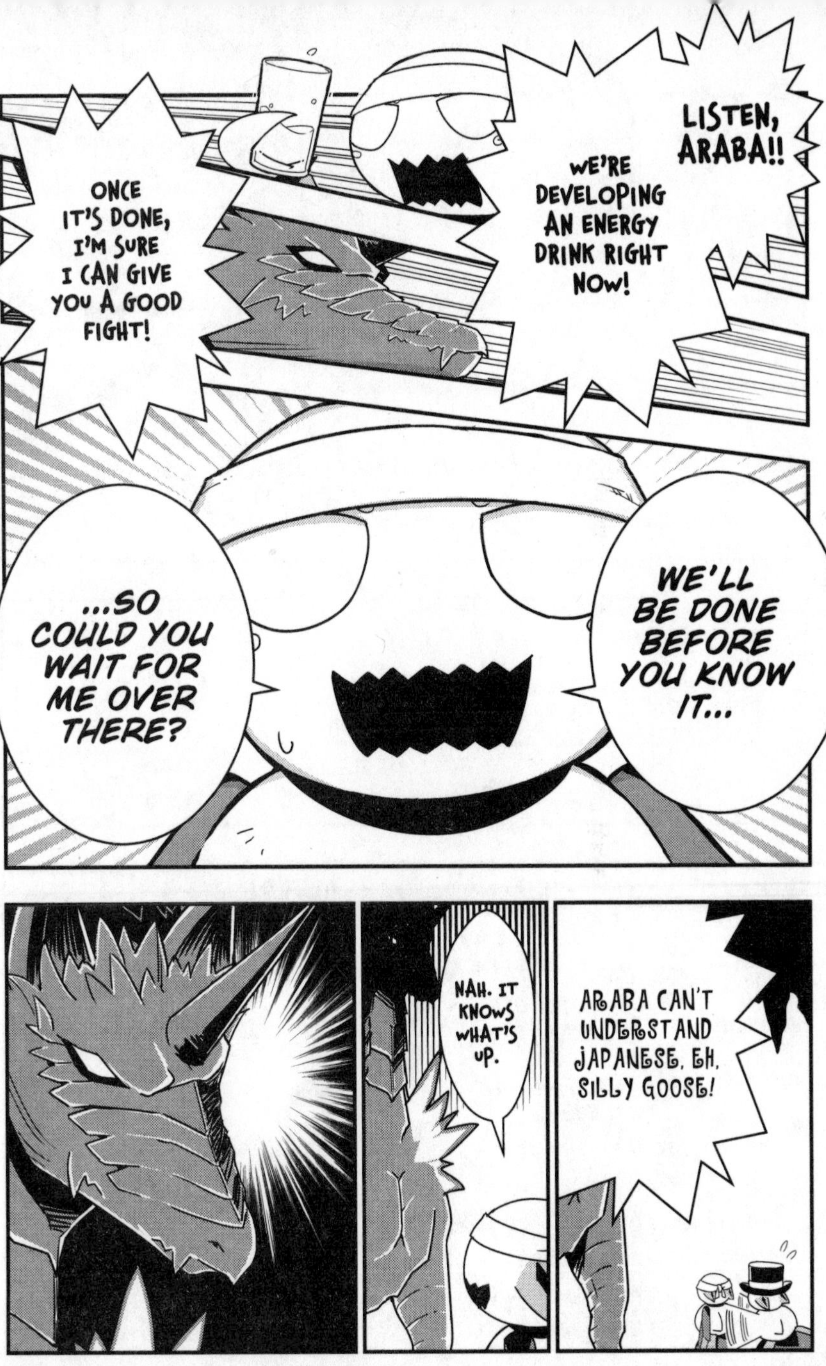
LISTEN, ARABA!!
WE'RE DEVELOPING AN ENERGY DRINK RIGHT NOW!
ONCE IT'S DONE, I'M SURE I CAN GIVE YOU A GOOD FIGHT!
WE'LL BE DONE BEFORE YOU KNOW IT...
...SO COULD YOU WAIT FOR ME OVER THERE?
ARABA CAN'T UNDERSTAND JAPANESE, EH, SILLY GOOSE!
NAH. IT KNOWS WHAT'S UP.

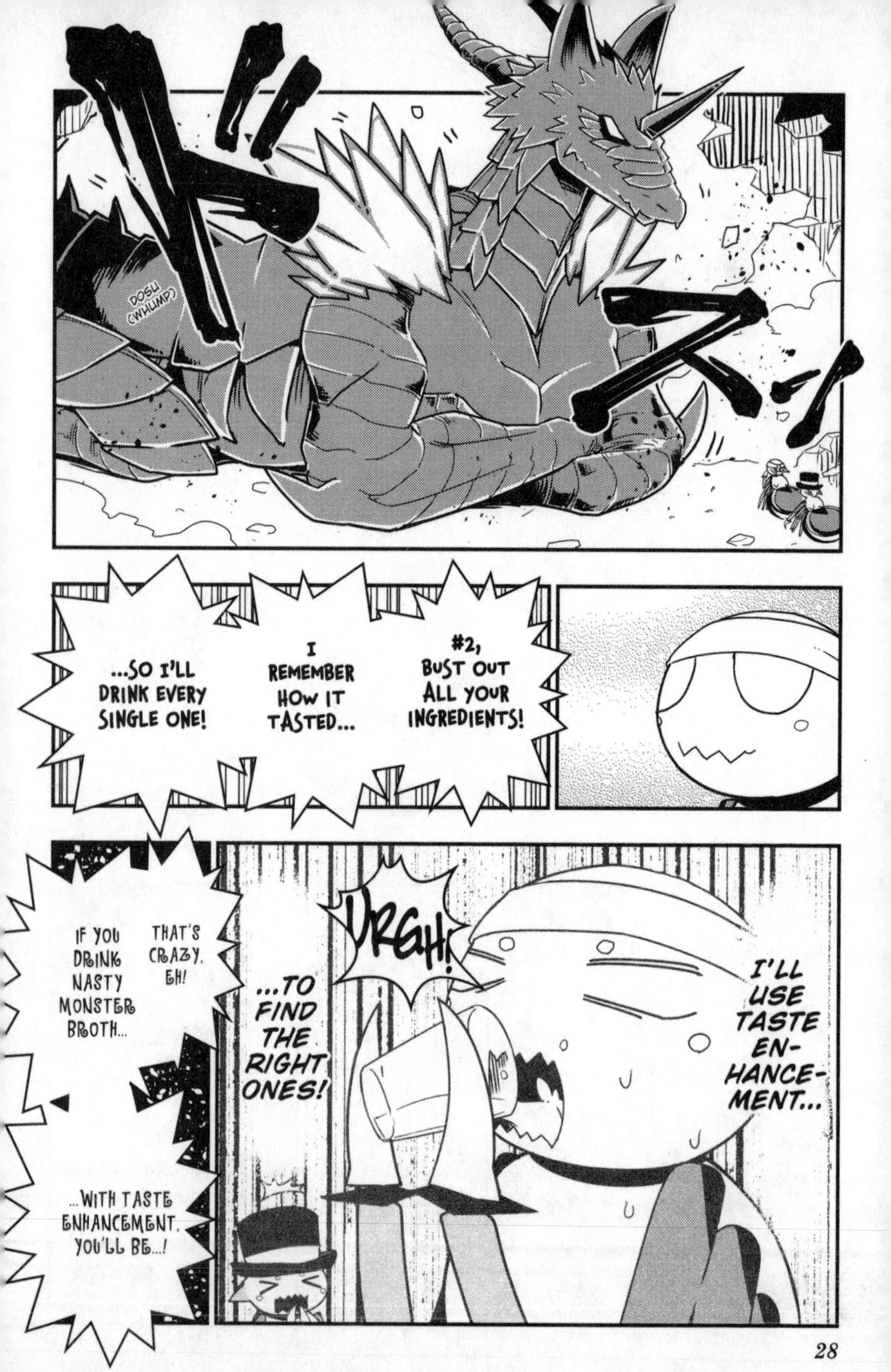
DOSU (WHUMP)
#2, BUST OUT ALL YOUR INGREDIENTS!
I REMEMBER HOW IT TASTED...
...SO I'LL DRINK EVERY SINGLE ONE!
I'LL USE TASTE EN-HANCE-MENT...
URGH!
...TO FIND THE RIGHT ONES!
THAT'S CRAZY, EH!
IF YOU DRINK NASTY MONSTER BROTH...
...WITH TASTE ENHANCEMENT, YOU'LL BE...!

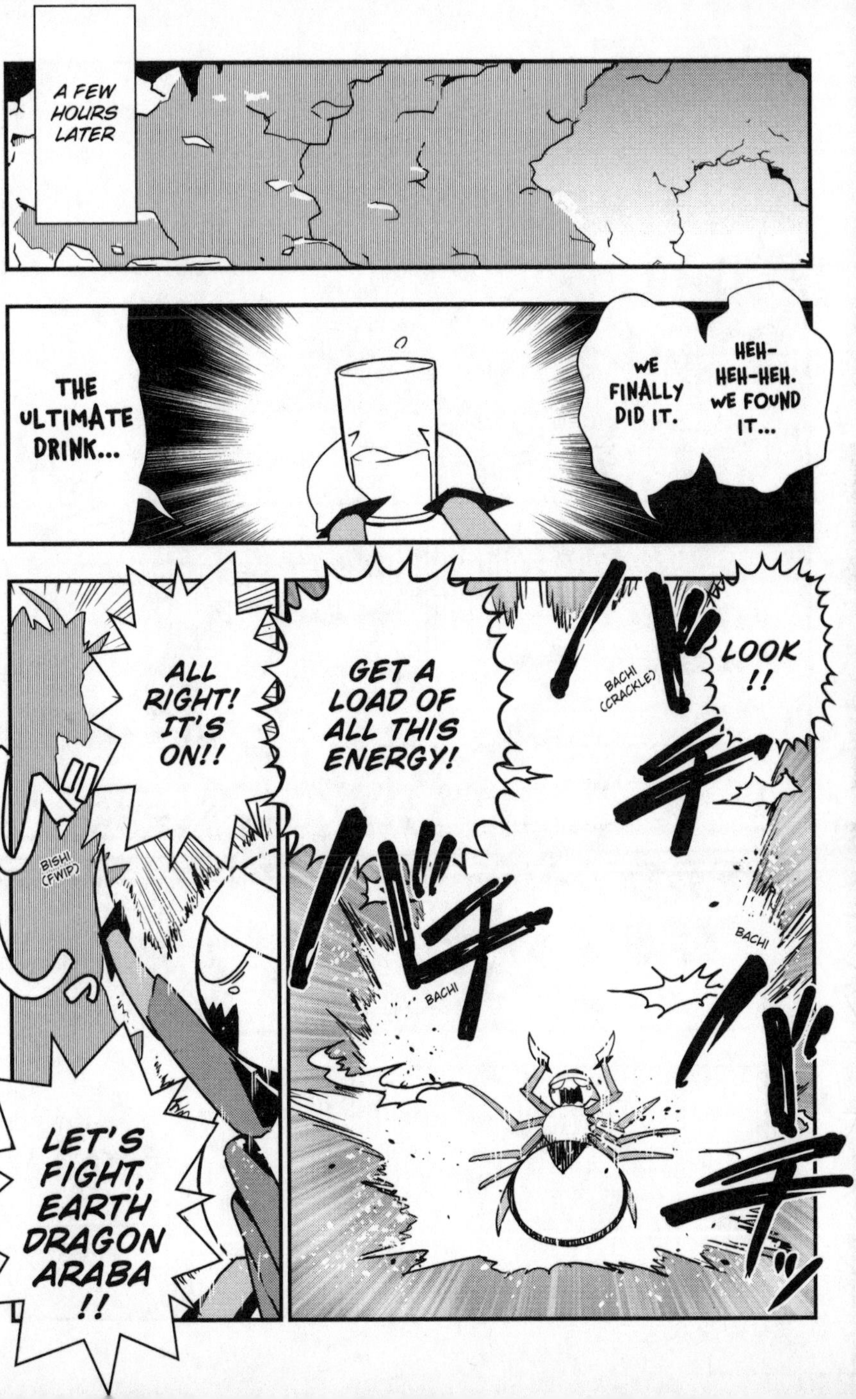
A FEW HOURS LATER
HEH-HEH-HEH. WE FOUND IT...
WE FINALLY DID IT.
THE ULTIMATE DRINK...
LOOK!!
BACHI (CRACKLE)
GET A LOAD OF ALL THIS ENERGY!
BACHI
BACHI
ALL RIGHT! IT'S ON!!
BISHI (FWIP)
LET'S FIGHT, EARTH DRAGON ARABA!!

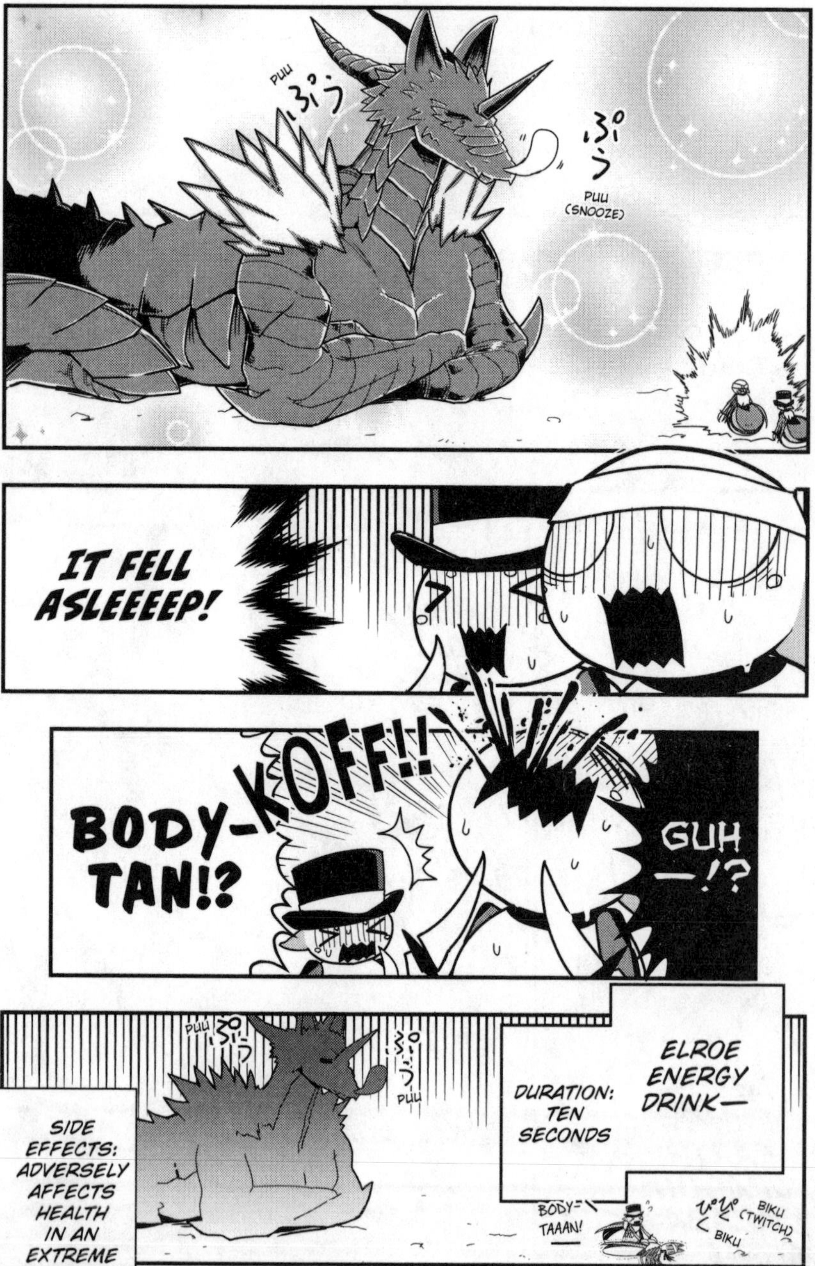
ぷう
PUU (SNOOZE)
PUU
ぷう
IT FELL ASLEEEEEP!
GUH—!?
KOFF!!
BODY-TAN!?
ELROE ENERGY DRINK—
DURATION: TEN SECONDS
ぴくぴく
BIKU (TWITCH) BIKU
BODY-TAAAN!
ぷう
PUU
PUU
ぷう
SIDE EFFECTS: ADVERSELY AFFECTS HEALTH IN AN EXTREME CAPACITY

So I'm a Spider so What?

THE DAILY LIVES OF THE KUMOKO SISTERS

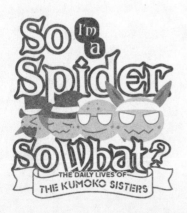

CHAPTER 21

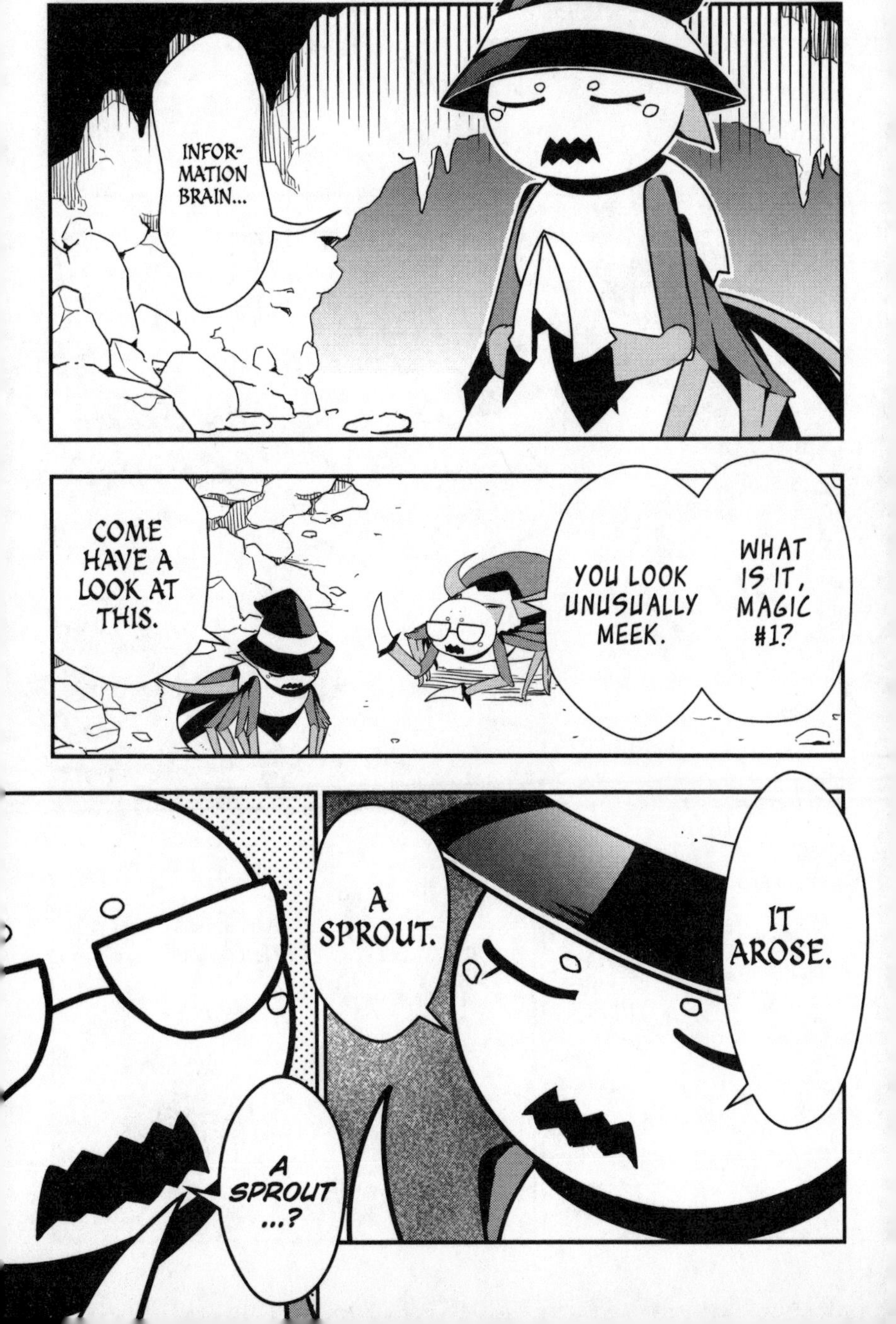
INFOR-MATION BRAIN...
WHAT IS IT, MAGIC #1?
YOU LOOK UNUSUALLY MEEK.
COME HAVE A LOOK AT THIS.
IT AROSE.
A SPROUT.
A SPROUT...?

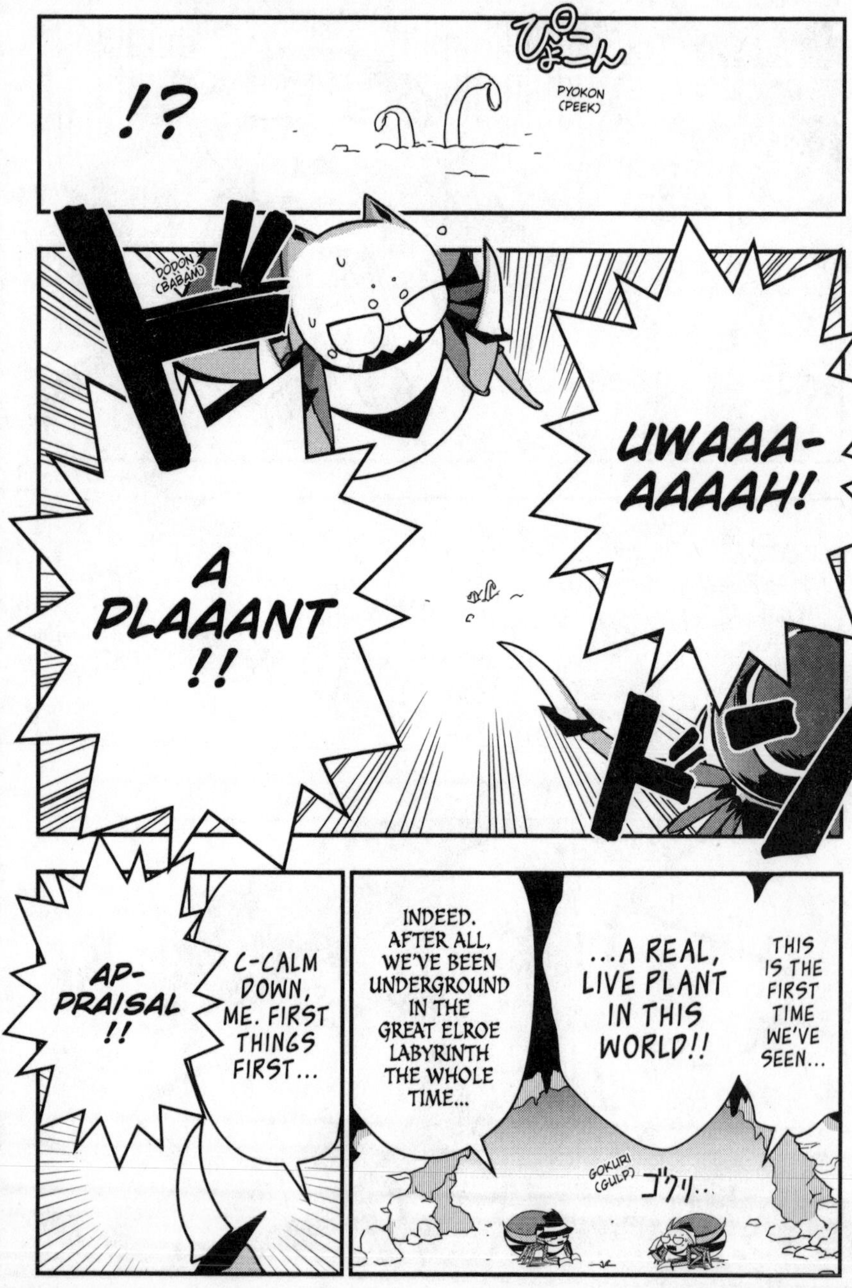
PYOKON (PEEK)
!?
UWAAA-AAAAH!
DODON (BABAM)
A PLAAANT!!
THIS IS THE FIRST TIME WE'VE SEEN...
...A REAL, LIVE PLANT IN THIS WORLD!!
INDEED. AFTER ALL, WE'VE BEEN UNDERGROUND IN THE GREAT ELROE LABYRINTH THE WHOLE TIME...
GOKURI (GULP)
ゴクリ…
C-CALM DOWN, ME. FIRST THINGS FIRST...
AP-PRAISAL!!

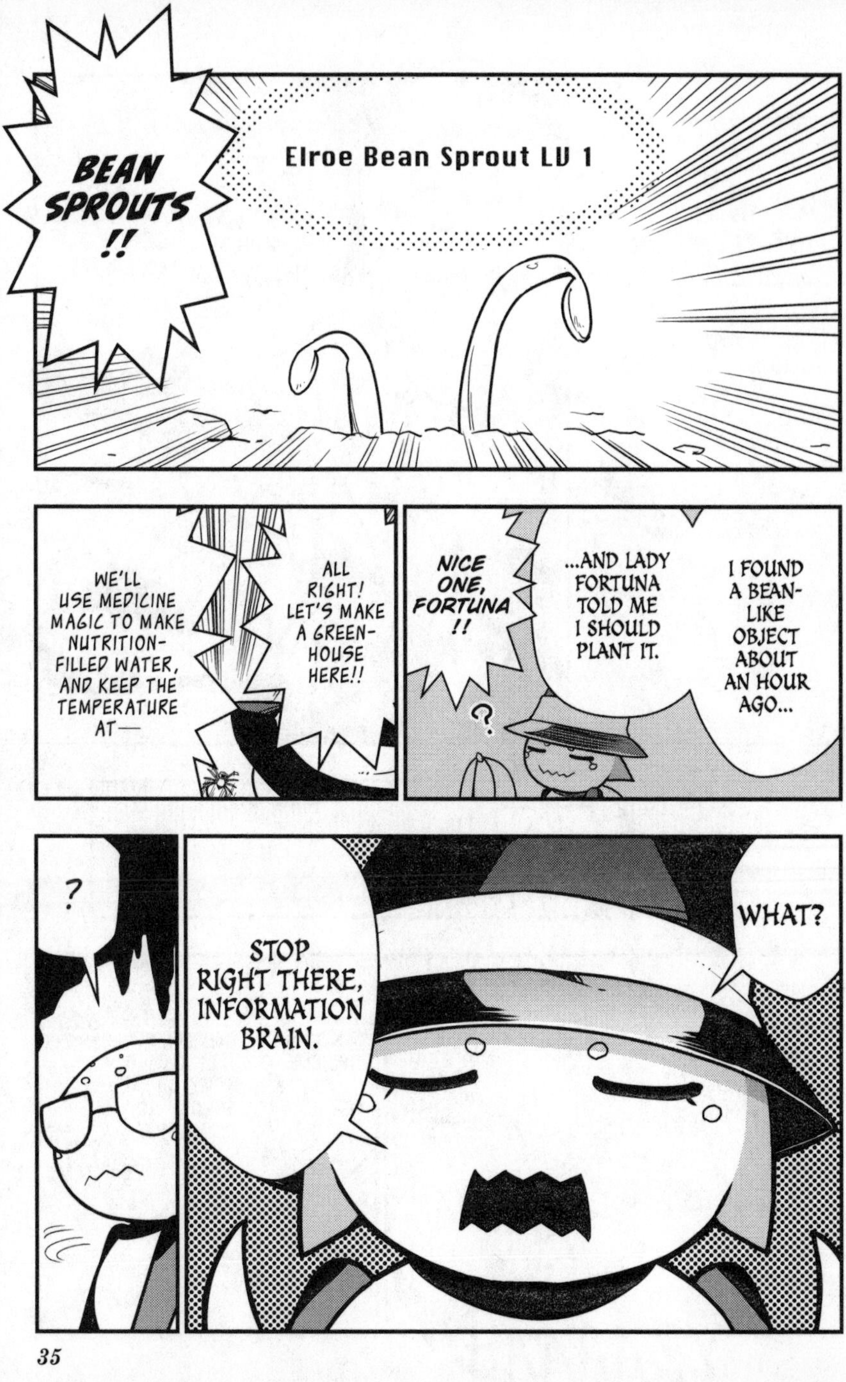
Elroe Bean Sprout LV 1
BEAN SPROUTS!!
I FOUND A BEAN-LIKE OBJECT ABOUT AN HOUR AGO...
...AND LADY FORTUNA TOLD ME I SHOULD PLANT IT.
NICE ONE, FORTUNA!!
?
ALL RIGHT! LET'S MAKE A GREEN-HOUSE HERE!!
WE'LL USE MEDICINE MAGIC TO MAKE NUTRITION-FILLED WATER, AND KEEP THE TEMPERATURE AT—
WHAT?
STOP RIGHT THERE, INFORMATION BRAIN.
?

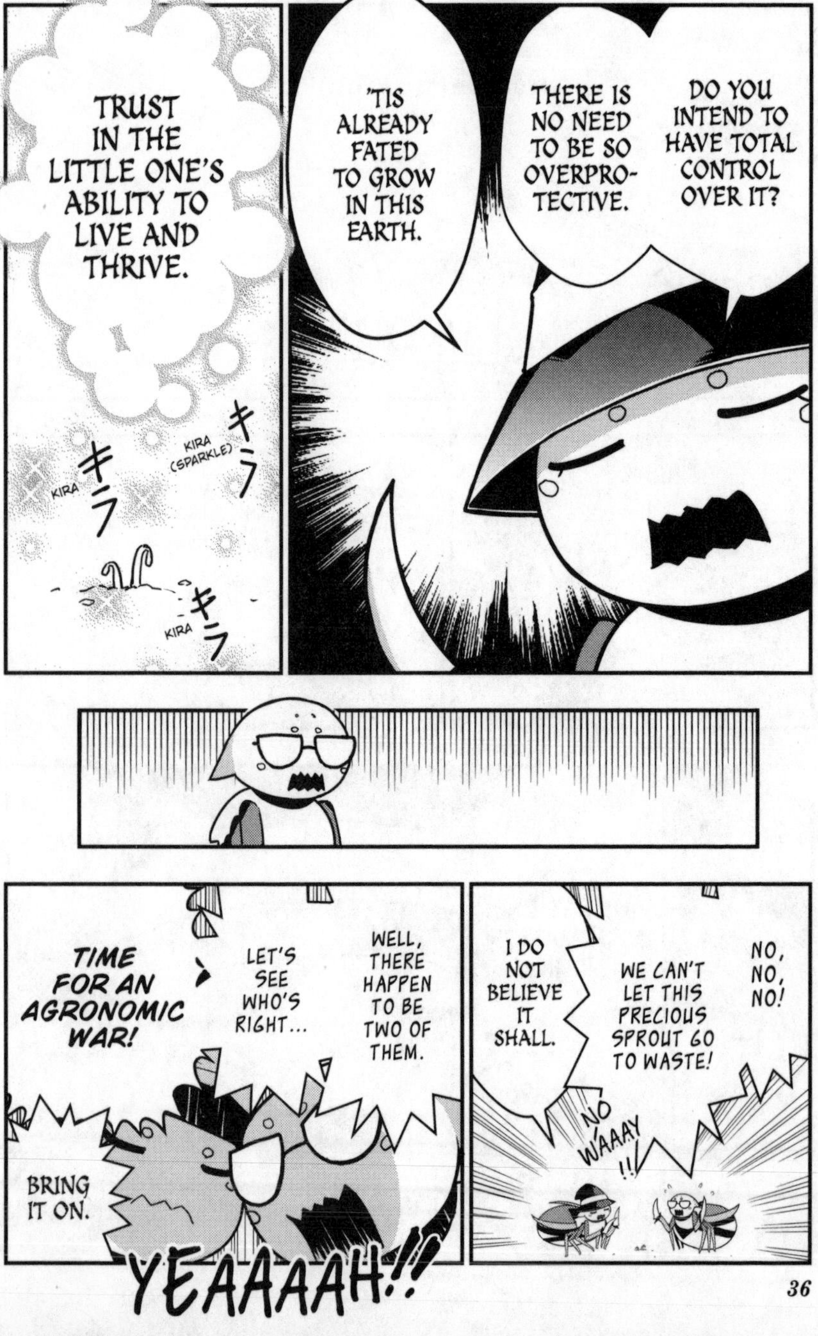
DO YOU INTEND TO HAVE TOTAL CONTROL OVER IT?
THERE IS NO NEED TO BE SO OVERPRO-TECTIVE.
'TIS ALREADY FATED TO GROW IN THIS EARTH.
TRUST IN THE LITTLE ONE'S ABILITY TO LIVE AND THRIVE.
キラ
KIRA (SPARKLE)
キラ
KIRA
キラ
KIRA
NO, NO, NO!
WE CAN'T LET THIS PRECIOUS SPROUT GO TO WASTE!
I DO NOT BELIEVE IT SHALL.
NO WAAAY!!
WELL, THERE HAPPEN TO BE TWO OF THEM.
LET'S SEE WHO'S RIGHT...
TIME FOR AN AGRONOMIC WAR!
BRING IT ON.
YEAAAAH!!

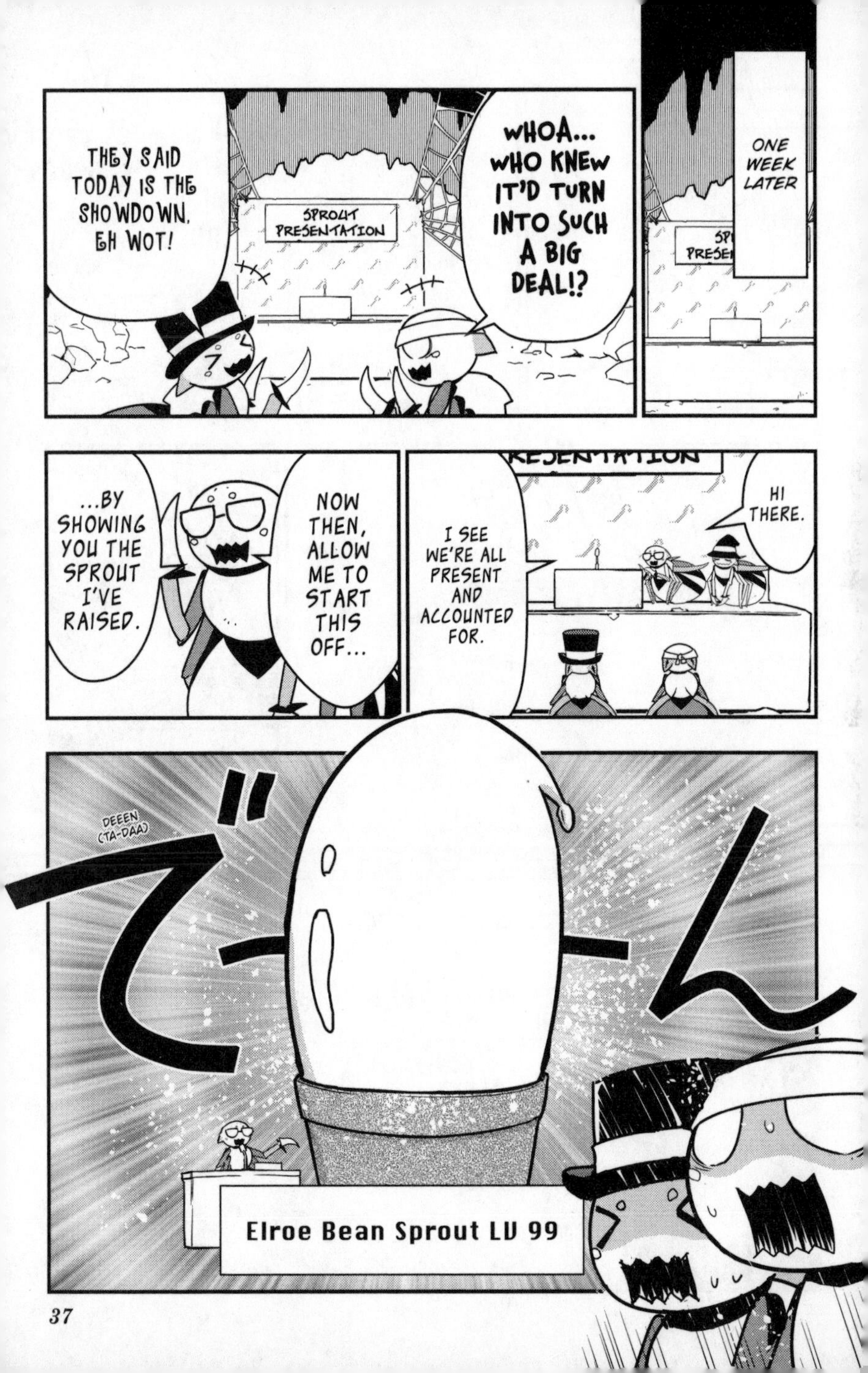
ONE WEEK LATER
SPROUT PRESENTATION
WHOA... WHO KNEW IT'D TURN INTO SUCH A BIG DEAL!?
THEY SAID TODAY IS THE SHOWDOWN, EH WOT!
HI THERE.
I SEE WE'RE ALL PRESENT AND ACCOUNTED FOR.
NOW THEN, ALLOW ME TO START THIS OFF...
...BY SHOWING YOU THE SPROUT I'VE RAISED.
DEEEN (TA-DAA)
Elroe Bean Sprout LV 99

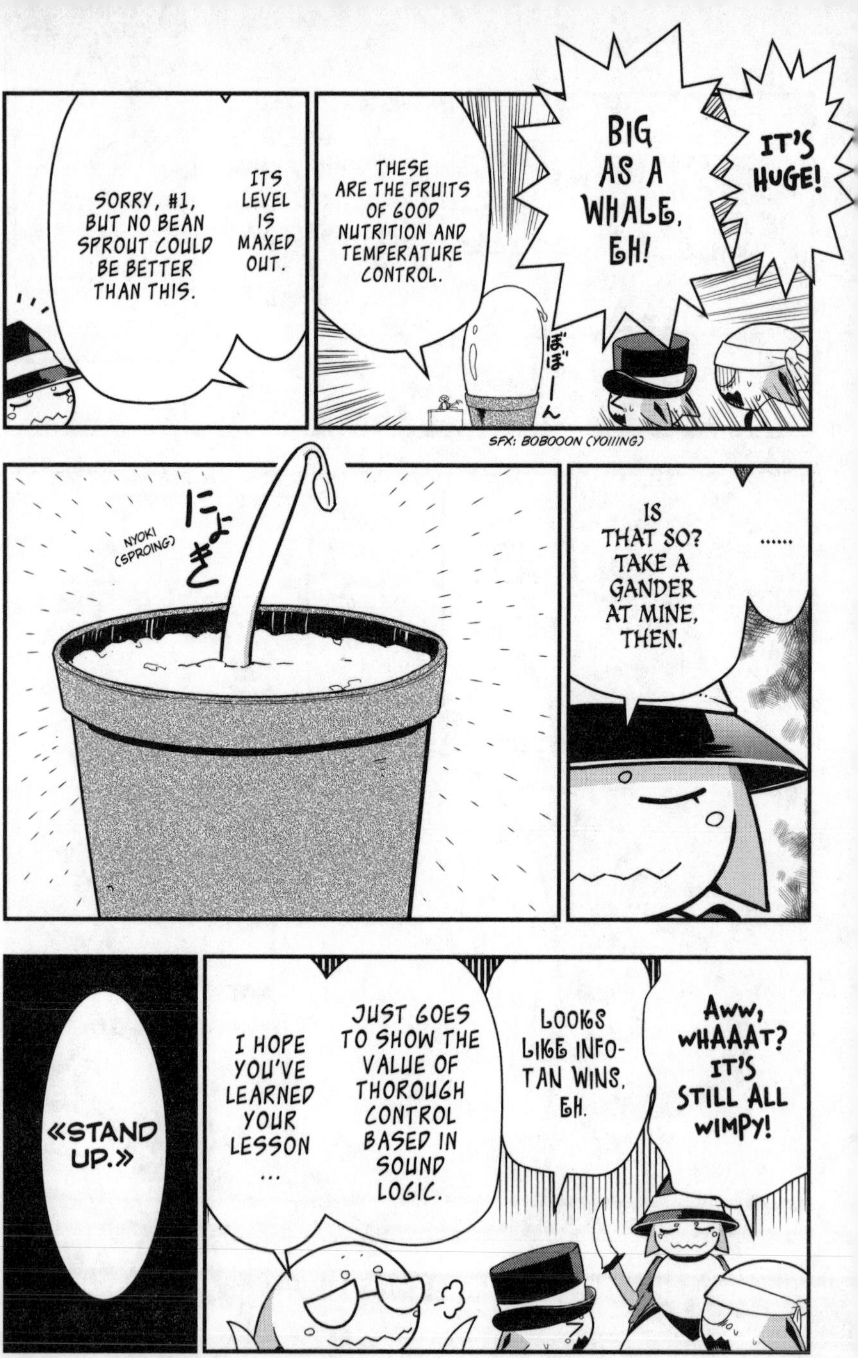
IT'S HUGE!
BIG AS A WHALE, EH!
THESE ARE THE FRUITS OF GOOD NUTRITION AND TEMPERATURE CONTROL.
ぼぼーん
SFX: BOBOOON (YOIIING)
ITS LEVEL IS MAXED OUT.
SORRY, #1, BUT NO BEAN SPROUT COULD BE BETTER THAN THIS.
......
IS THAT SO? TAKE A GANDER AT MINE, THEN.
にょき
NYOKI (SPROING)
Aww, WHAAAT? IT'S STILL ALL WIMPY!
LOOKS LIKE INFO-TAN WINS, EH.
JUST GOES TO SHOW THE VALUE OF THOROUGH CONTROL BASED IN SOUND LOGIC.
I HOPE YOU'VE LEARNED YOUR LESSON ...
«STAND UP.»

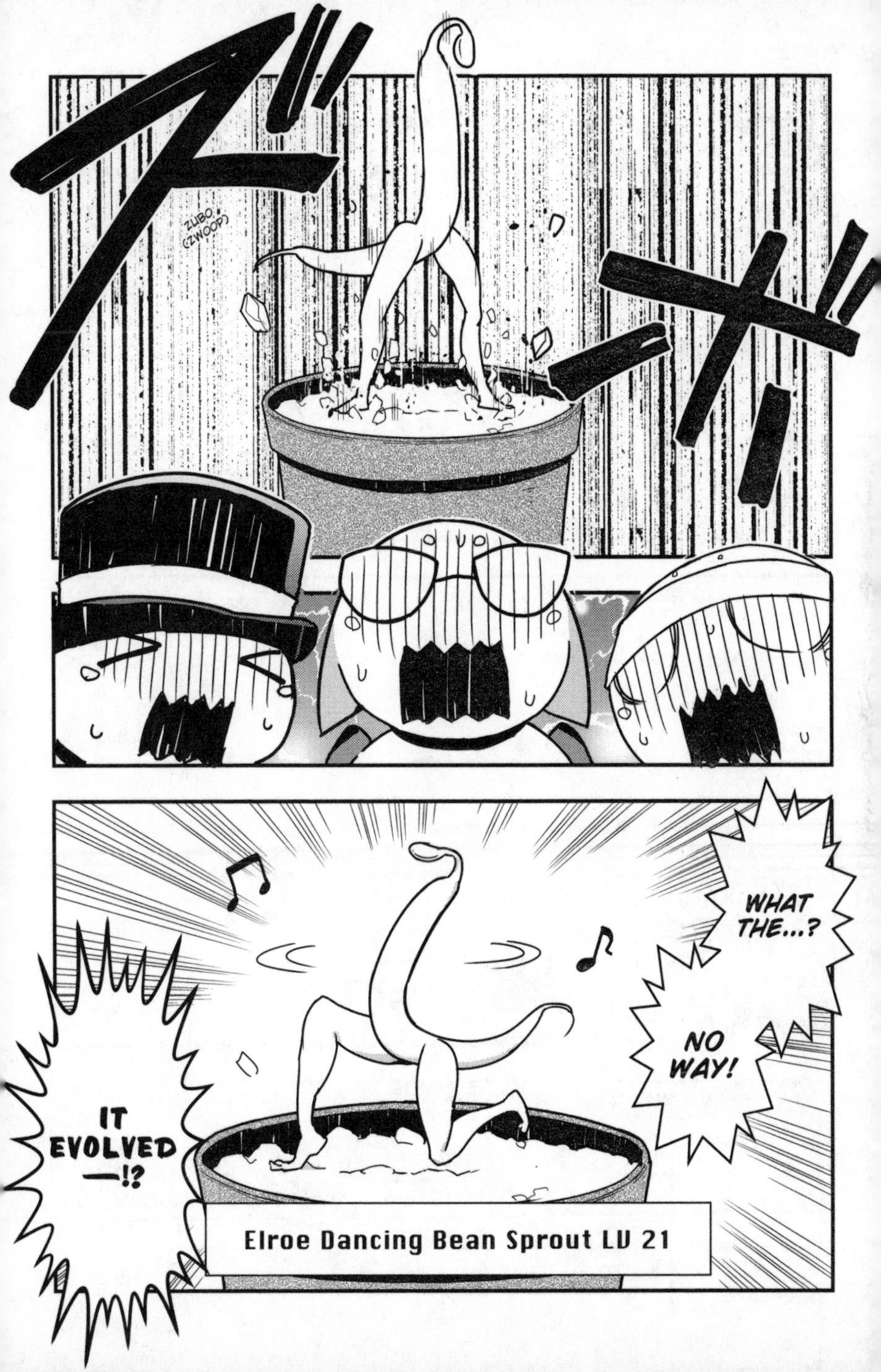
ZUBO (ZWOOP)
WHAT THE...?
NO WAY!
IT EVOLVED—!?
Elroe Dancing Bean Sprout LV 21

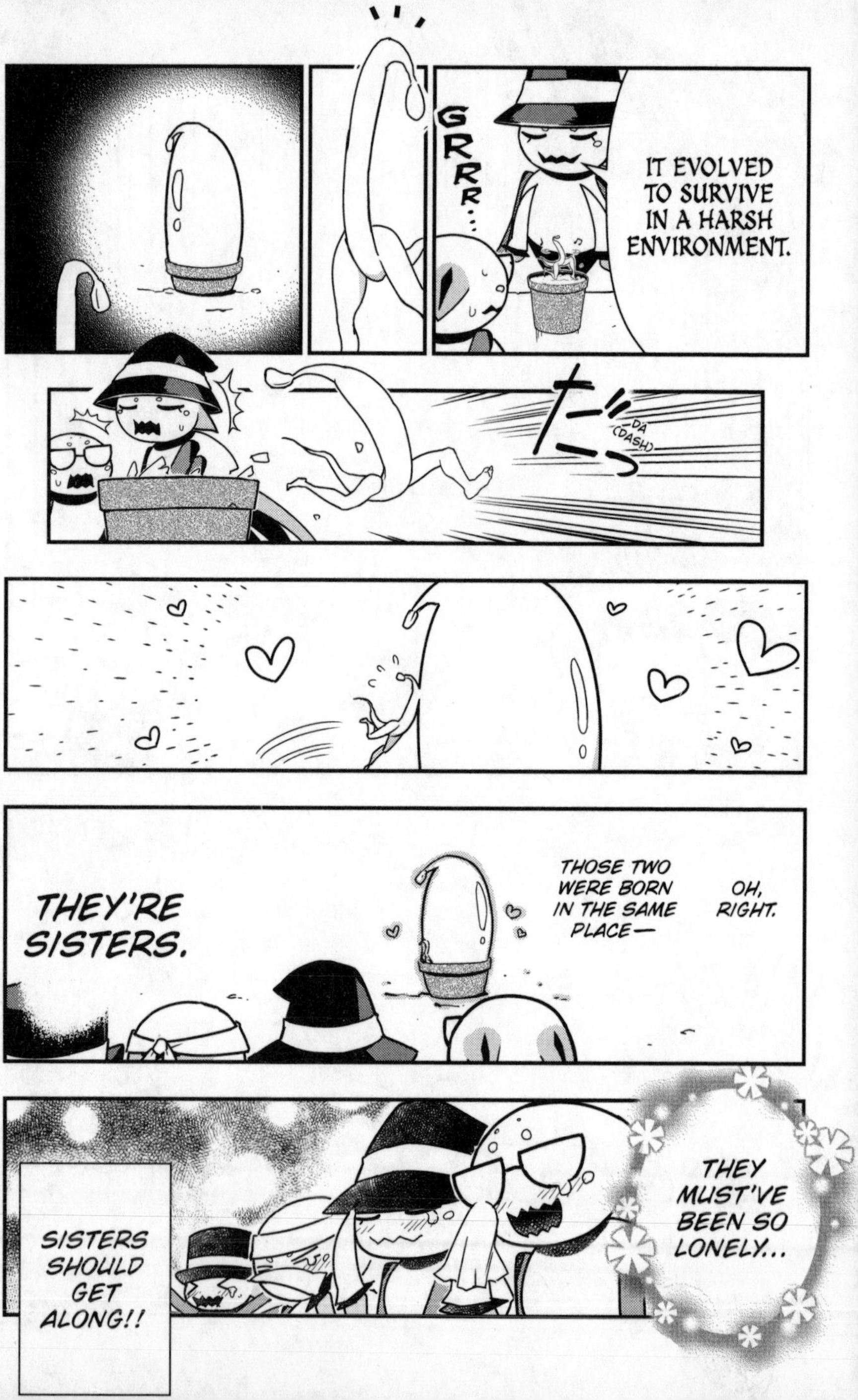
IT EVOLVED TO SURVIVE IN A HARSH ENVIRONMENT.
GRRR...
DA (DASH)
OH, RIGHT.
THOSE TWO WERE BORN IN THE SAME PLACE—
THEY'RE SISTERS.
THEY MUST'VE BEEN SO LONELY...
SISTERS SHOULD GET ALONG!!

So I'm a Spider so What?

THE DAILY LIVES OF THE KUMOKO SISTERS

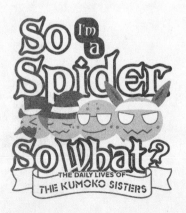

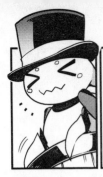

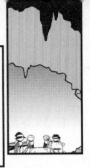

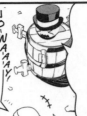

MY MAGIC TRICK FAILED AGAIN, EH WOT!!
NO-WAAAAY!
IT'S FINE. YOU'RE TOO CUTE TO STAY MAD AT, #2.
ACTUALLY, I'VE BEEN WONDERING—
WHICH SISTER IS THE CUTEST OF THEM ALL, EH?

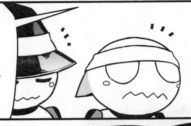

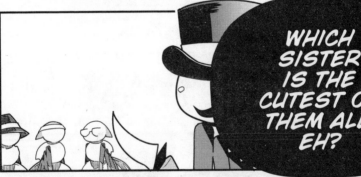

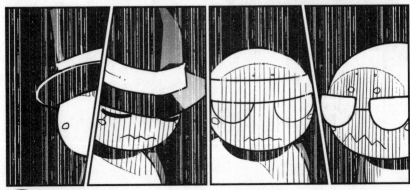

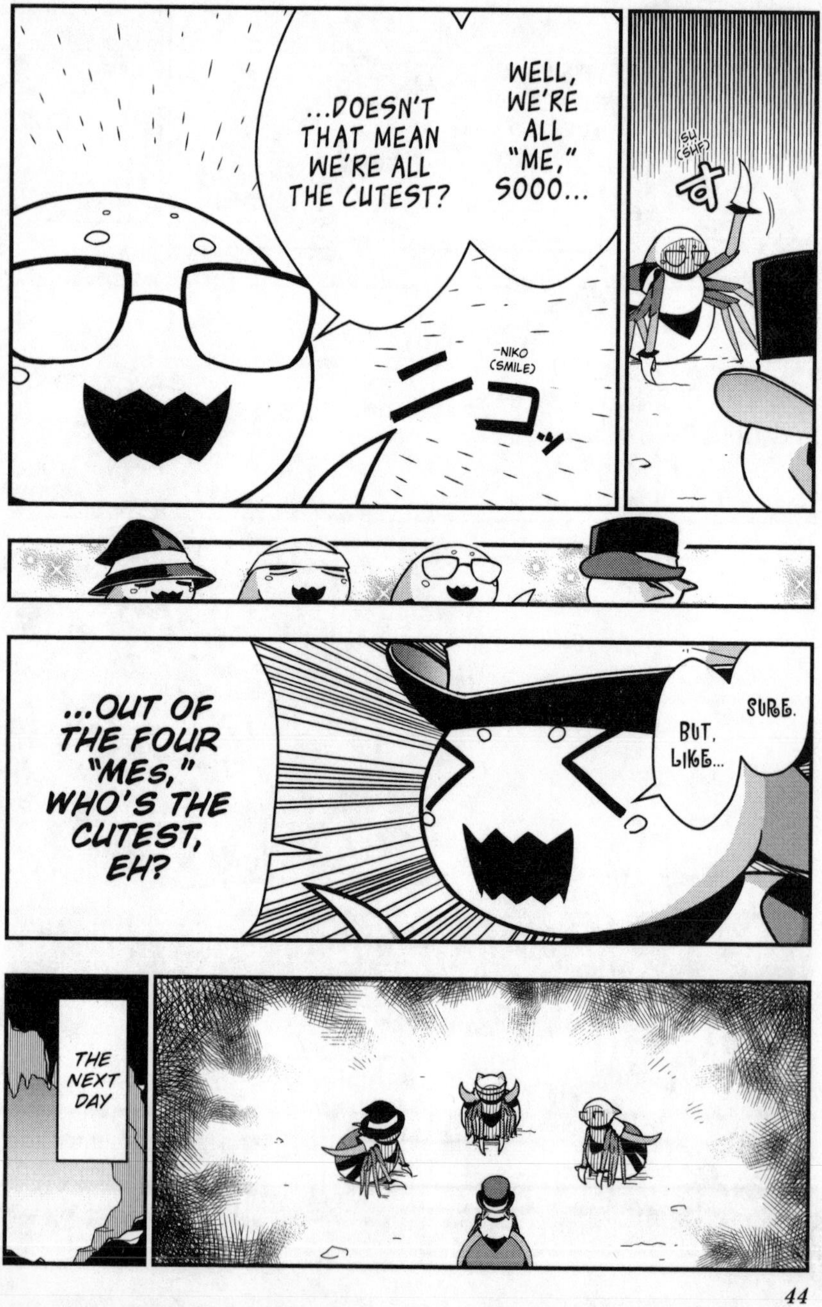
SU (SHF)
す
WELL, WE'RE ALL "ME," SOOO...
...DOESN'T THAT MEAN WE'RE ALL THE CUTEST?
NIKO (SMILE)
ニコッ
SURE.
BUT, LIKE...
...OUT OF THE FOUR "MES," WHO'S THE CUTEST, EH?
THE NEXT DAY

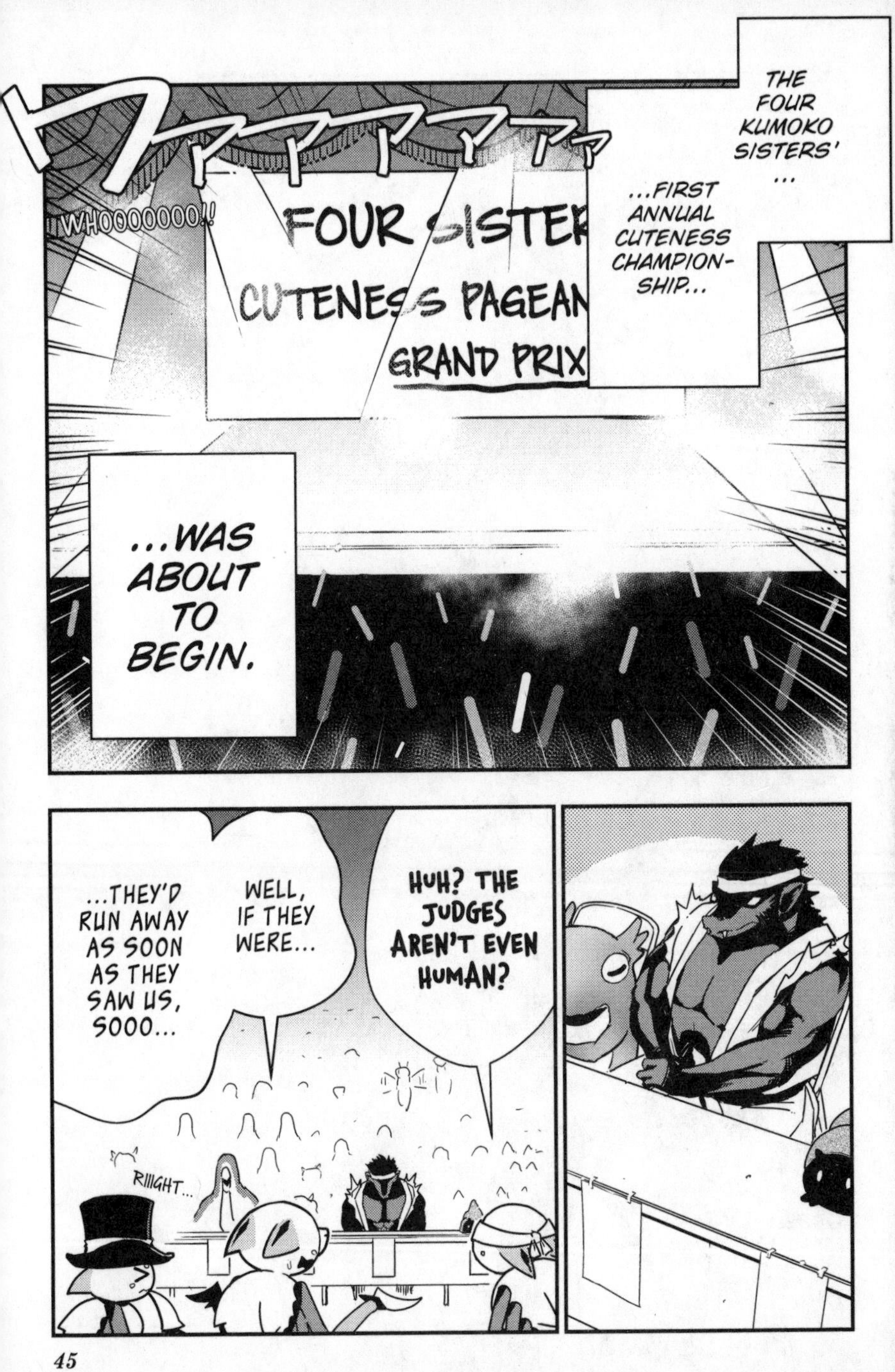
THE FOUR KUMOKO SISTERS' ...
...FIRST ANNUAL CUTENESS CHAMPION-SHIP...
WHOOOOOOO!!
FOUR SISTER
CUTENESS PAGEAN
GRAND PRIX
...WAS ABOUT TO BEGIN.
HUH? THE JUDGES AREN'T EVEN HUMAN?
WELL, IF THEY WERE...
...THEY'D RUN AWAY AS SOON AS THEY SAW US, SOOO...
RIIIGHT...

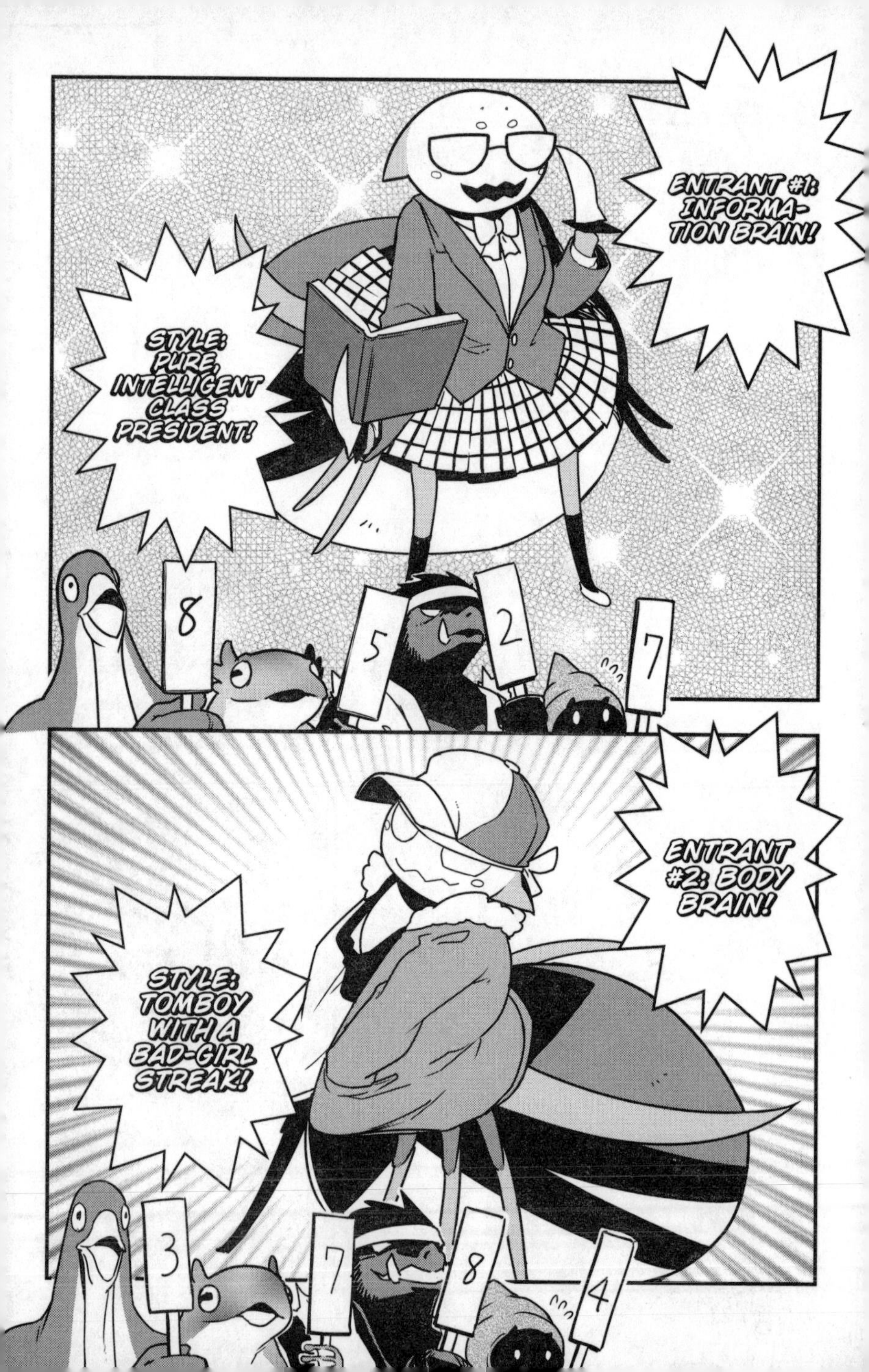
ENTRANT #1: INFORMATION BRAIN!
STYLE: PURE, INTELLIGENT CLASS PRESIDENT!
7
2
5
8
ENTRANT #2: BODY BRAIN!
STYLE: TOMBOY WITH A BAD-GIRL STREAK!
4
8
7
3

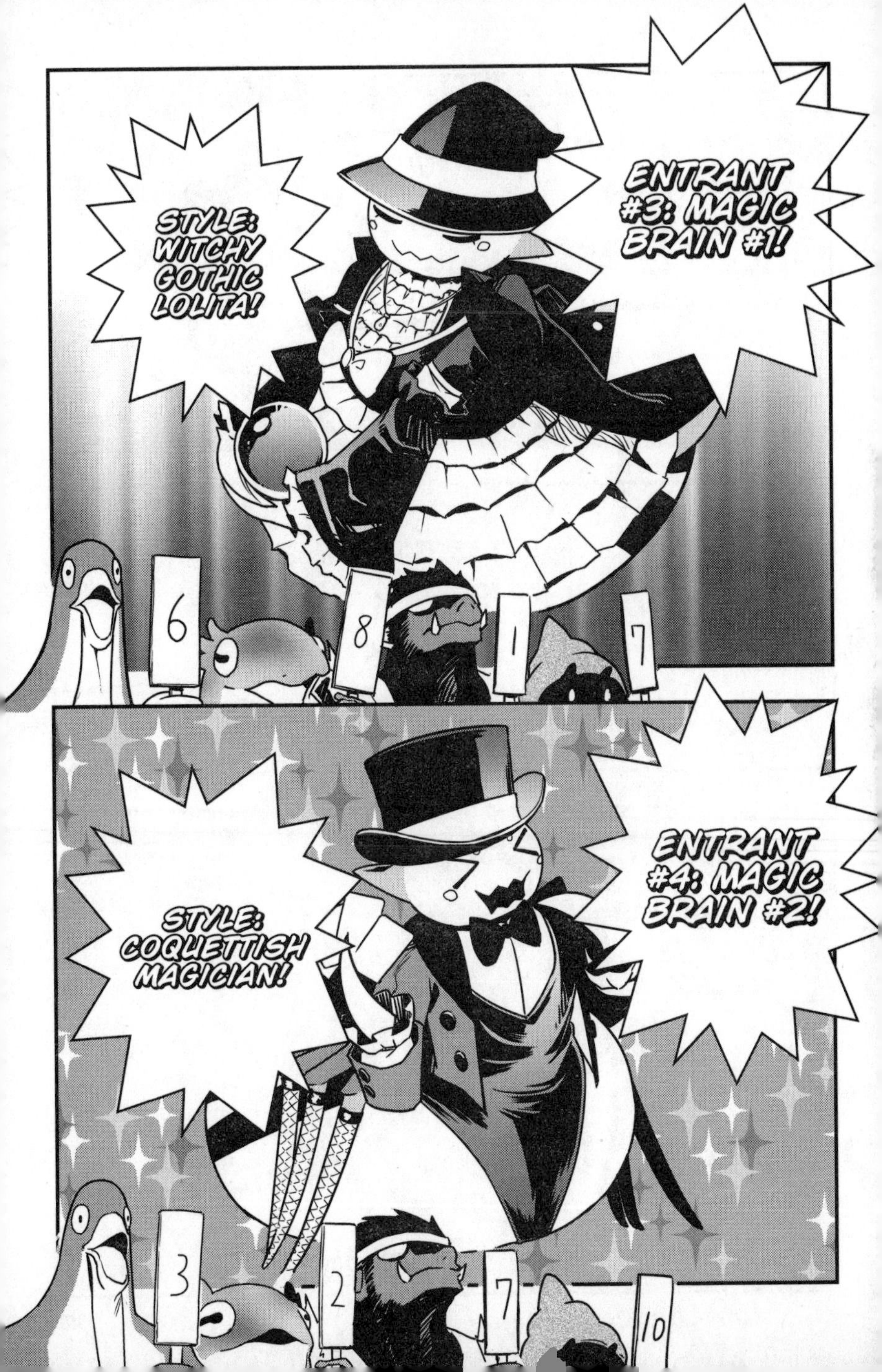
ENTRANT #3: MAGIC BRAIN #1!
STYLE: WITCHY GOTHIC LOLITA!
6
8
1
7
ENTRANT #4: MAGIC BRAIN #2!
STYLE: COQUETTISH MAGICIAN!
3
2
7
10

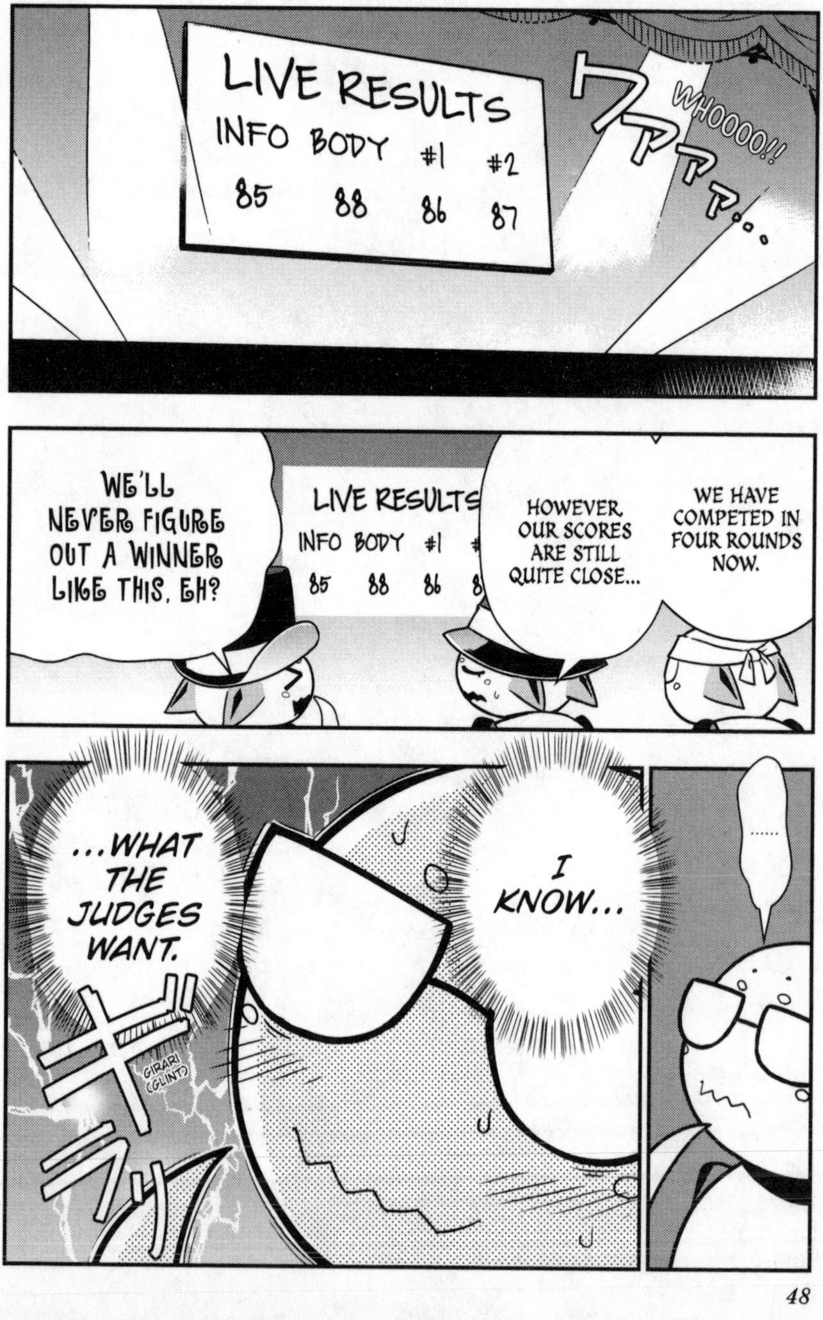
LIVE RESULTS
INFO BODY #1 #2
85 88 86 87
WHOOOOO!!
WE HAVE COMPETED IN FOUR ROUNDS NOW.
HOWEVER OUR SCORES ARE STILL QUITE CLOSE...
WE'LL NEVER FIGURE OUT A WINNER LIKE THIS, EH?
......
I KNOW...
...WHAT THE JUDGES WANT.
GIRARI (GLINT)

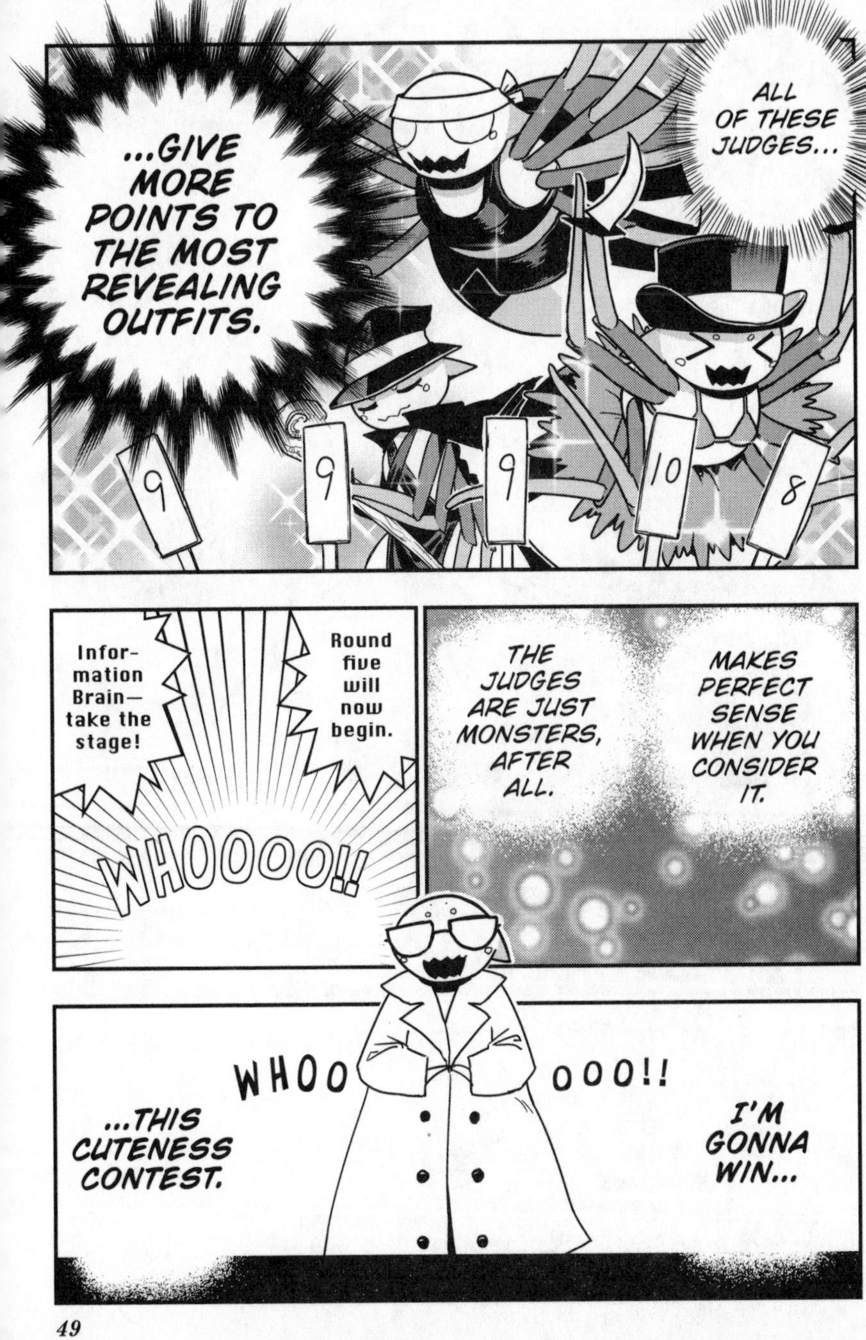
ALL OF THESE JUDGES...
...GIVE MORE POINTS TO THE MOST REVEALING OUTFITS.
MAKES PERFECT SENSE WHEN YOU CONSIDER IT.
THE JUDGES ARE JUST MONSTERS, AFTER ALL.
Round five will now begin.
Information Brain—take the stage!
WHOOOOO!!
WHOO OOO!!
I'M GONNA WIN...
...THIS CUTENESS CONTEST.

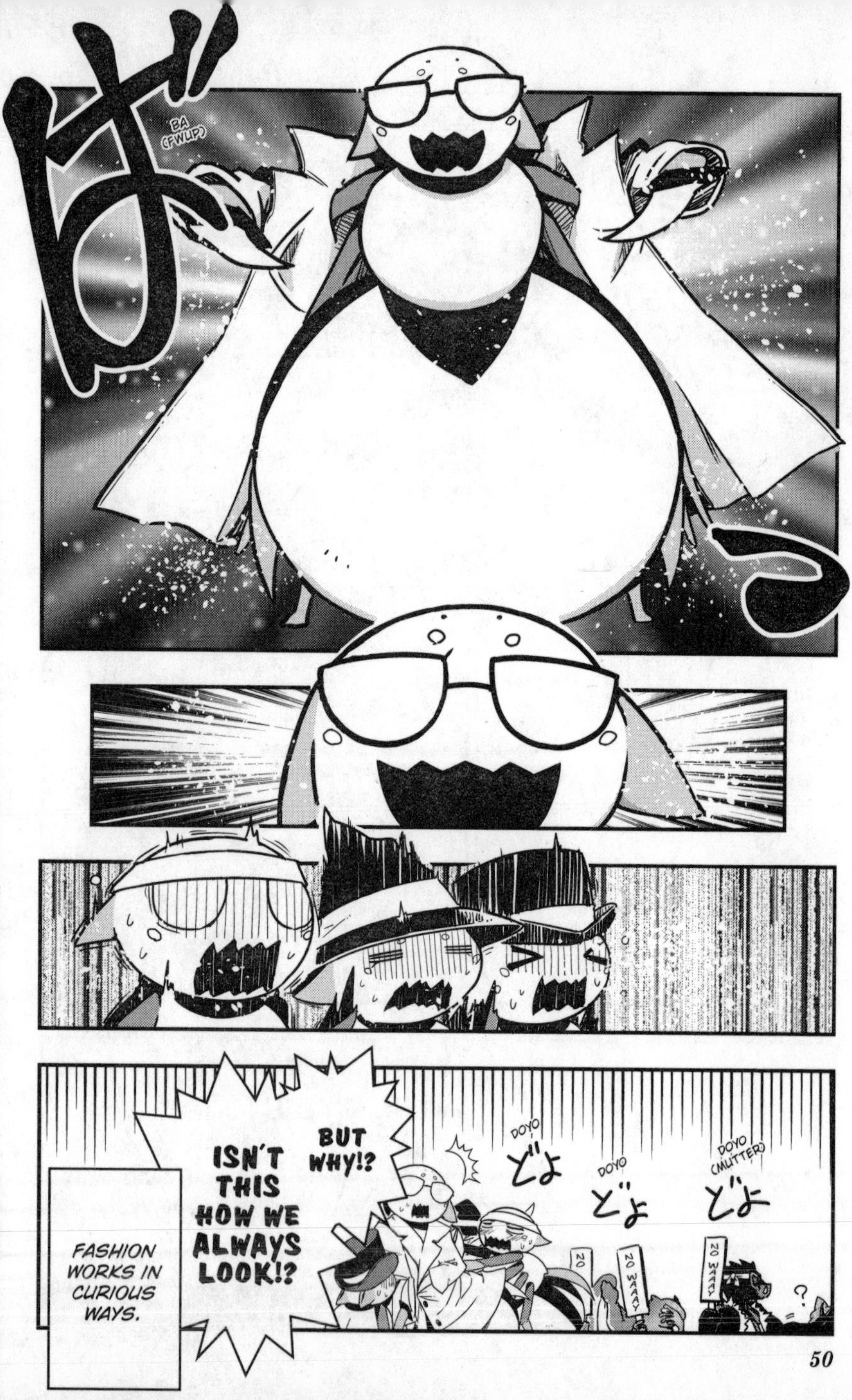
ば
BA (FWUP)
っ
DOYO (MUTTER)
どよ
NO WAAAY
DOYO
どよ
NO WAAAY
NO
DOYO
どよ
?
BUT WHY!?
ISN'T THIS HOW WE ALWAYS LOOK!?
FASHION WORKS IN CURIOUS WAYS.

So I'm a Spider, so What?

THE DAILY LIVES OF THE KUMOKO SISTERS

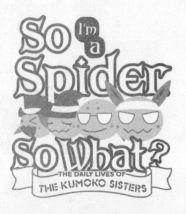

CHAPTER 23

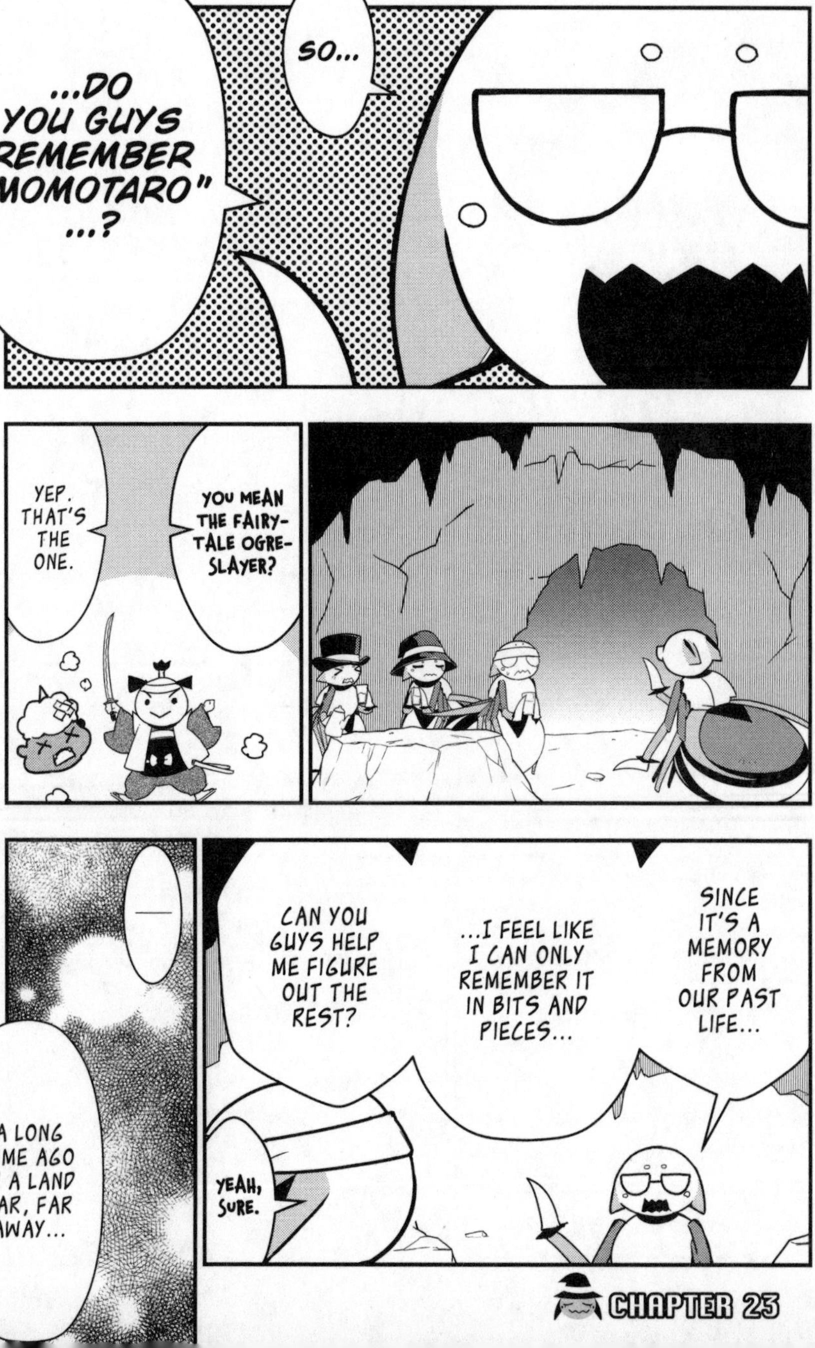
SO...
...DO YOU GUYS REMEMBER "MOMOTARO" ...?
YOU MEAN THE FAIRY-TALE OGRE-SLAYER?
YEP. THAT'S THE ONE.
SINCE IT'S A MEMORY FROM OUR PAST LIFE...
...I FEEL LIKE I CAN ONLY REMEMBER IT IN BITS AND PIECES...
CAN YOU GUYS HELP ME FIGURE OUT THE REST?
YEAH, SURE.
—
A LONG TIME AGO IN A LAND FAR, FAR AWAY...

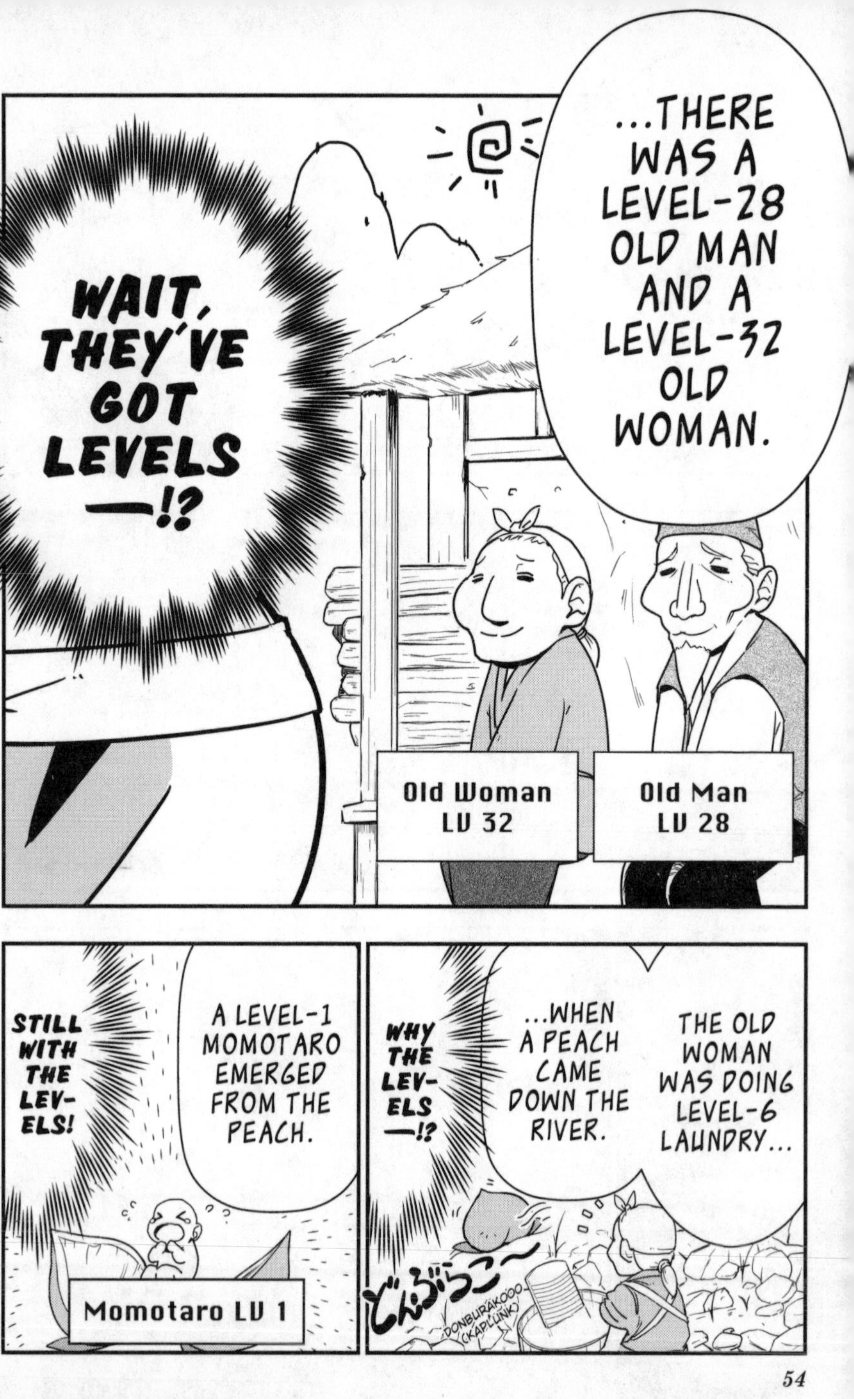
...THERE WAS A LEVEL-28 OLD MAN AND A LEVEL-32 OLD WOMAN.
Old Man LV 28
Old Woman LV 32
WAIT, THEY'VE GOT LEVELS—!?
THE OLD WOMAN WAS DOING LEVEL-6 LAUNDRY...
...WHEN A PEACH CAME DOWN THE RIVER.
どんぶらこ~
DONBURAKOOO (KAPLUNK)
WHY THE LEV-ELS—!?
A LEVEL-1 MOMOTARO EMERGED FROM THE PEACH.
Momotaro LV 1
STILL WITH THE LEV-ELS!

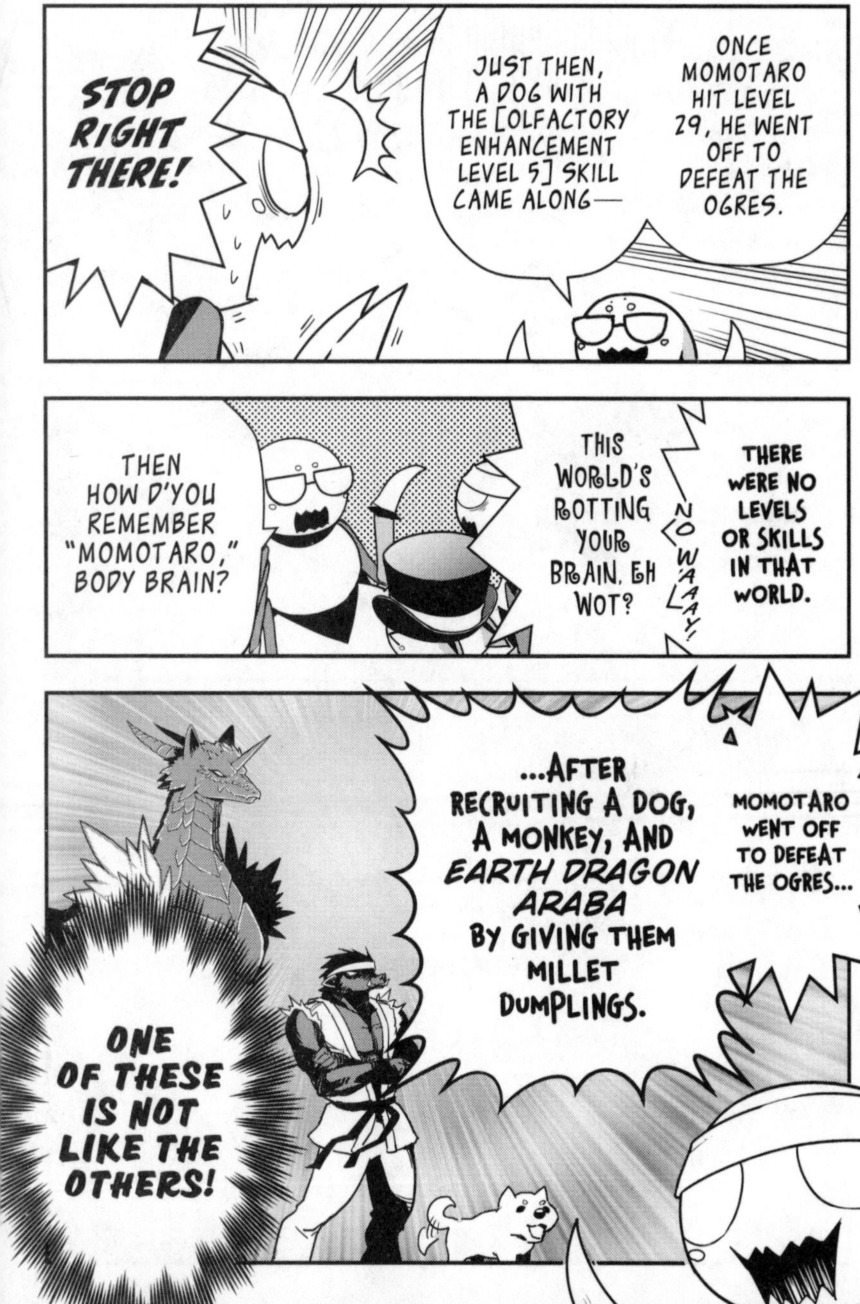
ONCE MOMOTARO HIT LEVEL 29, HE WENT OFF TO DEFEAT THE OGRES.
JUST THEN, A DOG WITH THE [OLFACTORY ENHANCEMENT LEVEL 5] SKILL CAME ALONG—
STOP RIGHT THERE!
THERE WERE NO LEVELS OR SKILLS IN THAT WORLD.
NO WAAAAY!
THIS WORLD'S ROTTING YOUR BRAIN, EH WOT?
THEN HOW D'YOU REMEMBER "MOMOTARO," BODY BRAIN?
MOMOTARO WENT OFF TO DEFEAT THE OGRES...
...AFTER RECRUITING A DOG, A MONKEY, AND *EARTH DRAGON ARABA* BY GIVING THEM MILLET DUMPLINGS.
ONE OF THESE IS NOT LIKE THE OTHERS!

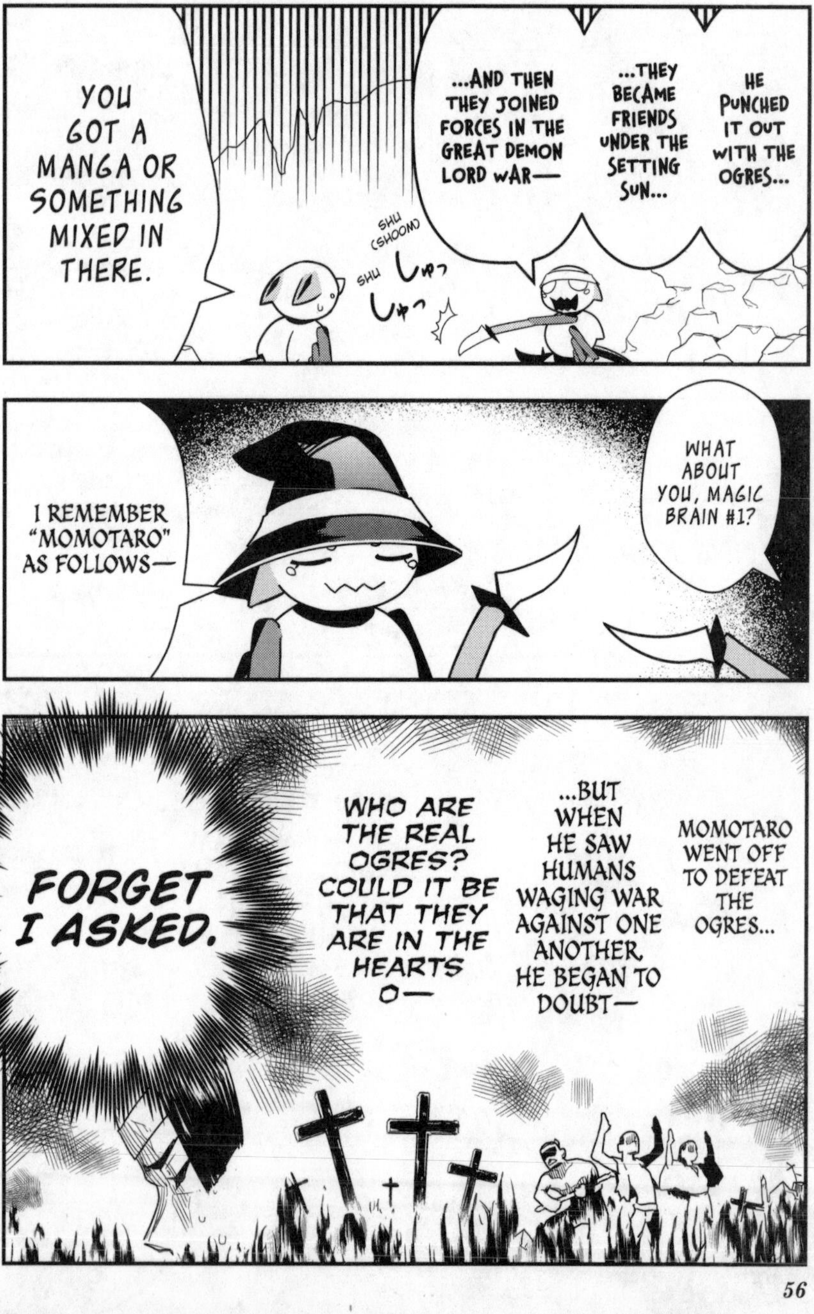
HE PUNCHED IT OUT WITH THE OGRES...
...THEY BECAME FRIENDS UNDER THE SETTING SUN...
...AND THEN THEY JOINED FORCES IN THE GREAT DEMON LORD WAR—
SHU (SHOOM)
しゅっ
SHU
しゅっ
YOU GOT A MANGA OR SOMETHING MIXED IN THERE.
WHAT ABOUT YOU, MAGIC BRAIN #1?
I REMEMBER "MOMOTARO" AS FOLLOWS—
MOMOTARO WENT OFF TO DEFEAT THE OGRES...
...BUT WHEN HE SAW HUMANS WAGING WAR AGAINST ONE ANOTHER HE BEGAN TO DOUBT—
WHO ARE THE REAL OGRES? COULD IT BE THAT THEY ARE IN THE HEARTS O—
FORGET I ASKED.

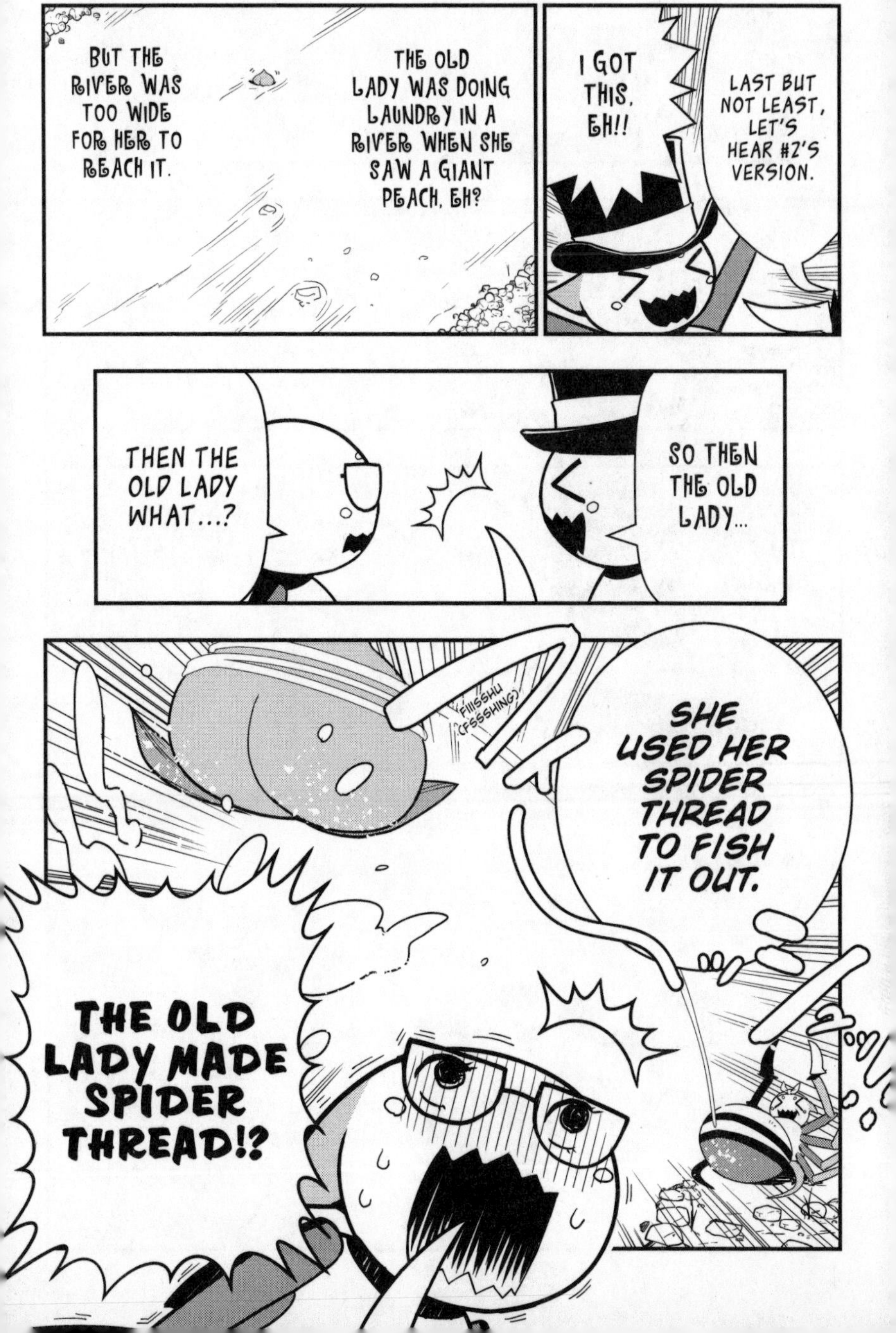

LAST BUT NOT LEAST, LET'S HEAR #2'S VERSION.
I GOT THIS, EH!!
THE OLD LADY WAS DOING LAUNDRY IN A RIVER WHEN SHE SAW A GIANT PEACH, EH?
BUT THE RIVER WAS TOO WIDE FOR HER TO REACH IT.
SO THEN THE OLD LADY...
THEN THE OLD LADY WHAT...?
SHE USED HER SPIDER THREAD TO FISH IT OUT.
FIIISSHU (FSSSHING)
THE OLD LADY MADE SPIDER THREAD!?

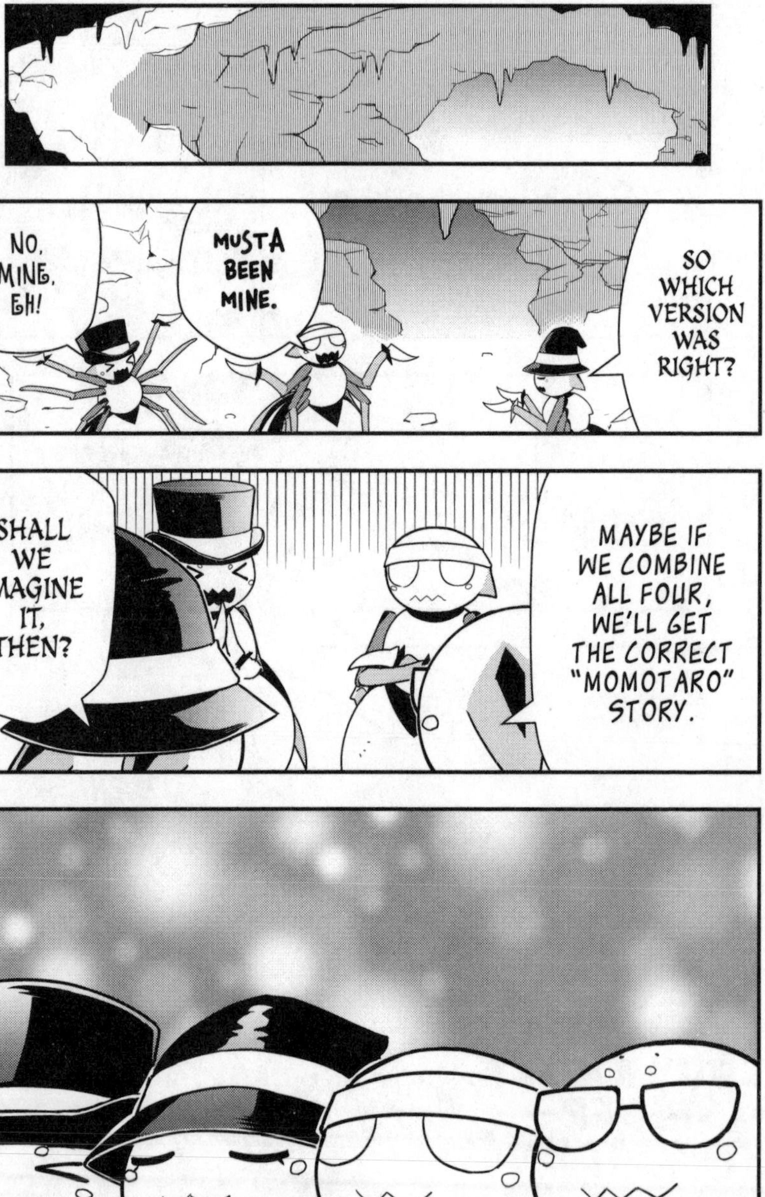
SO WHICH VERSION WAS RIGHT?
MUSTA BEEN MINE.
NO, MINE, EH!
MAYBE IF WE COMBINE ALL FOUR, WE'LL GET THE CORRECT "MOMOTARO" STORY.
SHALL WE IMAGINE IT, THEN?

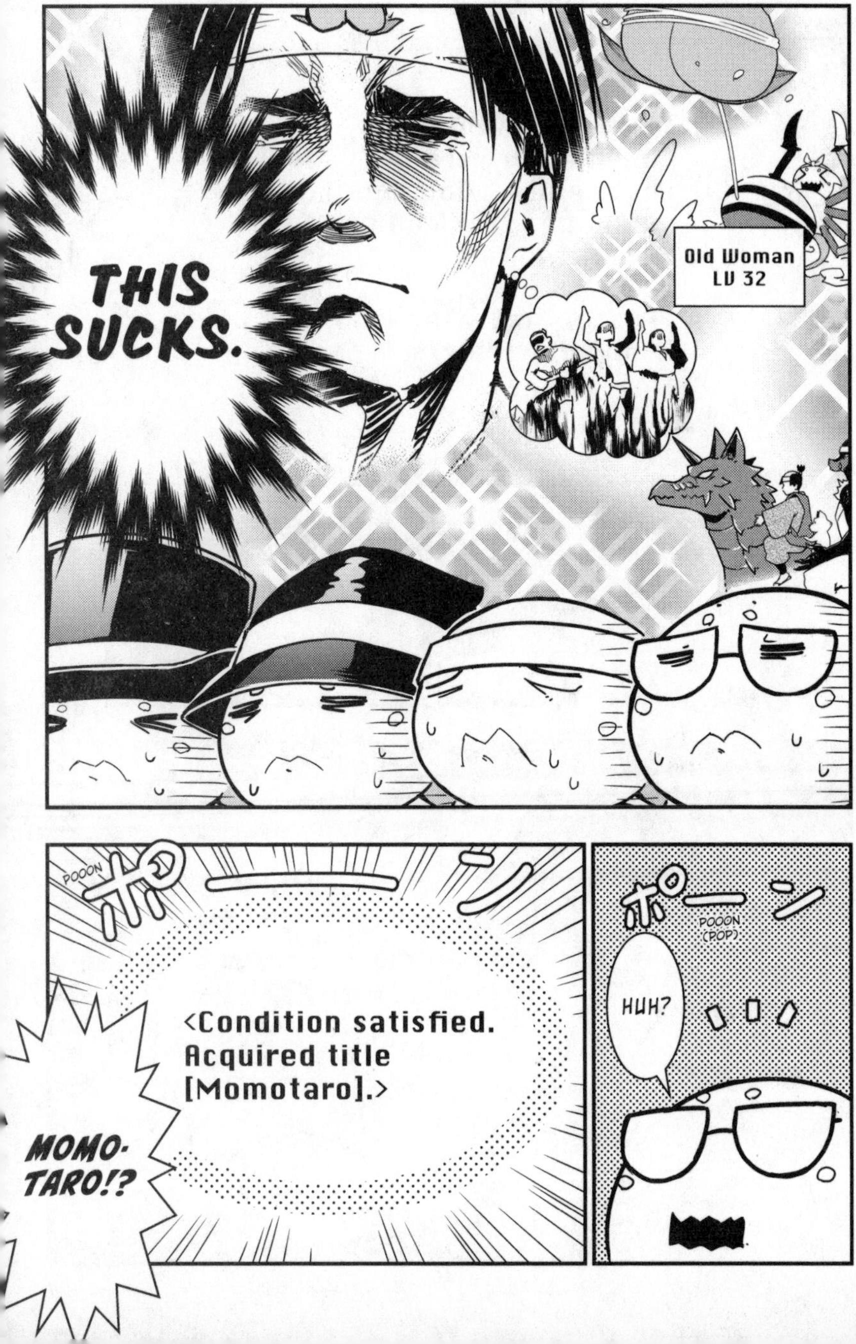
Old Woman
LV 32
THIS SUCKS.
ポーン
POOON (POP)
HUH?
ポーン
POOON
<Condition satisfied.
Acquired title
[Momotaro].>
MOMO-TARO!?

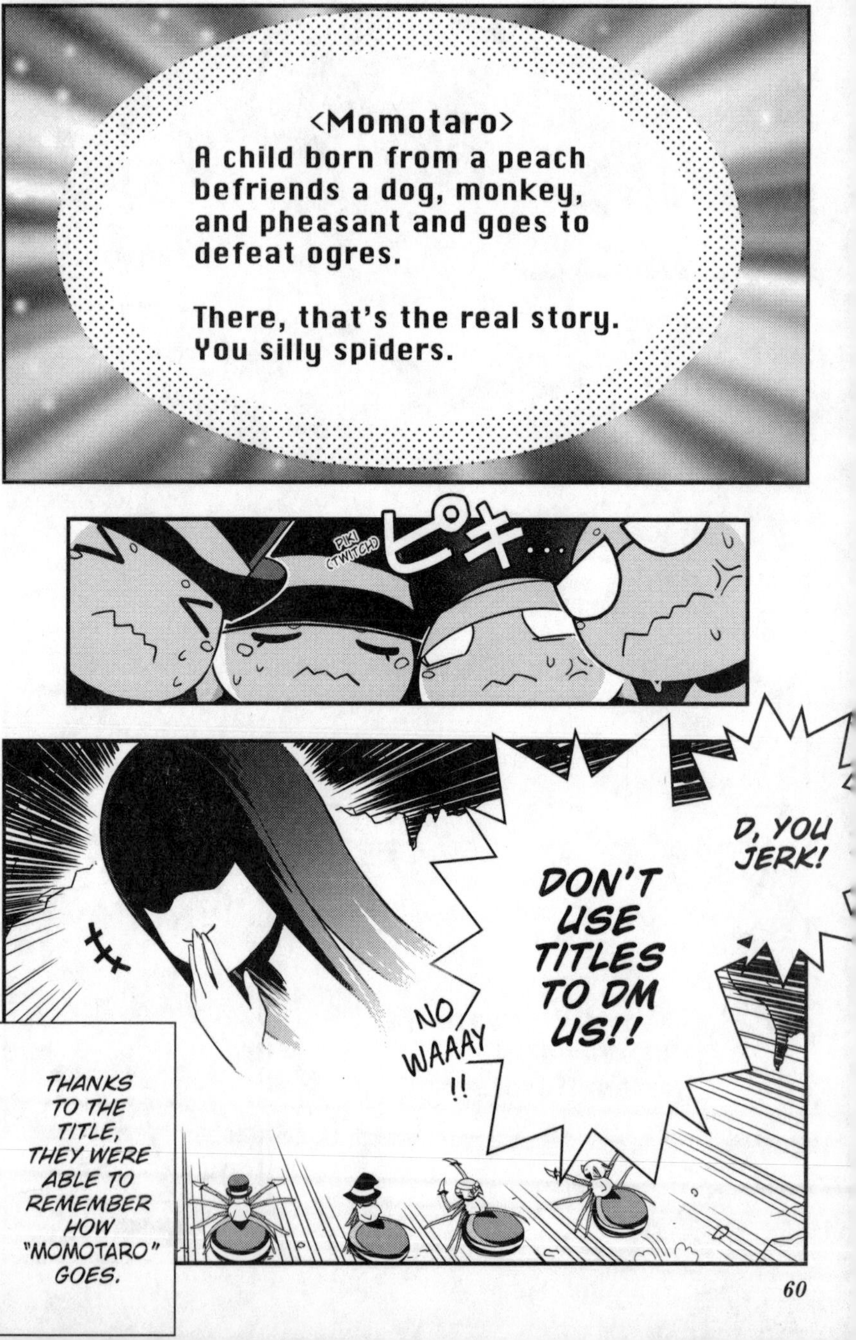
<Momotaro>
A child born from a peach befriends a dog, monkey, and pheasant and goes to defeat ogres.
There, that's the real story. You silly spiders.
PIKI (TWITCH)
ピキ…
D, YOU JERK!
DON'T USE TITLES TO DM US!!
NO WAAAY!!
THANKS TO THE TITLE, THEY WERE ABLE TO REMEMBER HOW "MOMOTARO" GOES.

So I'm a Spider, So What?

THE DAILY LIVES OF THE KUMOKO SISTERS

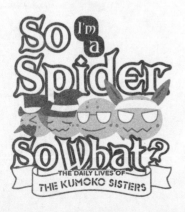

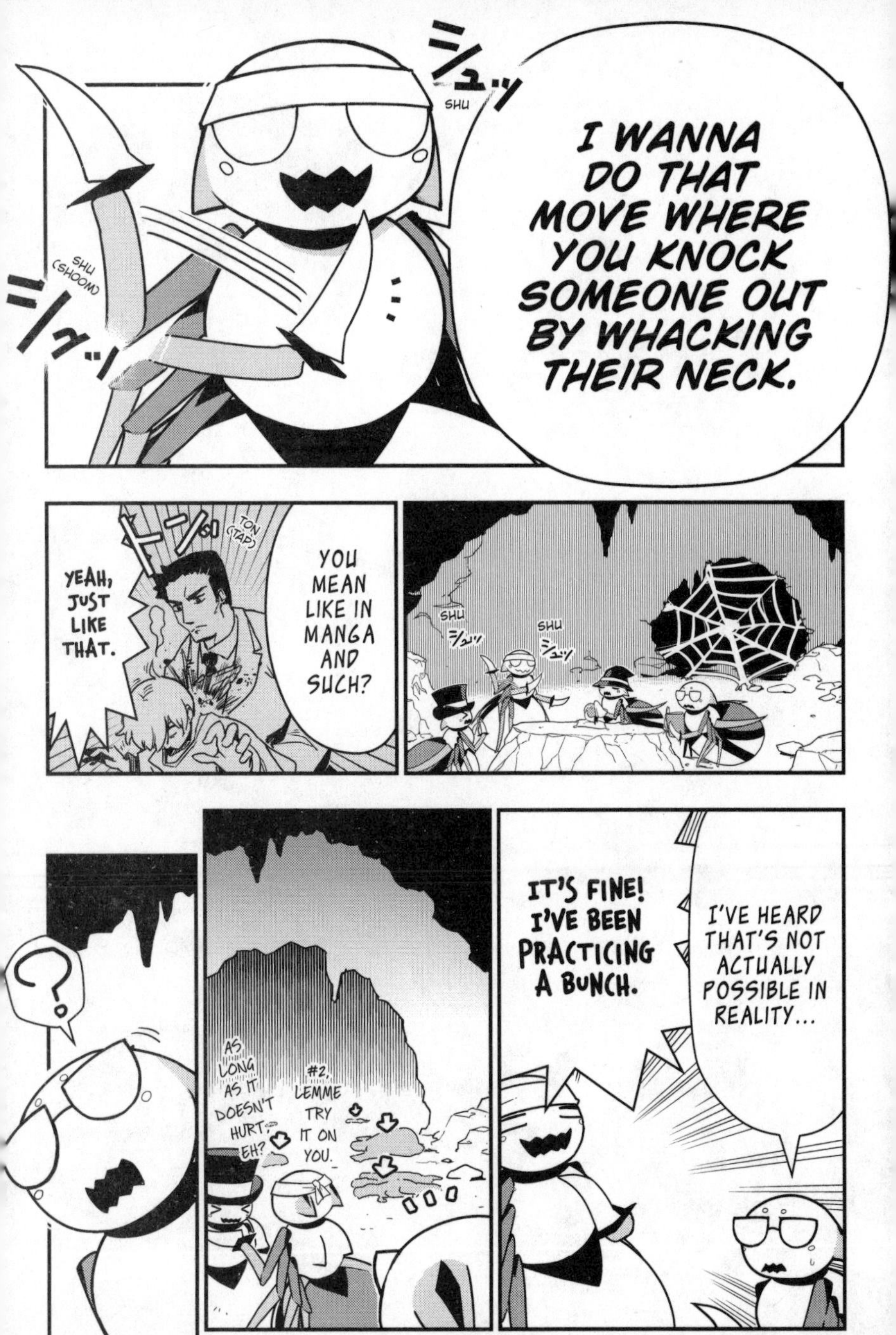
SHU
I WANNA DO THAT MOVE WHERE YOU KNOCK SOMEONE OUT BY WHACKING THEIR NECK.
SHU (SHOOM)
SHU
SHU
YOU MEAN LIKE IN MANGA AND SUCH?
TON (TAP)
YEAH, JUST LIKE THAT.
I'VE HEARD THAT'S NOT ACTUALLY POSSIBLE IN REALITY...
IT'S FINE! I'VE BEEN PRACTICING A BUNCH.
#2, LEMME TRY IT ON YOU.
AS LONG AS IT DOESN'T HURT, EH?
?

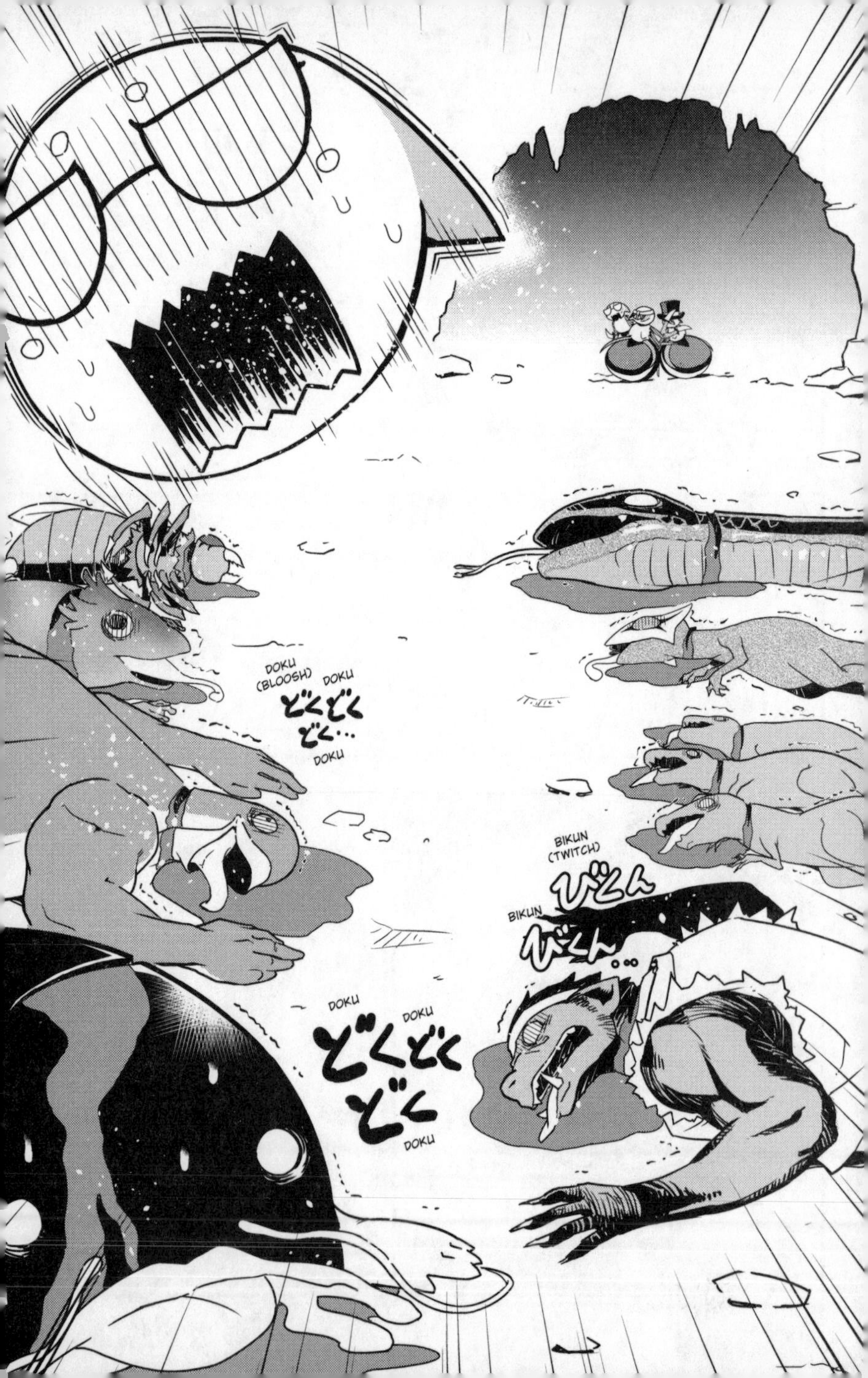
DOKU (BLOOSH) DOKU
どくどく
どく…
DOKU
BIKUN (TWITCH)
びくん
BIKUN
びくん…
DOKU DOKU
どくどく
どく
DOKU

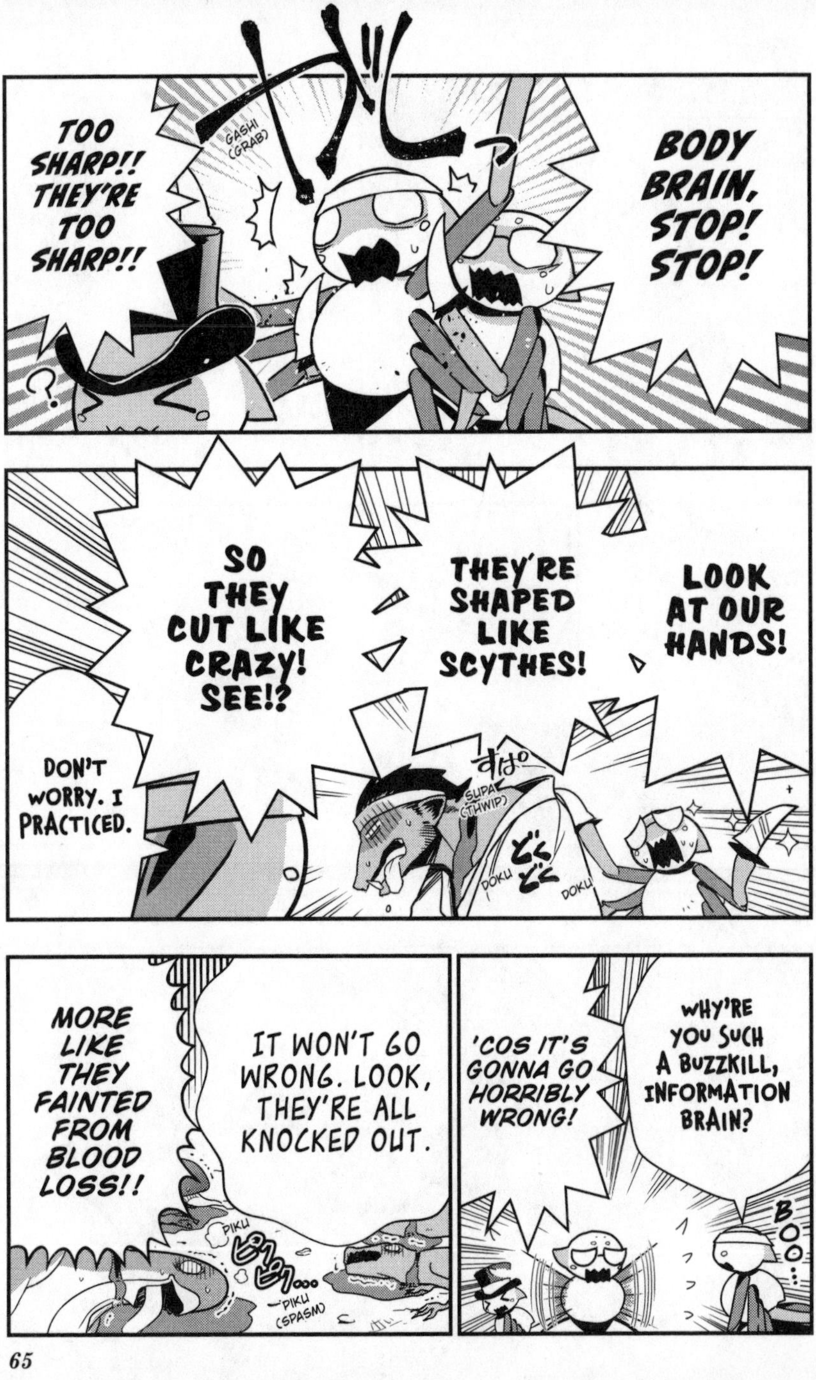
BODY BRAIN, STOP! STOP!
GASHI (GRAB)
TOO SHARP!! THEY'RE TOO SHARP!!
LOOK AT OUR HANDS!
THEY'RE SHAPED LIKE SCYTHES!
SO THEY CUT LIKE CRAZY! SEE!?
すぱ
SUPA (THWIP)
どくどく
DOKU DOKU
DON'T WORRY. I PRACTICED.
WHY'RE YOU SUCH A BUZZKILL, INFORMATION BRAIN?
'COS IT'S GONNA GO HORRIBLY WRONG!
BOO...
IT WON'T GO WRONG. LOOK, THEY'RE ALL KNOCKED OUT.
MORE LIKE THEY FAINTED FROM BLOOD LOSS!!
PIKU
ピクピク
PIKU (SPASM)

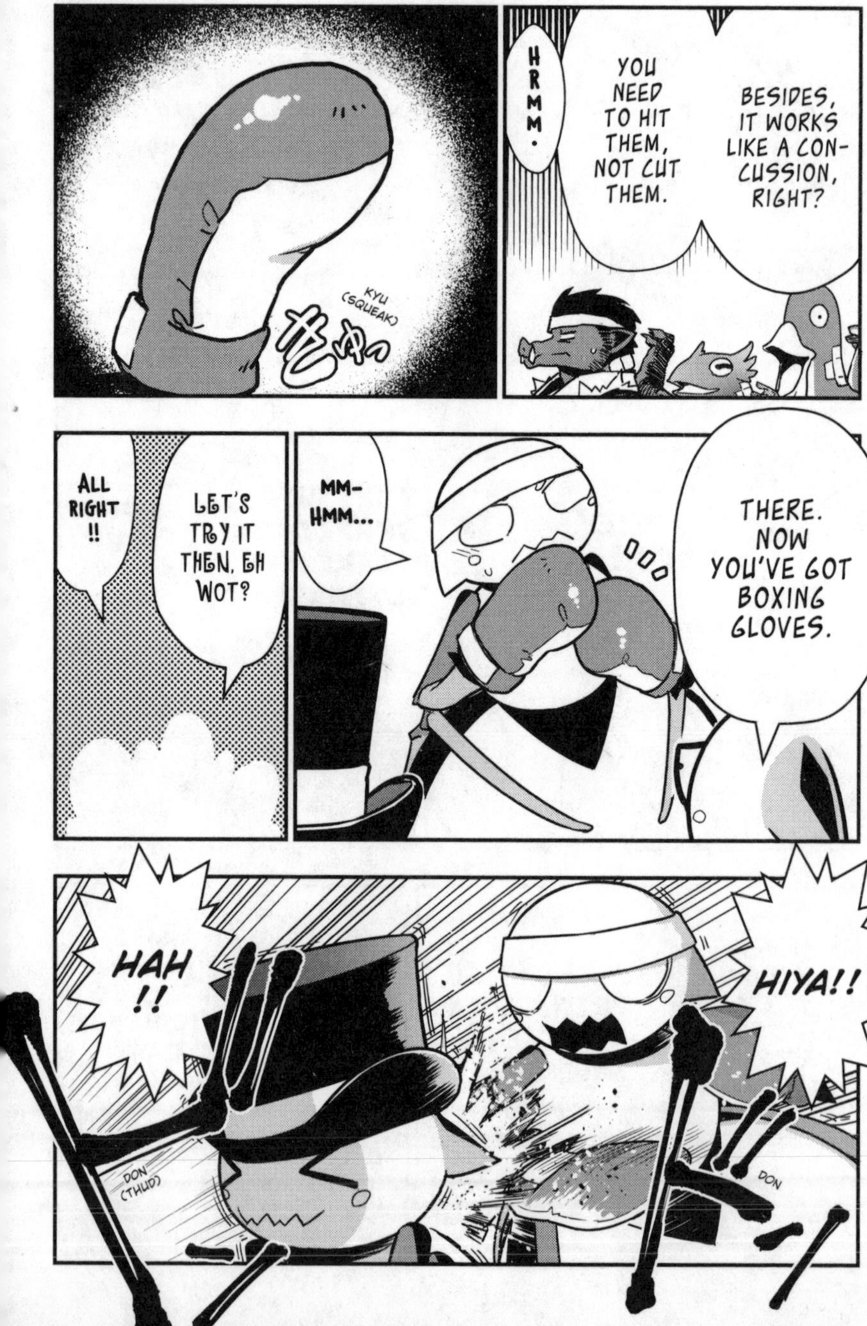
BESIDES, IT WORKS LIKE A CON-CUSSION, RIGHT?
YOU NEED TO HIT THEM, NOT CUT THEM.
HRMM.
KYU (SQUEAK)
THERE. NOW YOU'VE GOT BOXING GLOVES.
MM-HMM...
LET'S TRY IT THEN, EH WOT?
ALL RIGHT!!
HIYA!!
DON
HAH!!
DON (THUD)

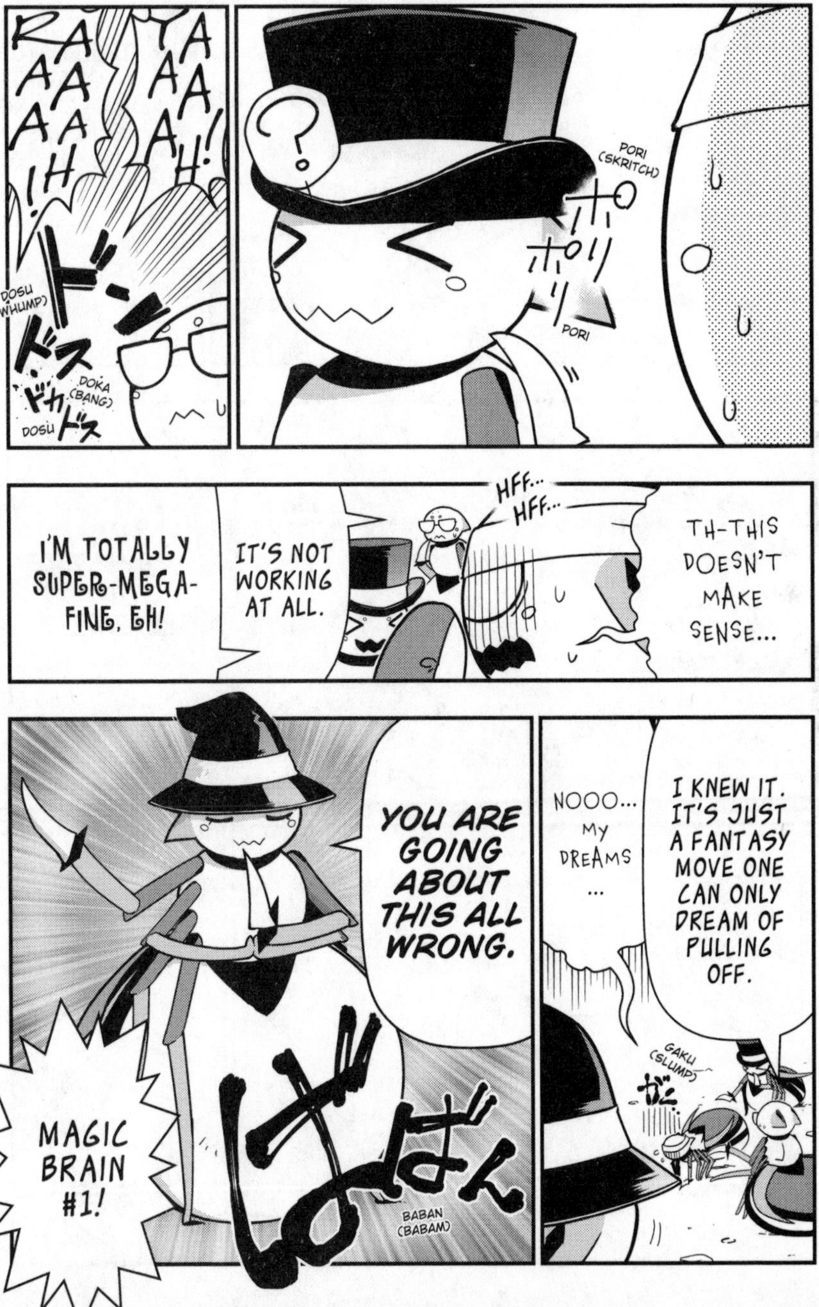
PORI (SKRITCH)
PORI
YAAAAH!
RAAAAH!
DOSU (WHUMP)
DOKA (BANG)
DOSU
TH-THIS DOESN'T MAKE SENSE...
HFF... HFF...
IT'S NOT WORKING AT ALL.
I'M TOTALLY SUPER-MEGA-FINE, EH!
I KNEW IT. IT'S JUST A FANTASY MOVE ONE CAN ONLY DREAM OF PULLING OFF.
NOOO... MY DREAMS ...
GAKU (SLUMP)
YOU ARE GOING ABOUT THIS ALL WRONG.
BABAN (BABAM)
MAGIC BRAIN #1!

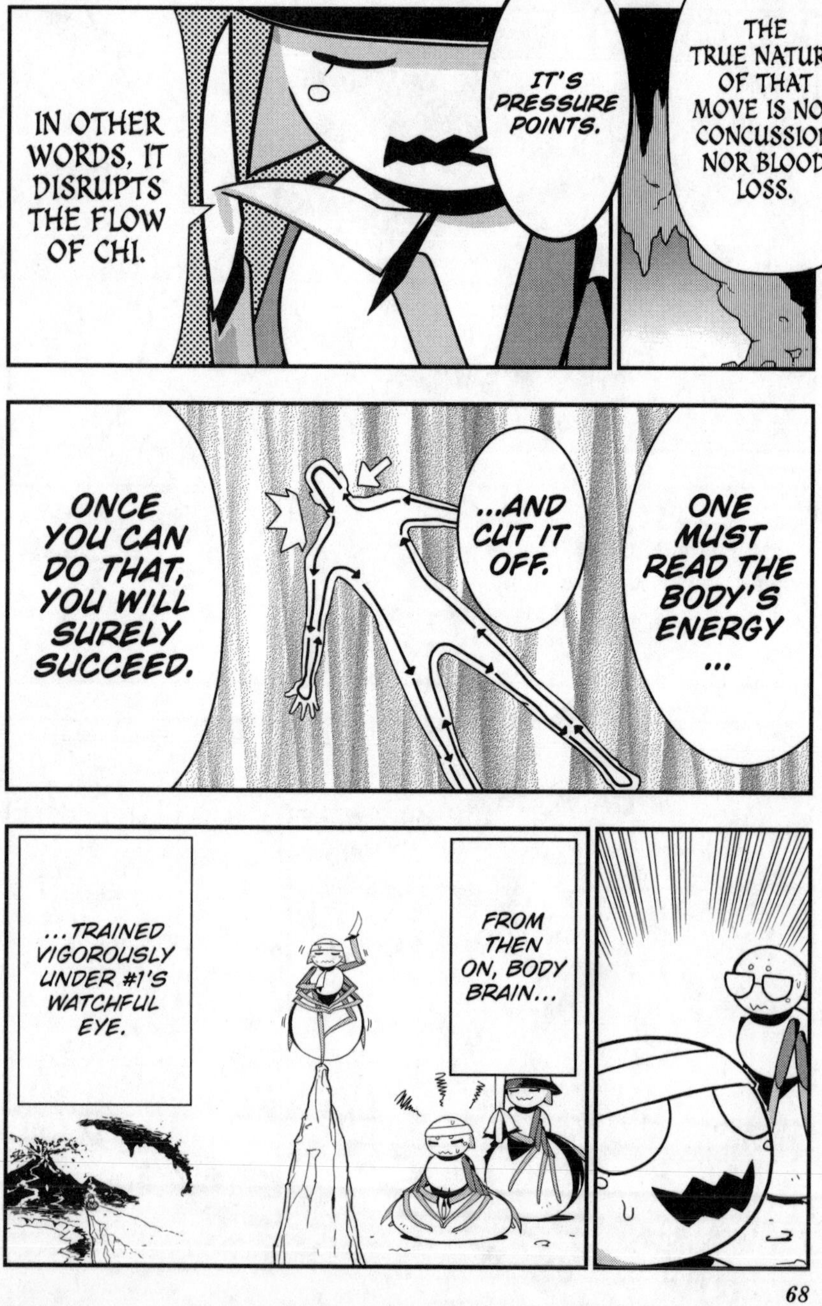
THE TRUE NATURE OF THAT MOVE IS NOT CONCUSSION NOR BLOOD LOSS.
IT'S PRESSURE POINTS.
IN OTHER WORDS, IT DISRUPTS THE FLOW OF CHI.
ONE MUST READ THE BODY'S ENERGY...
...AND CUT IT OFF.
ONCE YOU CAN DO THAT, YOU WILL SURELY SUCCEED.
FROM THEN ON, BODY BRAIN...
...TRAINED VIGOROUSLY UNDER #1'S WATCHFUL EYE.

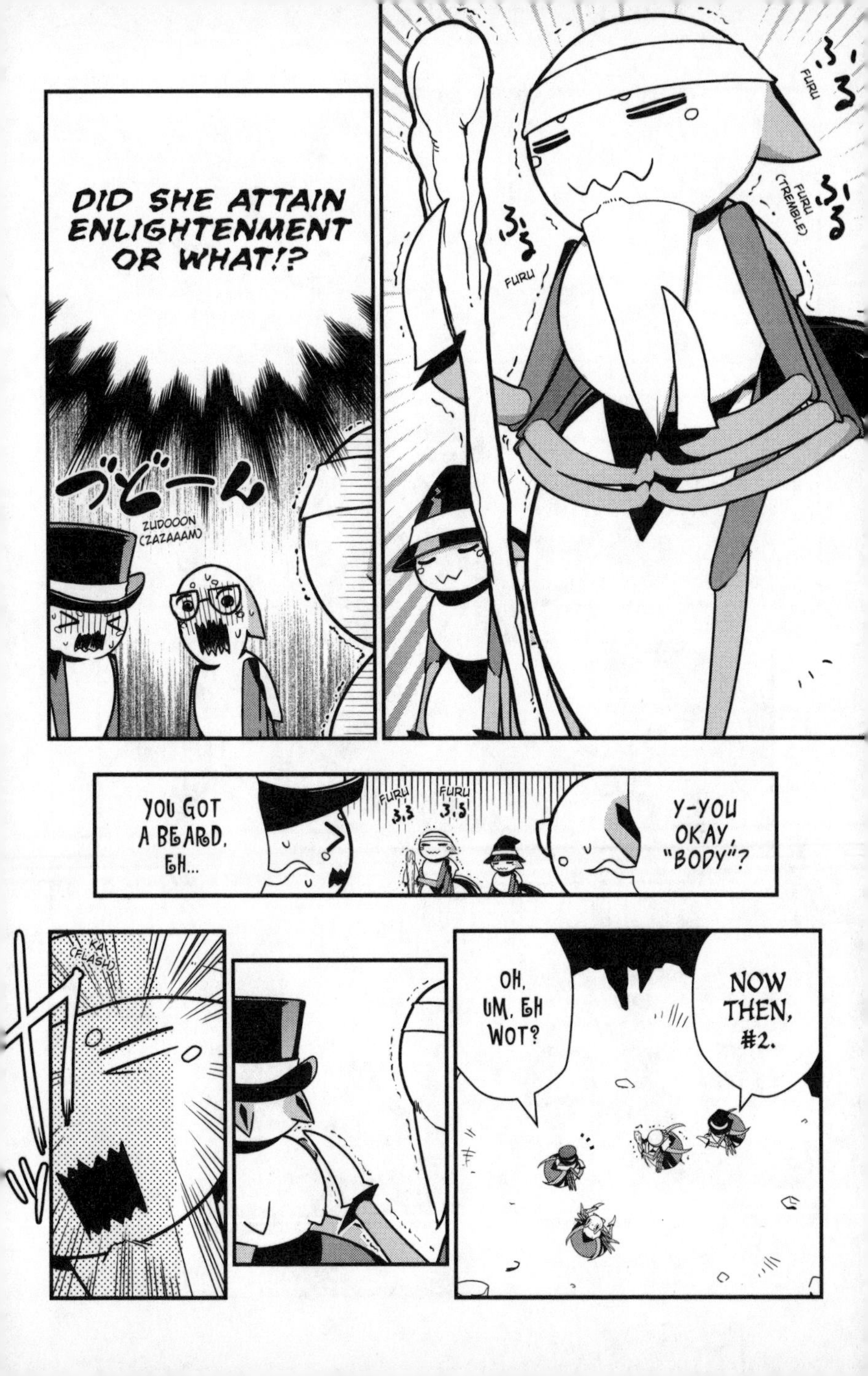
ふる
FURU
ふる
FURU (TREMBLE)
ふる
FURU
DID SHE ATTAIN ENLIGHTENMENT OR WHAT!?
づどーん
ZUDOOON (ZAZAAAM)
Y-YOU OKAY, "BODY"?
FURU
FURU
YOU GOT A BEARD, EH...
NOW THEN, #2.
OH, UM, EH WOT?
カッ
KA (FLASH)

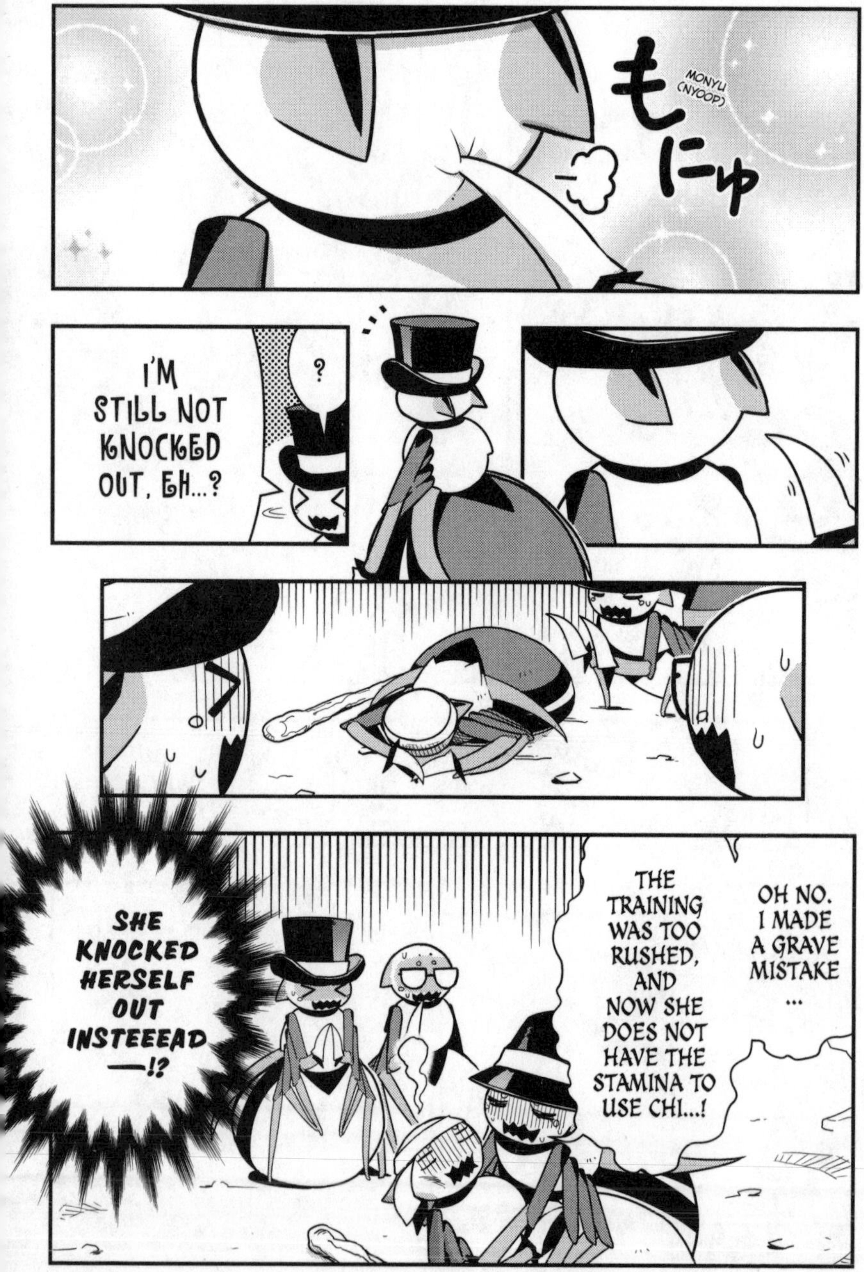
もにゅ
MONYU (NYOOP)
?
I'M STILL NOT KNOCKED OUT, EH...?
OH NO. I MADE A GRAVE MISTAKE...
THE TRAINING WAS TOO RUSHED, AND NOW SHE DOES NOT HAVE THE STAMINA TO USE CHI...!
SHE KNOCKED HERSELF OUT INSTEEEAD—!?

So I'm a Spider, So What?

THE DAILY LIVES OF

THE KUMOKO SISTERS

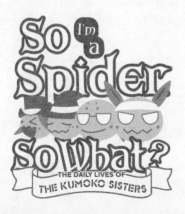

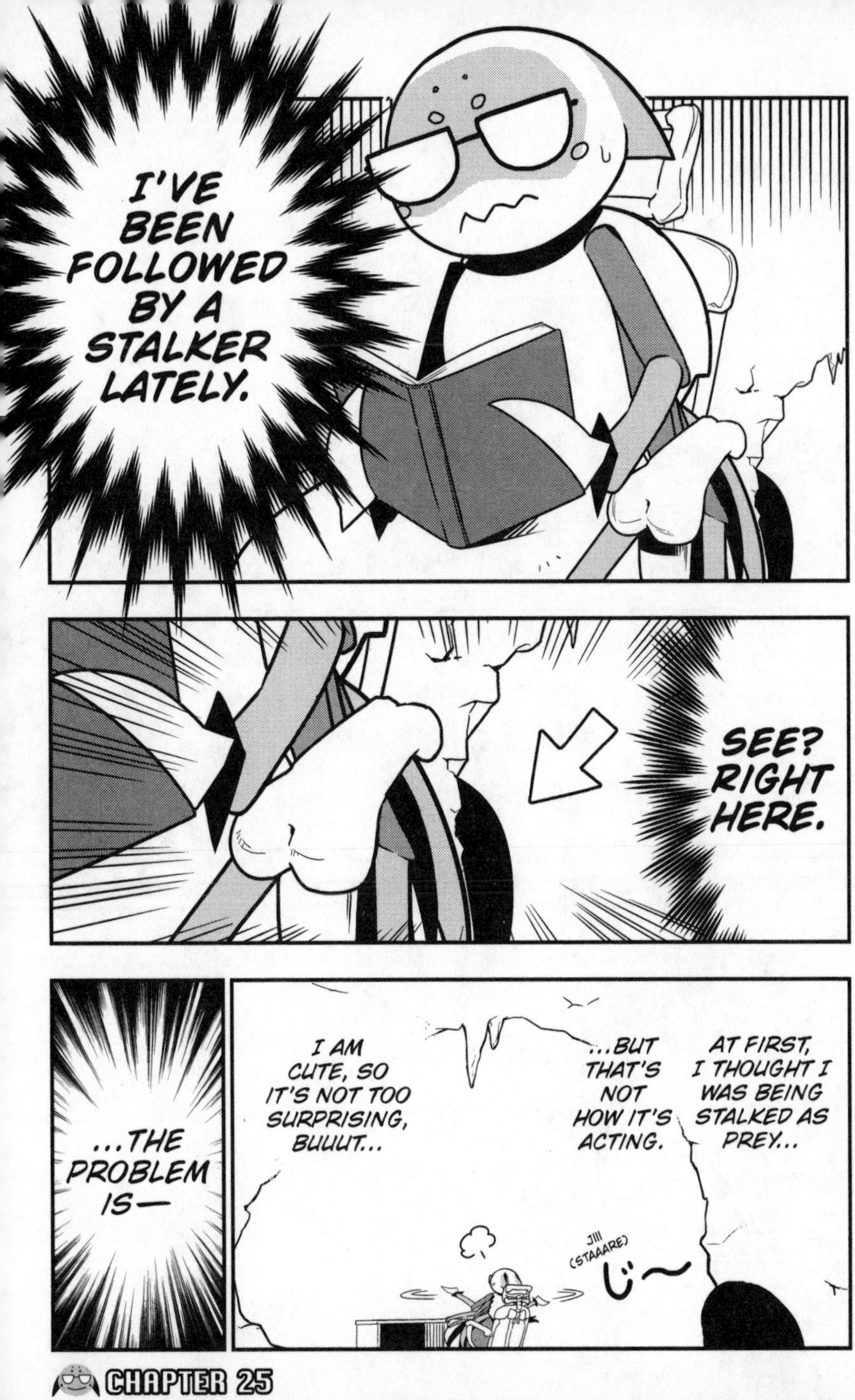
I'VE BEEN FOLLOWED BY A STALKER LATELY.
SEE? RIGHT HERE.
AT FIRST, I THOUGHT I WAS BEING STALKED AS PREY...
...BUT THAT'S NOT HOW IT'S ACTING.
I AM CUTE, SO IT'S NOT TOO SURPRISING, BUUUT...
JIII (STAAARE)
じ～
...THE PROBLEM IS—

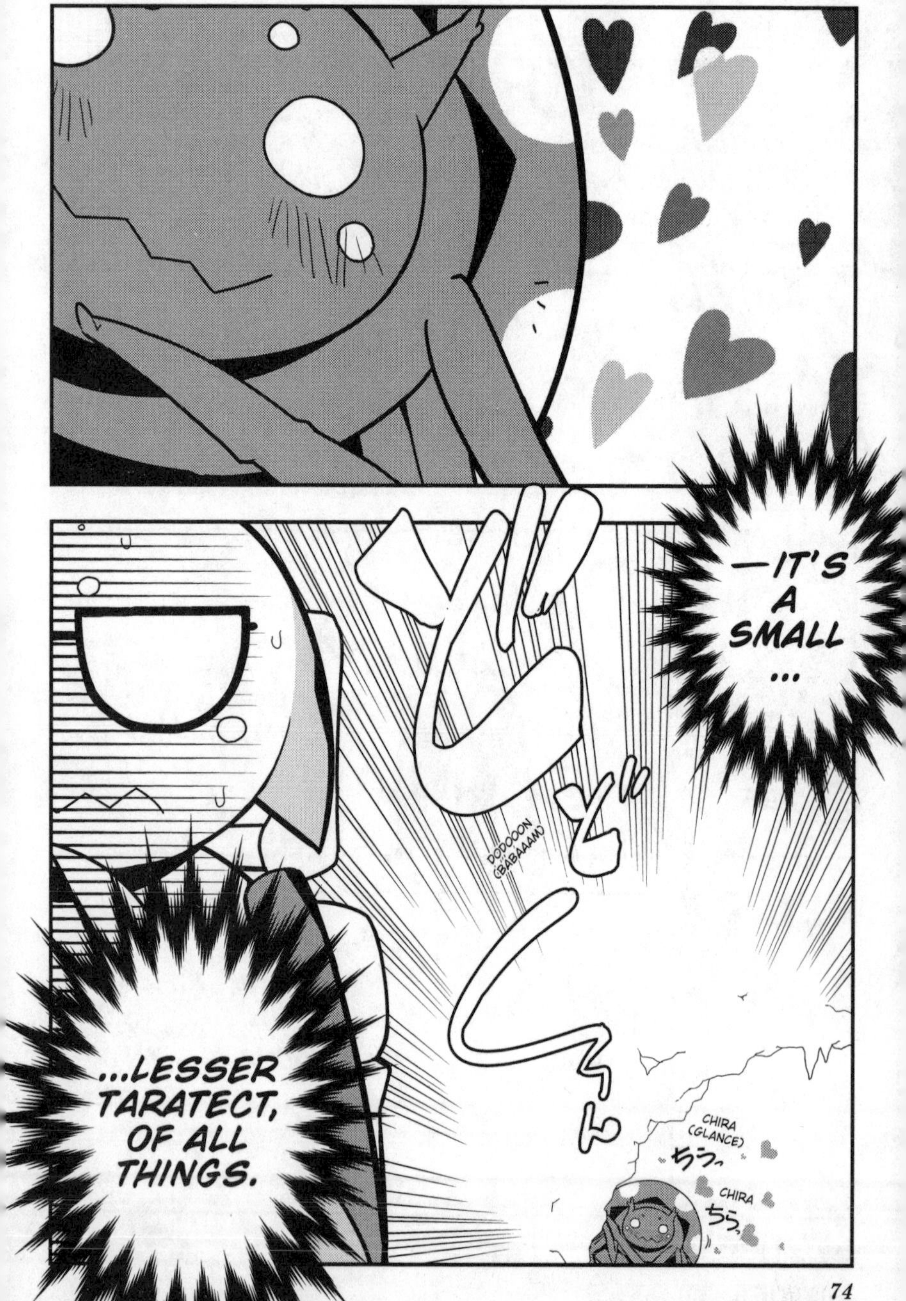
—IT'S A SMALL ...
DODOOON (BABAAAM)
...LESSER TARATECT, OF ALL THINGS.
CHIRA (GLANCE)
ちらっ
CHIRA
ちらっ

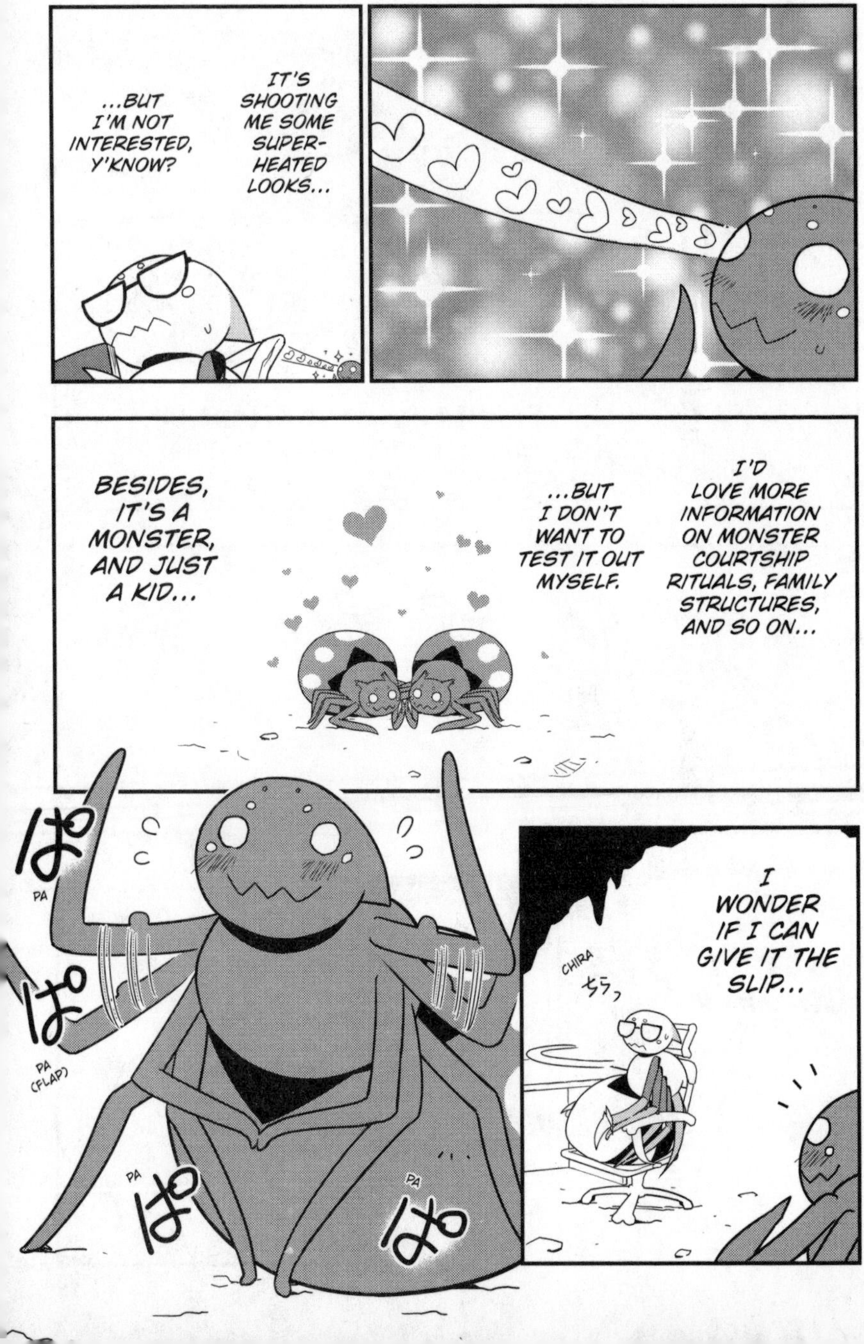
IT'S SHOOTING ME SOME SUPER-HEATED LOOKS...
...BUT I'M NOT INTERESTED, Y'KNOW?
I'D LOVE MORE INFORMATION ON MONSTER COURTSHIP RITUALS, FAMILY STRUCTURES, AND SO ON...
...BUT I DON'T WANT TO TEST IT OUT MYSELF.
BESIDES, IT'S A MONSTER, AND JUST A KID...
I WONDER IF I CAN GIVE IT THE SLIP...
ちらっ
CHIRA
ぱ
PA
ぱ
PA (FLAP)
ぱ
PA
ぱ
PA

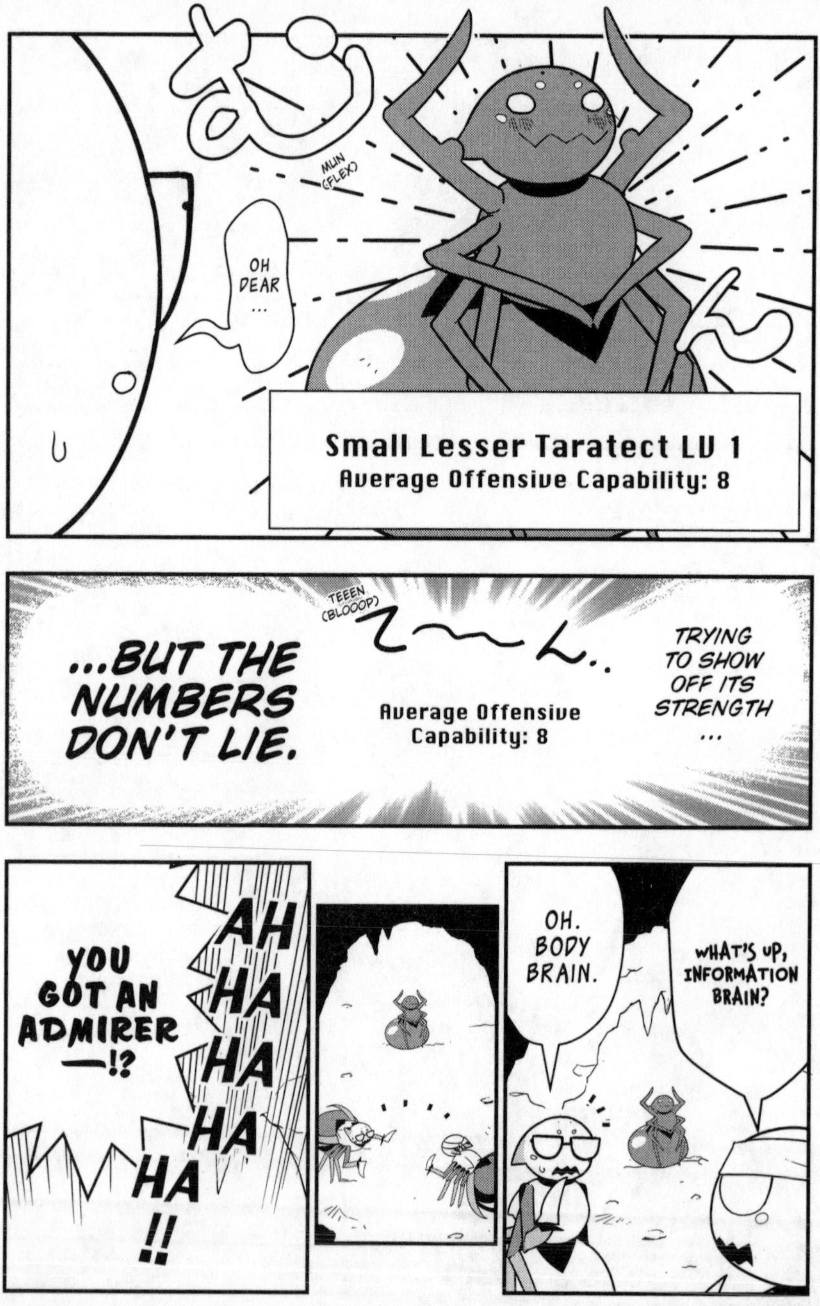
MUN (FLEX)
OH DEAR ...
Small Lesser Taratect LV 1
Average Offensive Capability: 8
TRYING TO SHOW OFF ITS STRENGTH ...
TEEEN (BLOOOP)
Average Offensive Capability: 8
...BUT THE NUMBERS DON'T LIE.
WHAT'S UP, INFORMATION BRAIN?
OH. BODY BRAIN.
AH HA HA HA HA HA !!
YOU GOT AN ADMIRER—!?

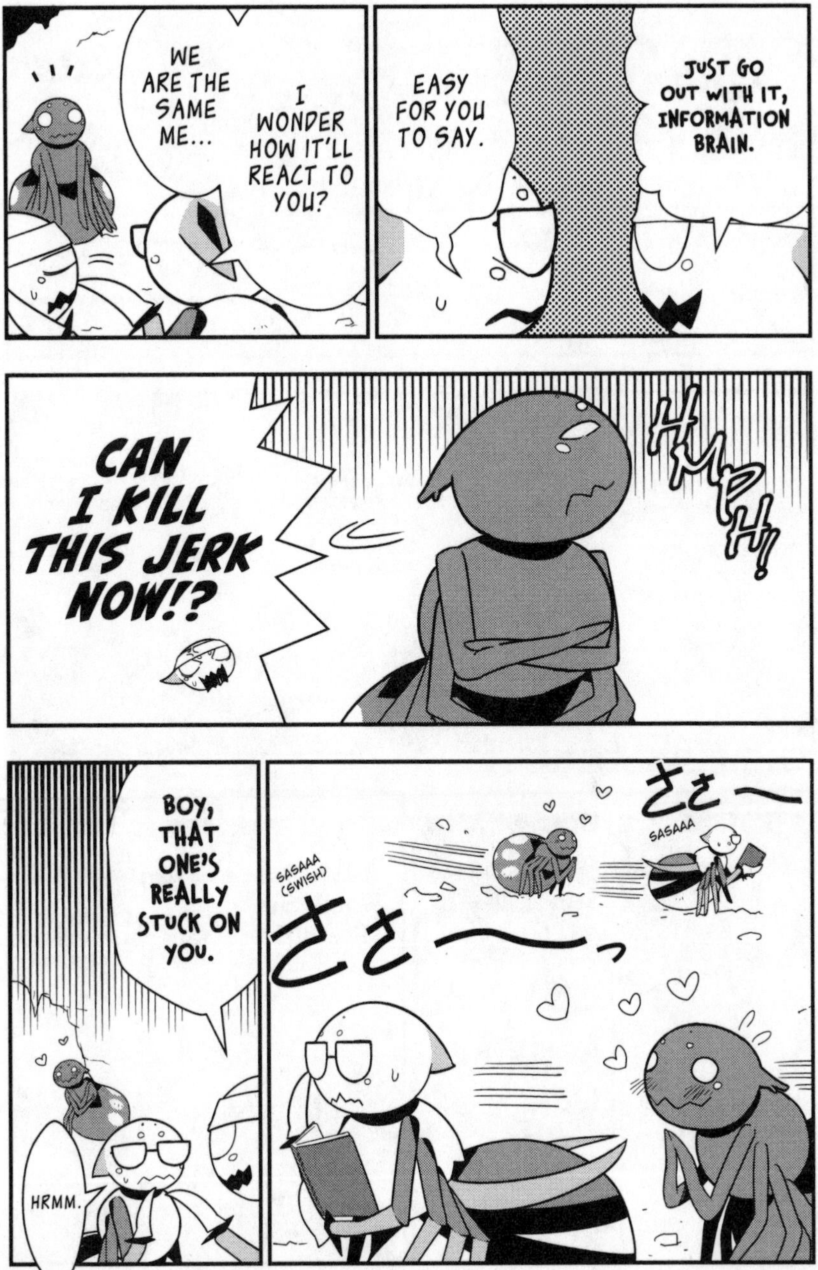
JUST GO OUT WITH IT, INFORMATION BRAIN.
EASY FOR YOU TO SAY.
WE ARE THE SAME ME...
I WONDER HOW IT'LL REACT TO YOU?
HMPH!
CAN I KILL THIS JERK NOW!?
さ さー
SASAAA
SASAAA (SWISH)
さ さーーっ
BOY, THAT ONE'S REALLY STUCK ON YOU.
HRMM.

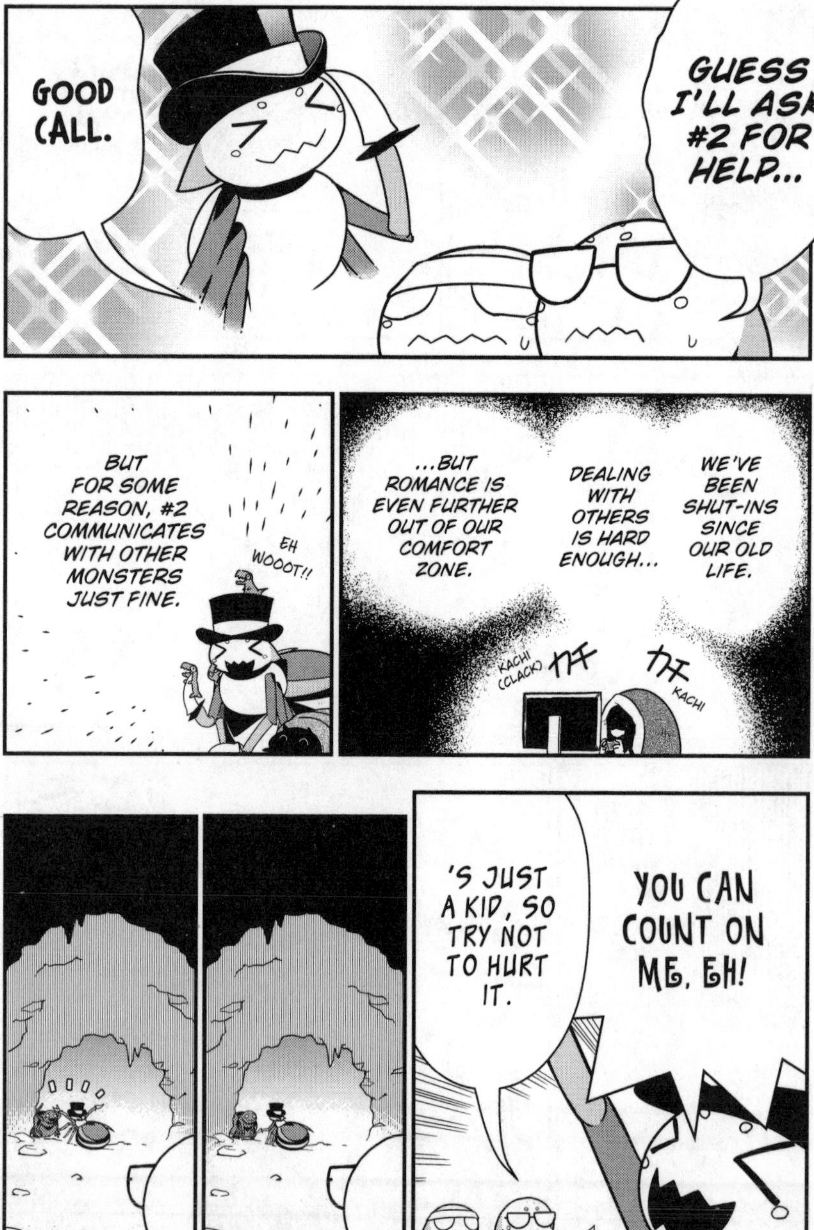
GUESS I'LL ASK #2 FOR HELP...
GOOD CALL.
WE'VE BEEN SHUT-INS SINCE OUR OLD LIFE.
DEALING WITH OTHERS IS HARD ENOUGH...
...BUT ROMANCE IS EVEN FURTHER OUT OF OUR COMFORT ZONE.
カチ
KACHI
カチ
KACHI (CLACK)
BUT FOR SOME REASON, #2 COMMUNICATES WITH OTHER MONSTERS JUST FINE.
EH WOOOT!!
YOU CAN COUNT ON ME, EH!
'S JUST A KID, SO TRY NOT TO HURT IT.

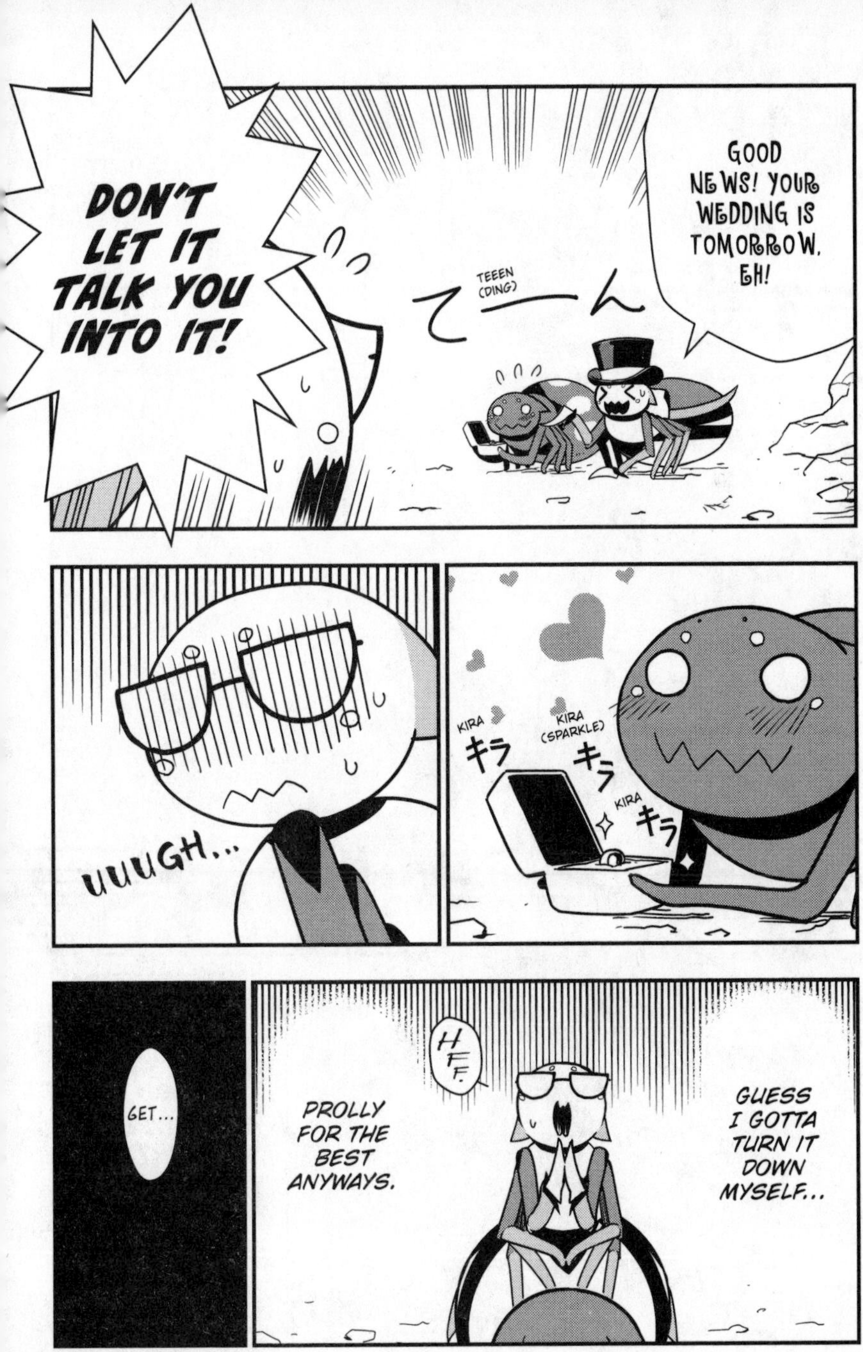
GOOD NEWS! YOUR WEDDING IS TOMORROW, EH!
TEEEN (DING)
てーん
DON'T LET IT TALK YOU INTO IT!
KIRA (SPARKLE)
キラ
KIRA
キラ
KIRA
キラ
UUUGH...
GUESS I GOTTA TURN IT DOWN MYSELF...
HFF.
PROLLY FOR THE BEST ANYWAYS.
GET...

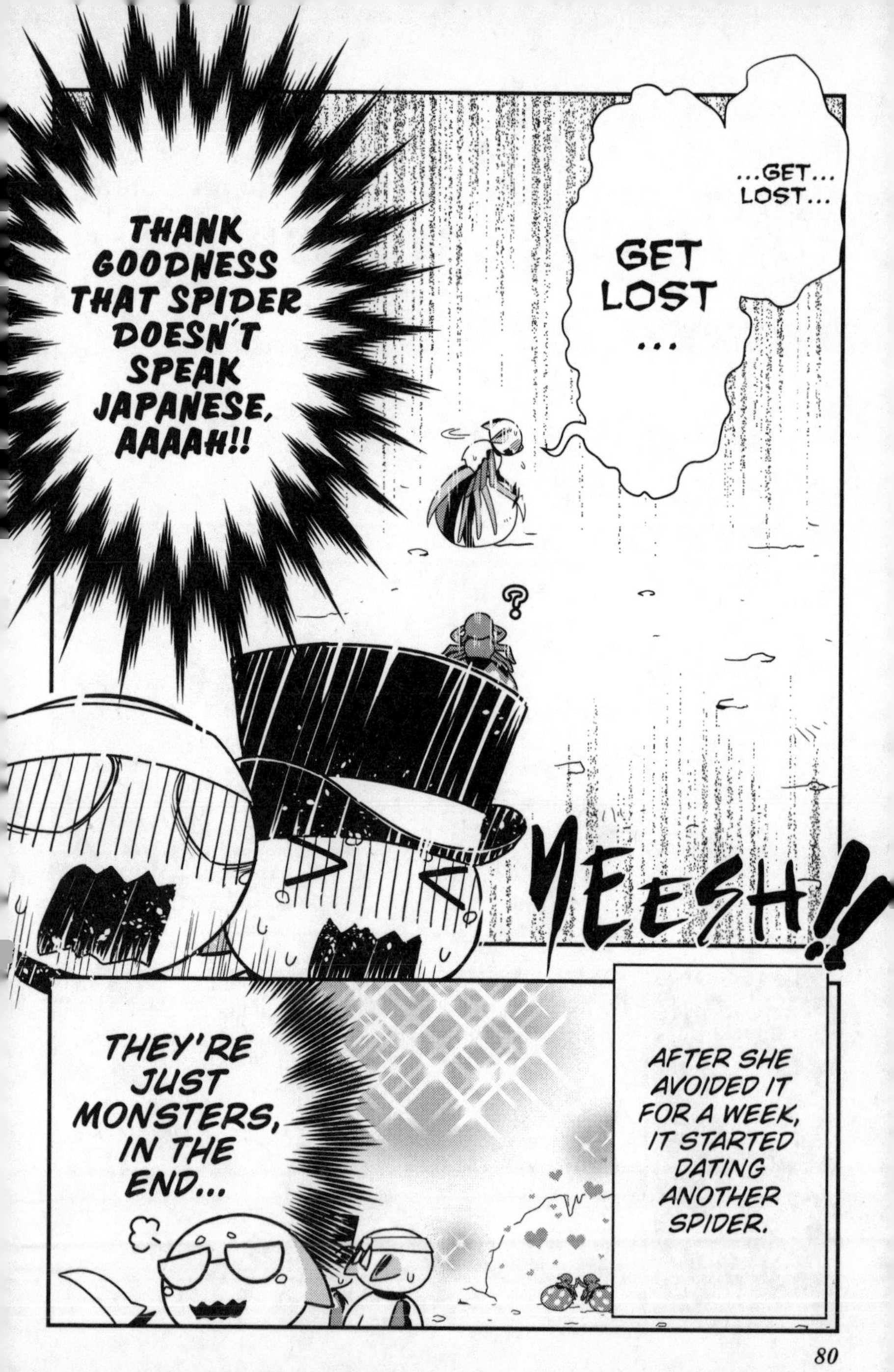
...GET... LOST...
GET LOST ...
THANK GOODNESS THAT SPIDER DOESN'T SPEAK JAPANESE, AAAAH!!
YEESH!!
AFTER SHE AVOIDED IT FOR A WEEK, IT STARTED DATING ANOTHER SPIDER.
THEY'RE JUST MONSTERS, IN THE END...

So I'm a Spider, so What?
THE DAILY LIVES OF
THE KUMOKO SISTERS

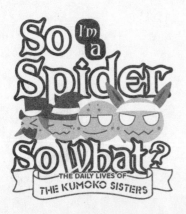

CHAPTER 26

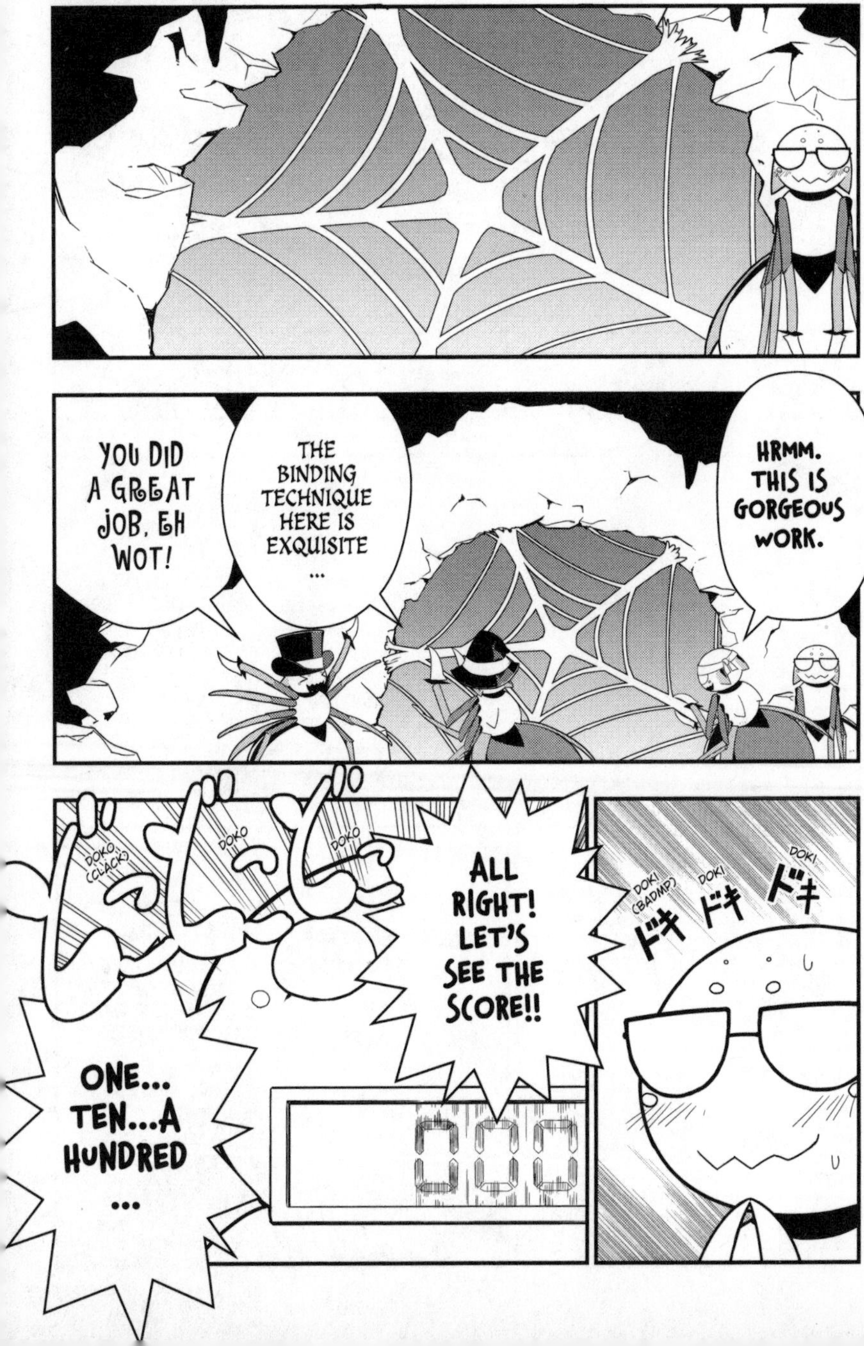

HRMM. THIS IS GORGEOUS WORK.
THE BINDING TECHNIQUE HERE IS EXQUISITE ...
YOU DID A GREAT JOB, EH WOT!
DOKI (BADMP) DOKI DOKI
ドキ ドキ ドキ
ALL RIGHT! LET'S SEE THE SCORE!!
DOKO (CLACK) DOKO DOKO
000
ONE... TEN...A HUNDRED ...

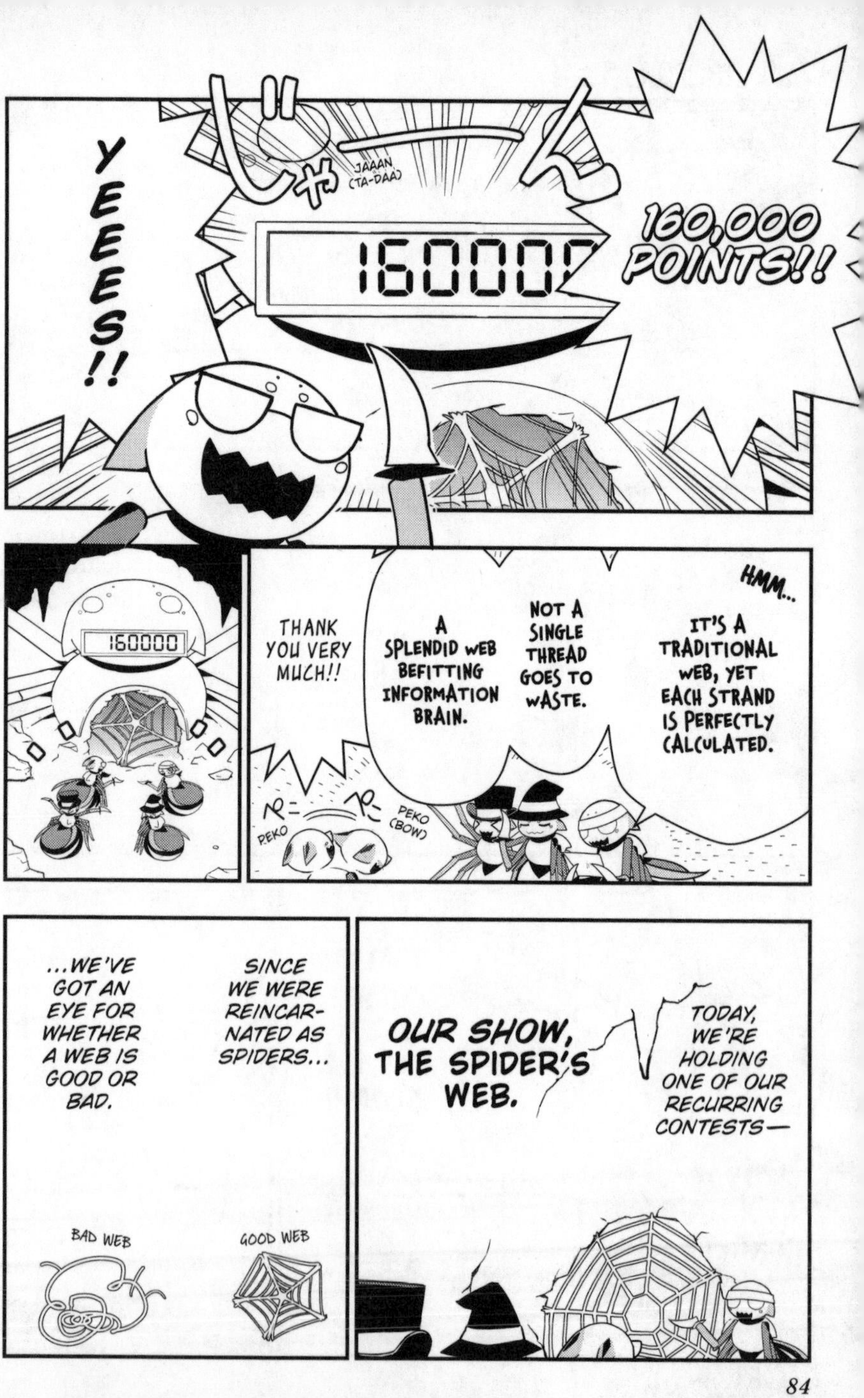
160,000 POINTS!!
じゃーん
JAAAN (TA-DAA)
YEEES!!
HMM...
IT'S A TRADITIONAL WEB, YET EACH STRAND IS PERFECTLY CALCULATED.
NOT A SINGLE THREAD GOES TO WASTE.
A SPLENDID WEB BEFITTING INFORMATION BRAIN.
THANK YOU VERY MUCH!!
ぺこ
PEKO (BOW)
ぺこ
PEKO
160000
TODAY, WE'RE HOLDING ONE OF OUR RECURRING CONTESTS—
OUR SHOW, THE SPIDER'S WEB.
SINCE WE WERE REINCARNATED AS SPIDERS...
...WE'VE GOT AN EYE FOR WHETHER A WEB IS GOOD OR BAD.
GOOD WEB
BAD WEB

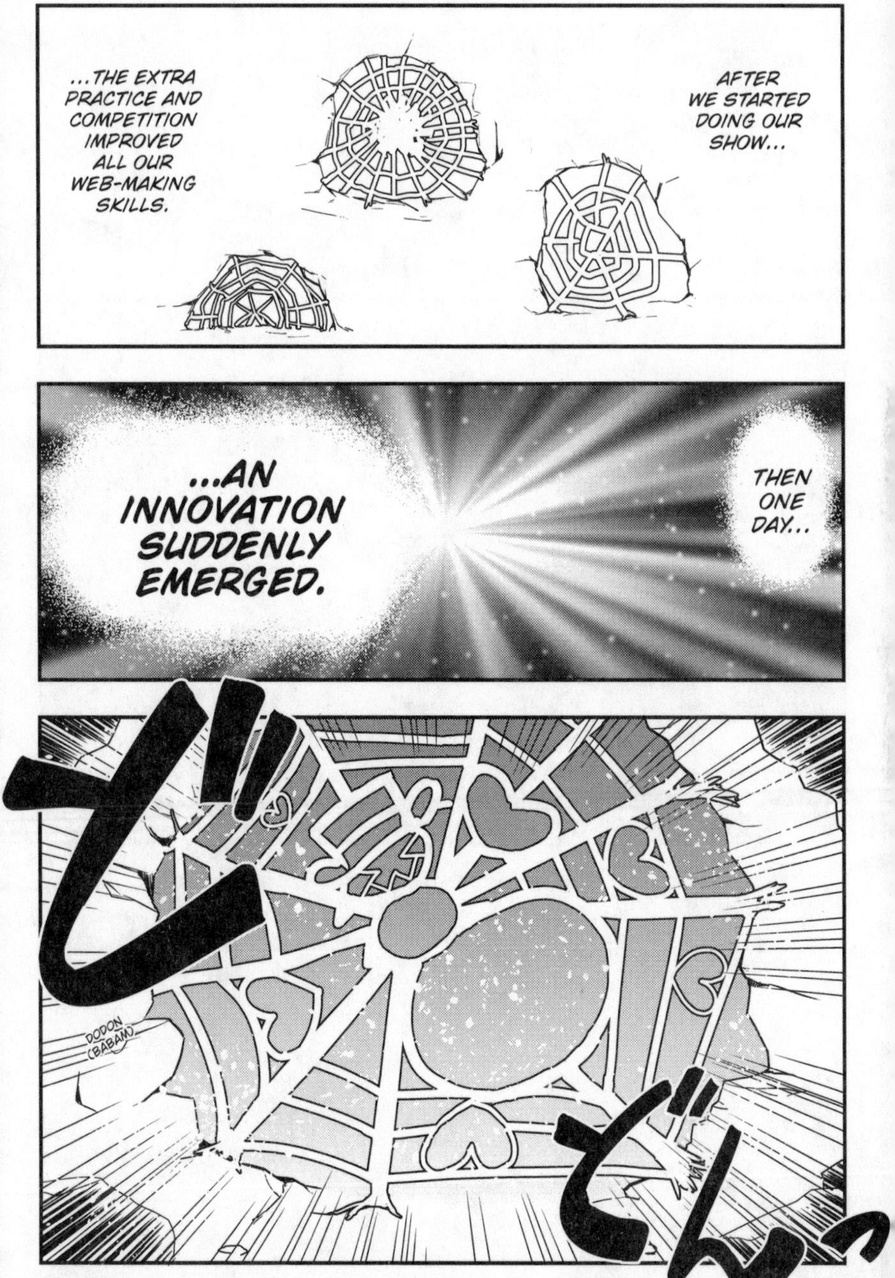
AFTER WE STARTED DOING OUR SHOW...
...THE EXTRA PRACTICE AND COMPETITION IMPROVED ALL OUR WEB-MAKING SKILLS.
THEN ONE DAY...
...AN INNOVATION SUDDENLY EMERGED.
ど
DODON (BABAM)
どん

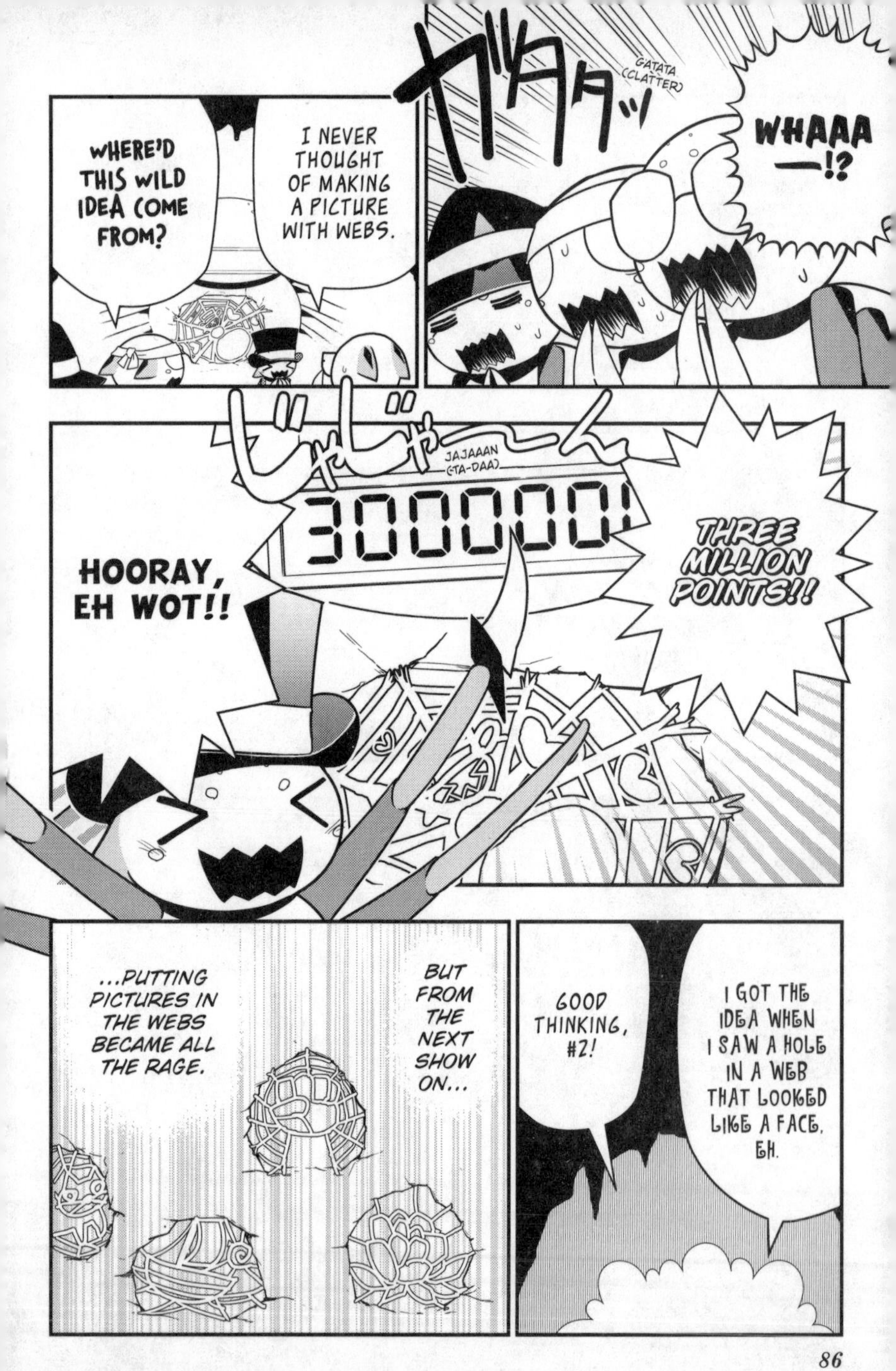
ガタタッ
GATATA (CLATTER)
WHAAA—!?
I NEVER THOUGHT OF MAKING A PICTURE WITH WEBS.
WHERE'D THIS WILD IDEA COME FROM?
じゃじゃーん
JAJAAAN (TA-DAA)
300000!
THREE MILLION POINTS!!
HOORAY, EH WOT!!
I GOT THE IDEA WHEN I SAW A HOLE IN A WEB THAT LOOKED LIKE A FACE, EH.
GOOD THINKING, #2!
BUT FROM THE NEXT SHOW ON...
...PUTTING PICTURES IN THE WEBS BECAME ALL THE RAGE.

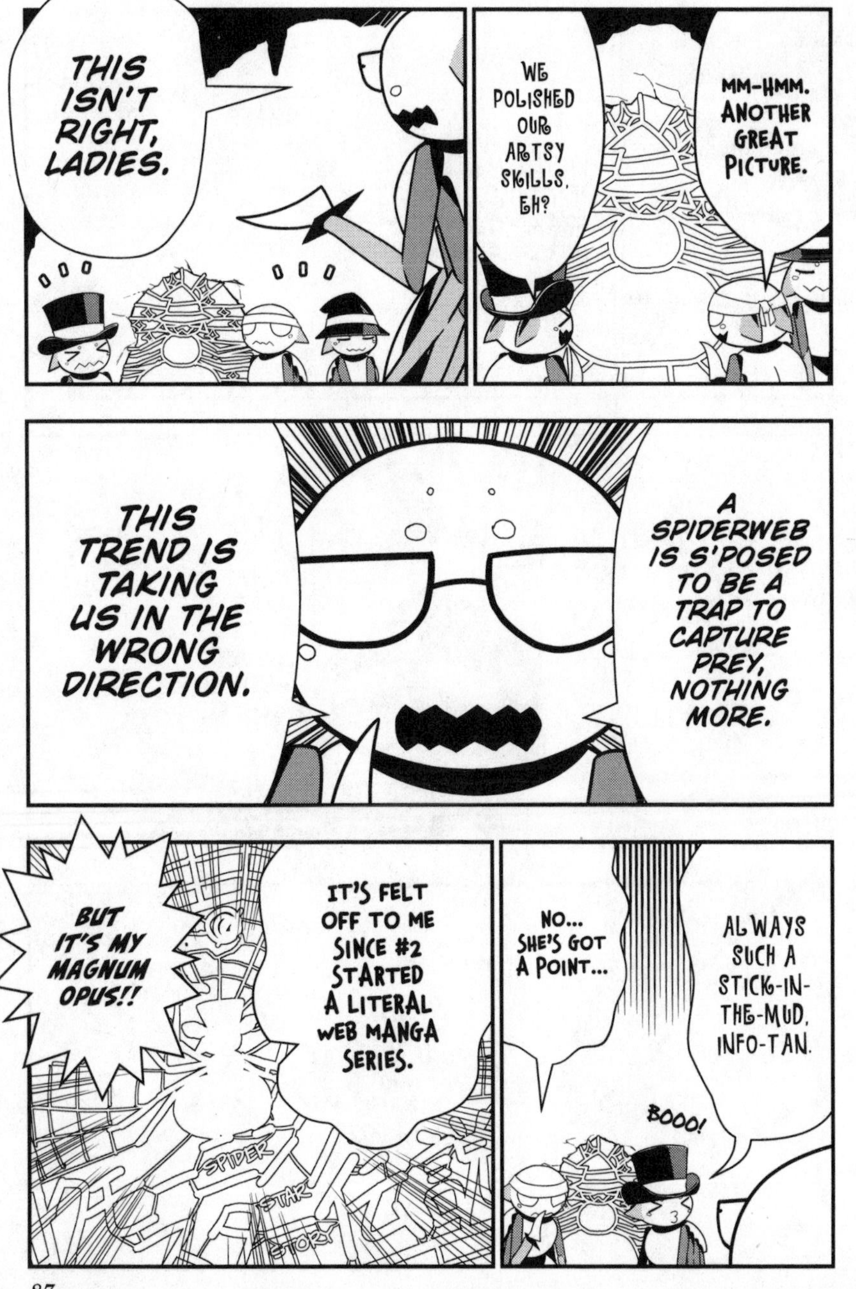
MM-HMM. ANOTHER GREAT PICTURE.
WE POLISHED OUR ARTSY SKILLS, EH?
THIS ISN'T RIGHT, LADIES.
A SPIDERWEB IS S'POSED TO BE A TRAP TO CAPTURE PREY, NOTHING MORE.
THIS TREND IS TAKING US IN THE WRONG DIRECTION.
ALWAYS SUCH A STICK-IN-THE-MUD, INFO-TAN.
NO... SHE'S GOT A POINT...
BOOO!
IT'S FELT OFF TO ME SINCE #2 STARTED A LITERAL WEB MANGA SERIES.
BUT IT'S MY MAGNUM OPUS!!
SPIDER
STAR
STORY

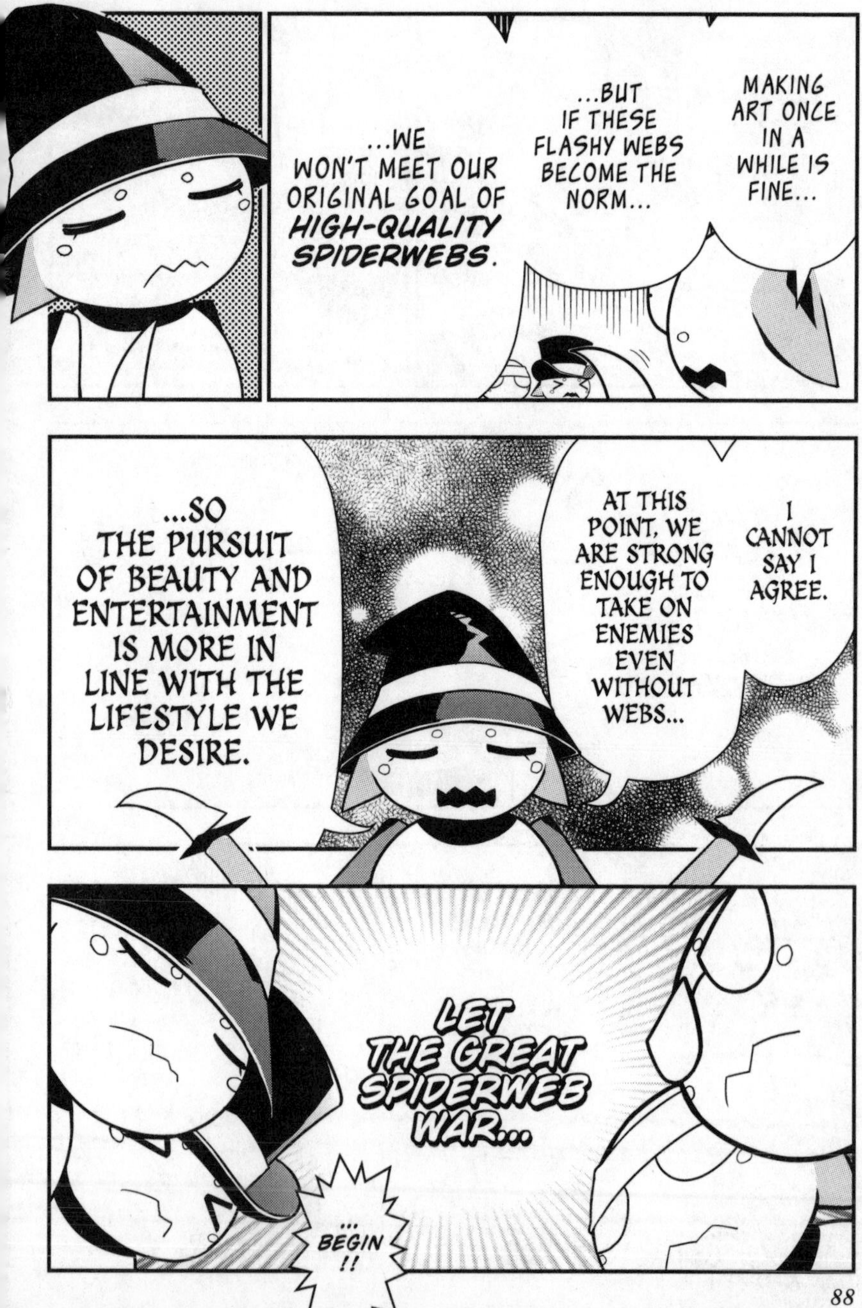
MAKING ART ONCE IN A WHILE IS FINE...
...BUT IF THESE FLASHY WEBS BECOME THE NORM...
...WE WON'T MEET OUR ORIGINAL GOAL OF HIGH-QUALITY SPIDERWEBS.
I CANNOT SAY I AGREE.
AT THIS POINT, WE ARE STRONG ENOUGH TO TAKE ON ENEMIES EVEN WITHOUT WEBS...
...SO THE PURSUIT OF BEAUTY AND ENTERTAINMENT IS MORE IN LINE WITH THE LIFESTYLE WE DESIRE.
LET THE GREAT SPIDERWEB WAR...
...BEGIN!!

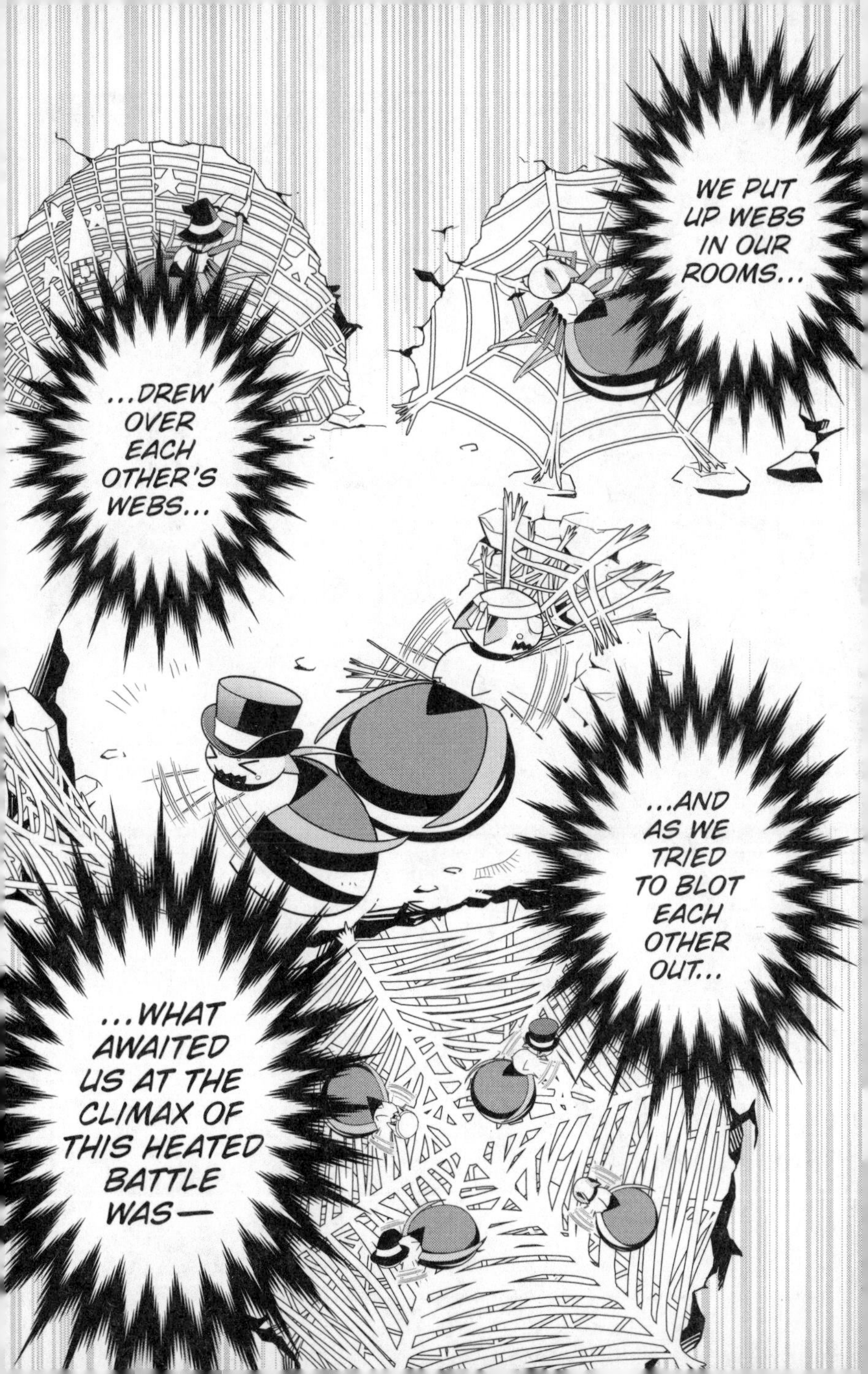
WE PUT UP WEBS IN OUR ROOMS...
...DREW OVER EACH OTHER'S WEBS...
...AND AS WE TRIED TO BLOT EACH OTHER OUT...
...WHAT AWAITED US AT THE CLIMAX OF THIS HEATED BATTLE WAS—

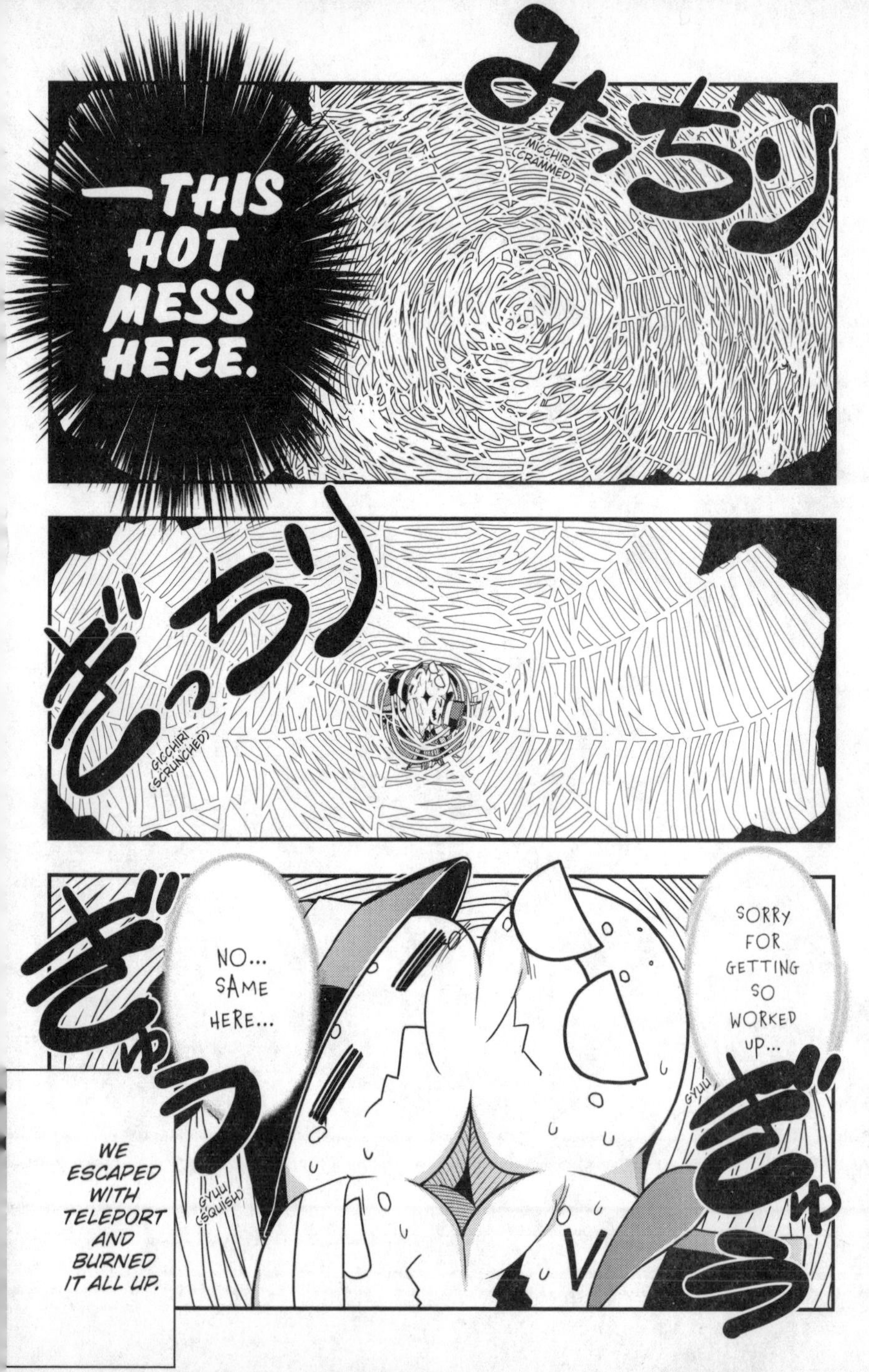
みっちり
MICCHIRI (CRAMMED)
—THIS HOT MESS HERE.
ぎっちり
GICCHIRI (SCRUNCHED)
SORRY FOR GETTING SO WORKED UP...
ぎゅう
GYUU
NO... SAME HERE...
ぎゅう
GYUU (SQUISH)
WE ESCAPED WITH TELEPORT AND BURNED IT ALL UP.

So I'm a Spider, so What?

THE DAILY LIVES OF THE KUMOKO SISTERS

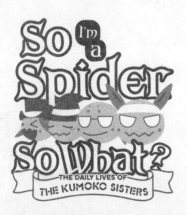

CHAPTER 27

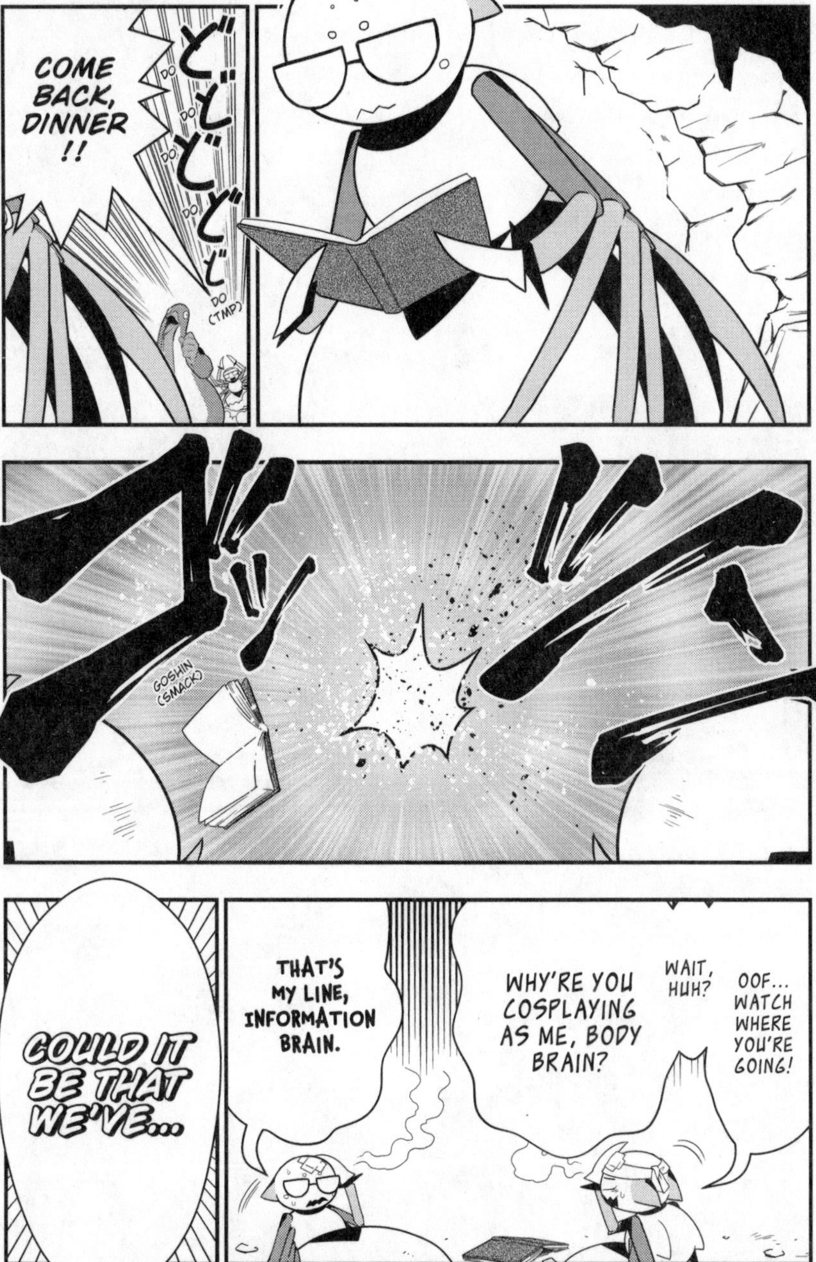
COME BACK, DINNER!!
どどどどど
DO DO DO DO DO (TMP)
GOSHIN (SMACK)
OOF... WATCH WHERE YOU'RE GOING!
WAIT, HUH?
WHY'RE YOU COSPLAYING AS ME, BODY BRAIN?
THAT'S MY LINE, INFORMATION BRAIN.
COULD IT BE THAT WE'VE...

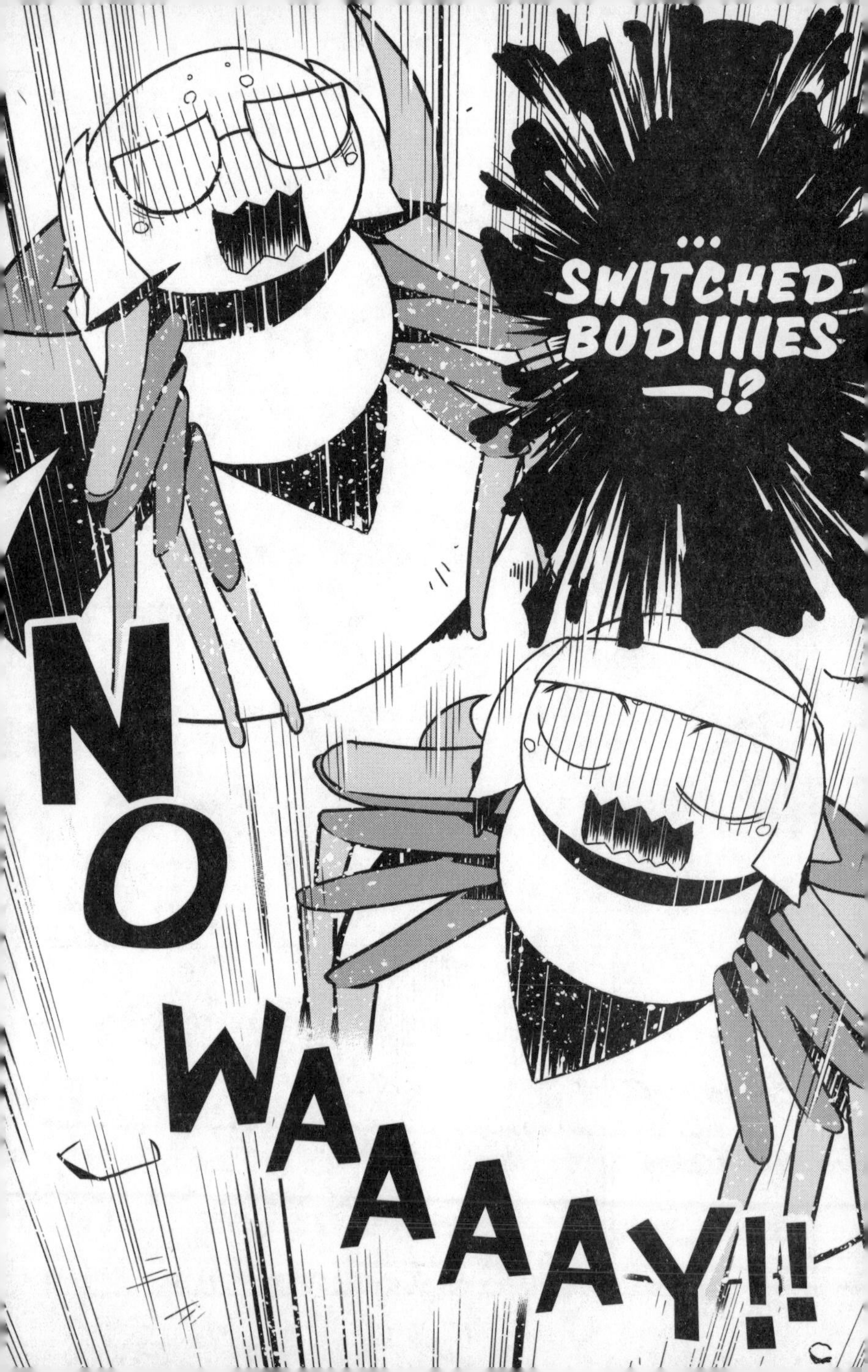
...SWITCHED BODIIIIES—!?
NO WAAAAAY!!

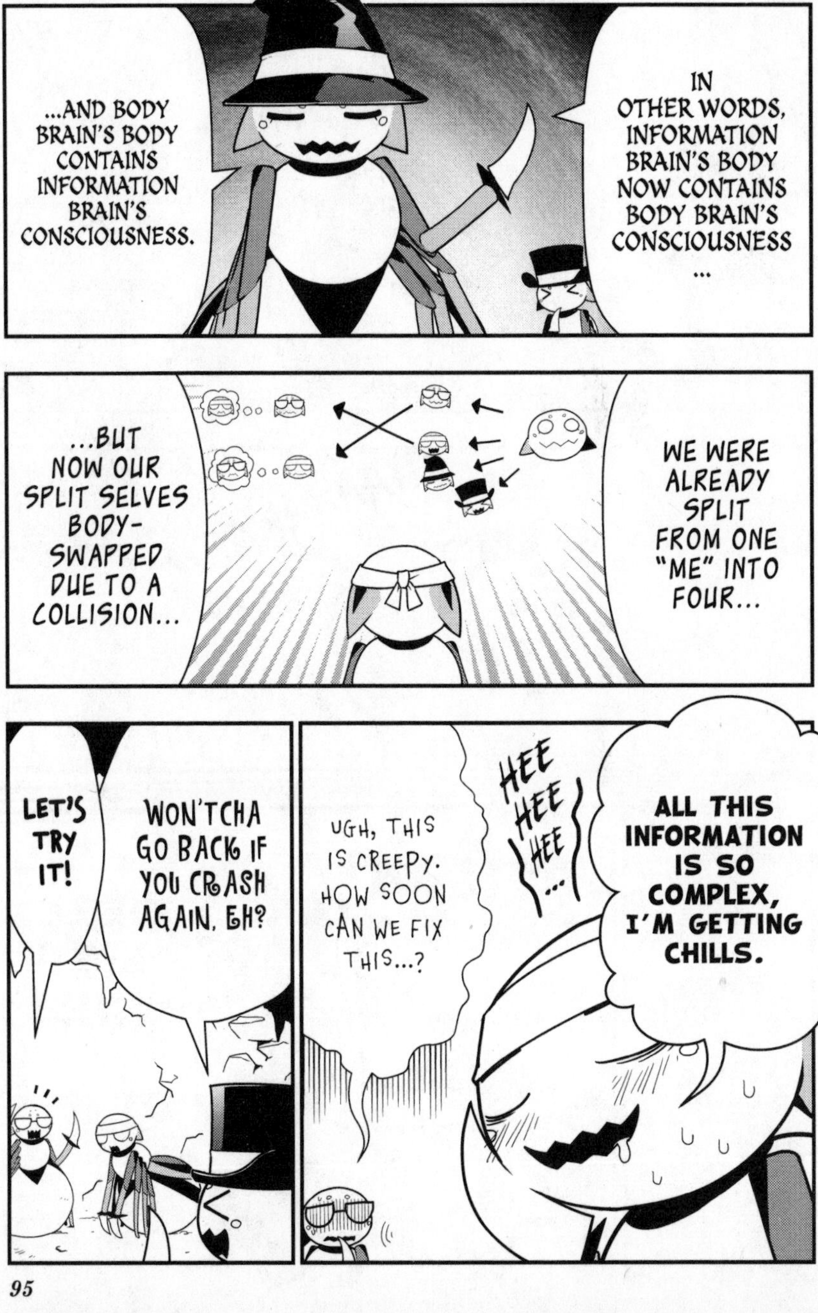
IN OTHER WORDS, INFORMATION BRAIN'S BODY NOW CONTAINS BODY BRAIN'S CONSCIOUSNESS ...
...AND BODY BRAIN'S BODY CONTAINS INFORMATION BRAIN'S CONSCIOUSNESS.
WE WERE ALREADY SPLIT FROM ONE "ME" INTO FOUR...
...BUT NOW OUR SPLIT SELVES BODY-SWAPPED DUE TO A COLLISION...
ALL THIS INFORMATION IS SO COMPLEX, I'M GETTING CHILLS.
HEE HEE HEE...
UGH, THIS IS CREEPY. HOW SOON CAN WE FIX THIS...?
WON'TCHA GO BACK IF YOU CRASH AGAIN, EH?
LET'S TRY IT!

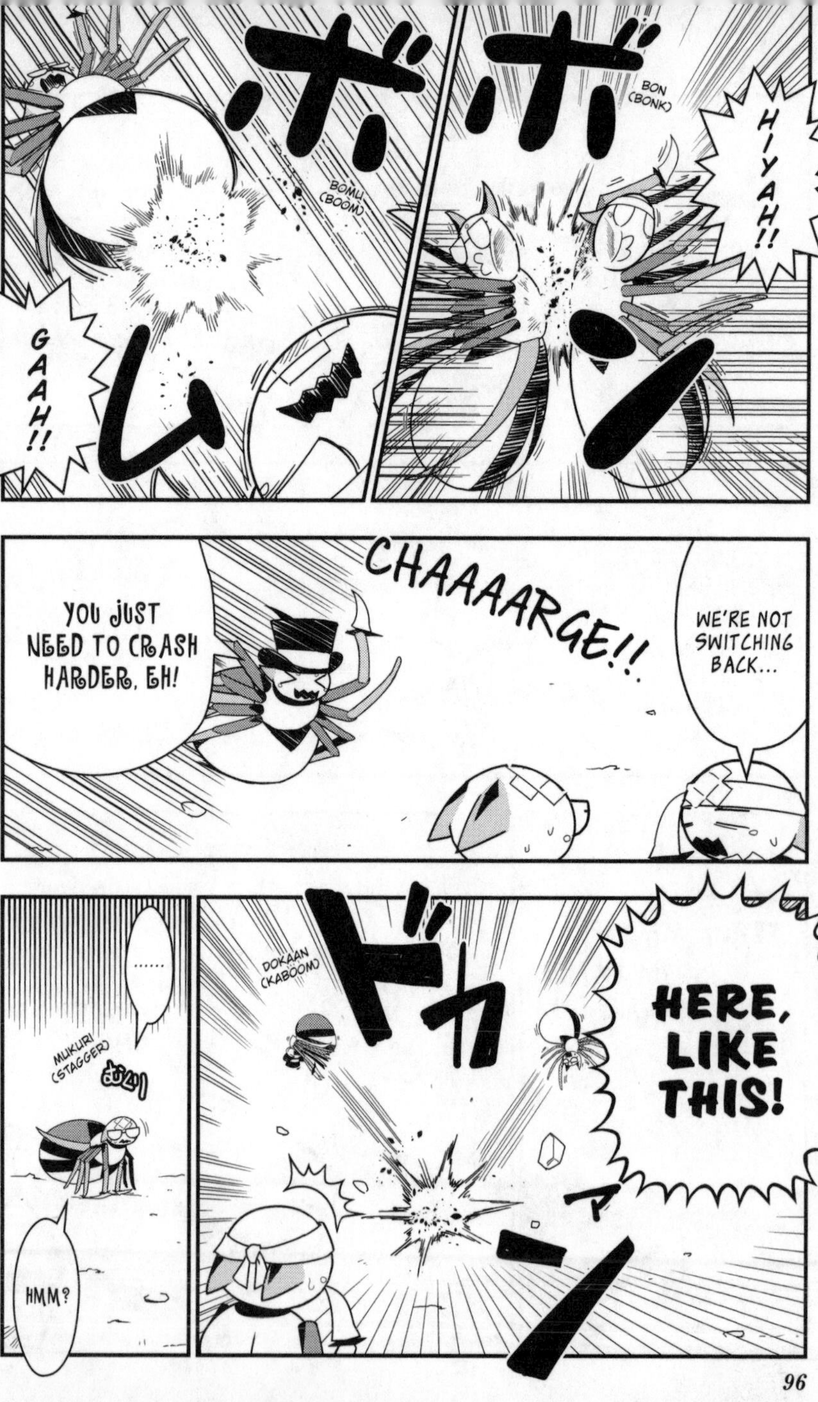
BON (BONK)
HIYAH!!
BOMU (BOOM)
GAAH!!
WE'RE NOT SWITCHING BACK...
CHAAAARGE!!
YOU JUST NEED TO CRASH HARDER, EH!
HERE, LIKE THIS!
DOKAAN (KABOOM)
......
MUKURI (STAGGER)
HMM?

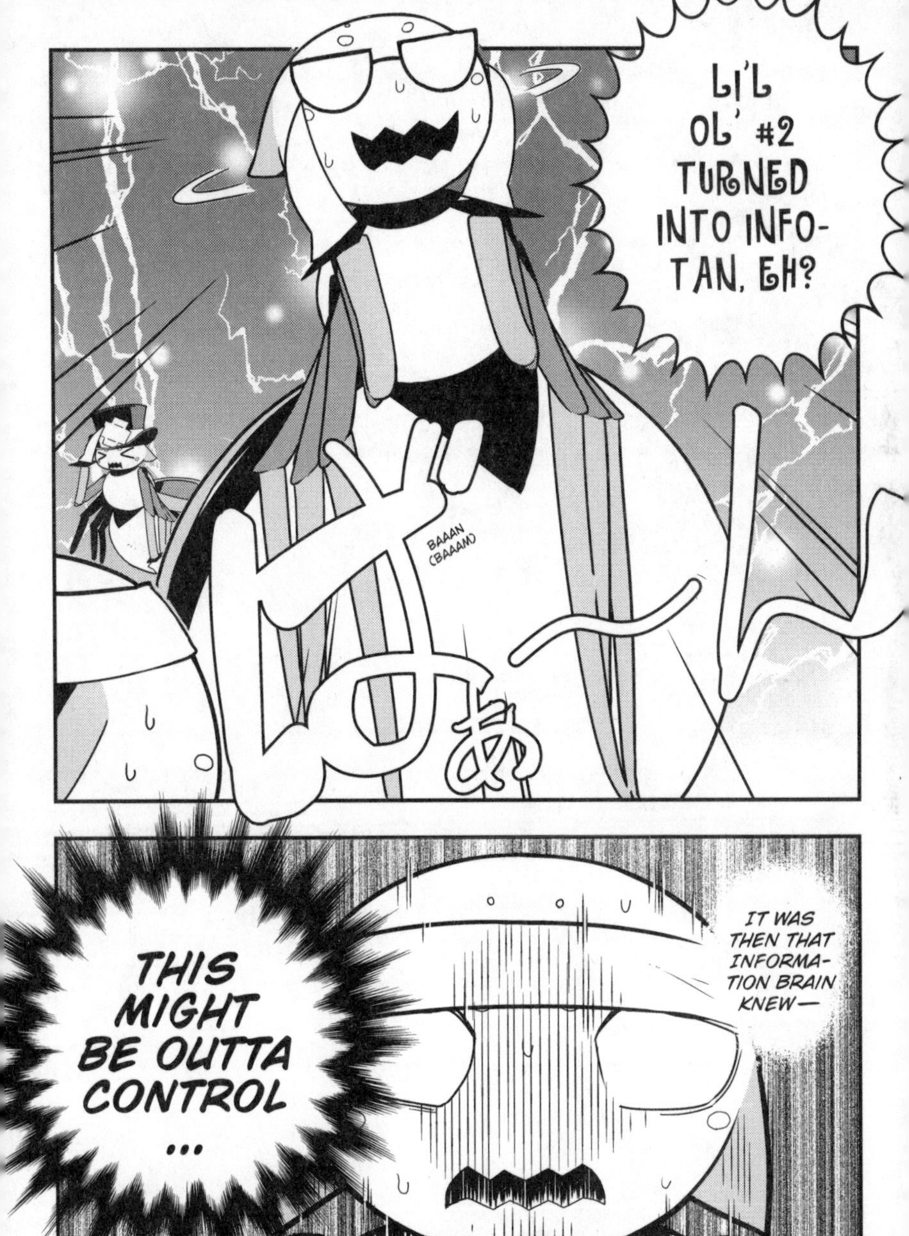
LI'L OL' #2 TURNED INTO INFO-TAN, EH?
BAAAN (BAAAM)
IT WAS THEN THAT INFORMATION BRAIN KNEW—
THIS MIGHT BE OUTTA CONTROL ...

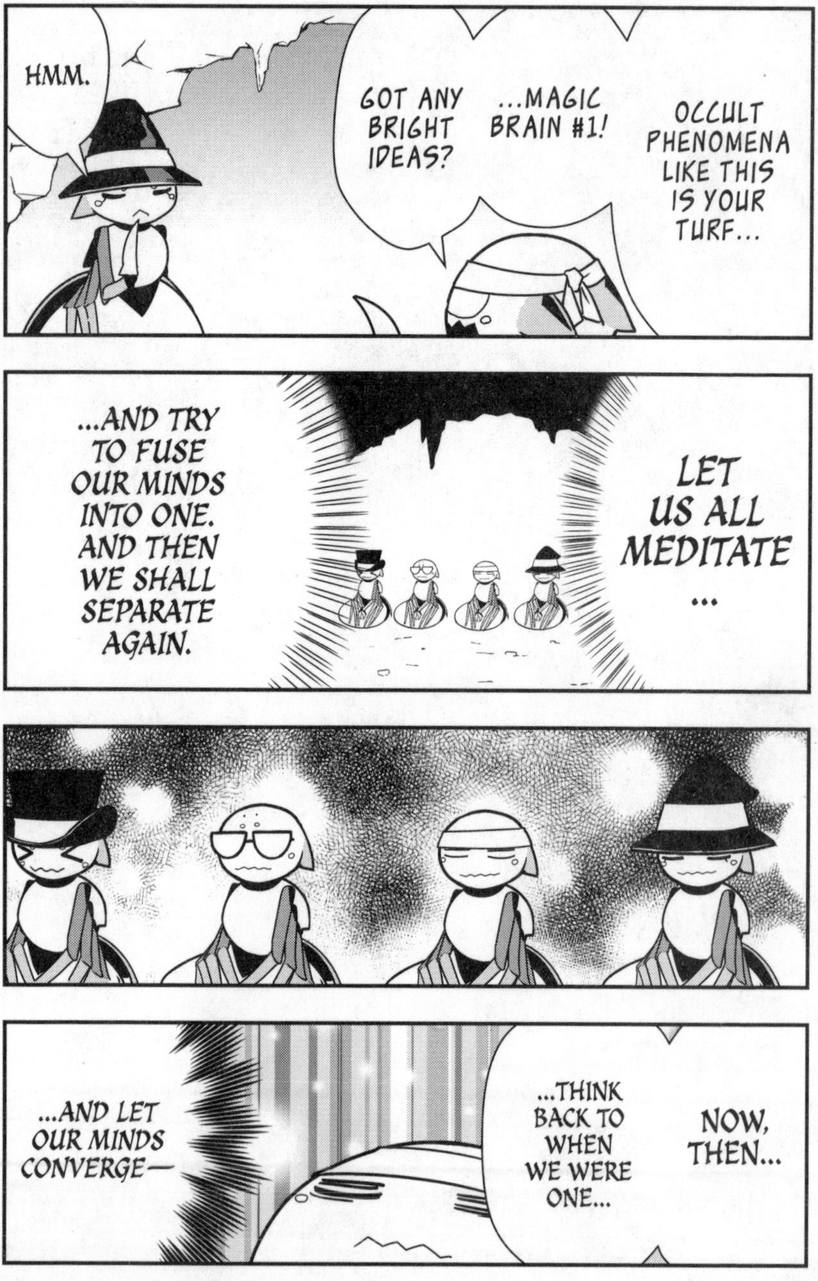
OCCULT PHENOMENA LIKE THIS IS YOUR TURF...
...MAGIC BRAIN #1!
GOT ANY BRIGHT IDEAS?
HMM.
LET US ALL MEDITATE ...
...AND TRY TO FUSE OUR MINDS INTO ONE. AND THEN WE SHALL SEPARATE AGAIN.
NOW, THEN...
...THINK BACK TO WHEN WE WERE ONE...
...AND LET OUR MINDS CONVERGE—

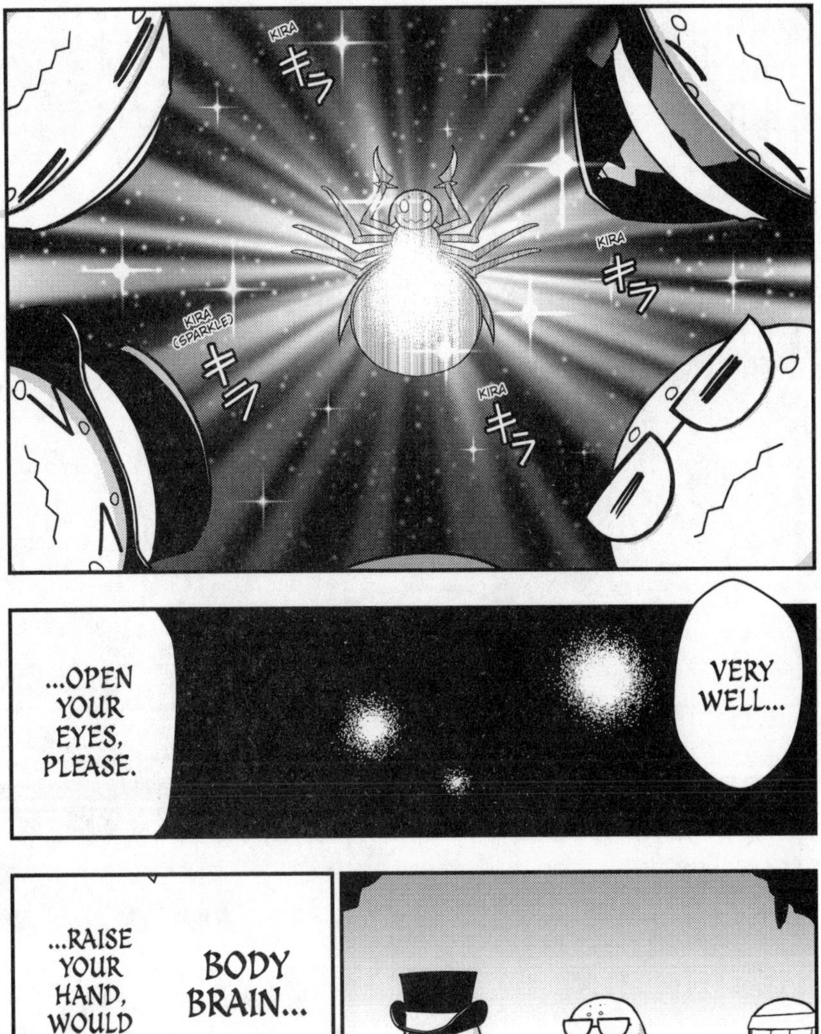
KIRA
キラ
KIRA
キラ
KIRA (SPARKLE)
キラ
KIRA
キラ
VERY WELL...
...OPEN YOUR EYES, PLEASE.
BODY BRAIN...
...RAISE YOUR HAND, WOULD YOU?

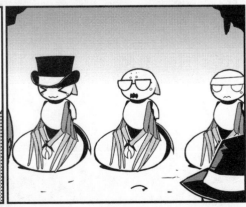

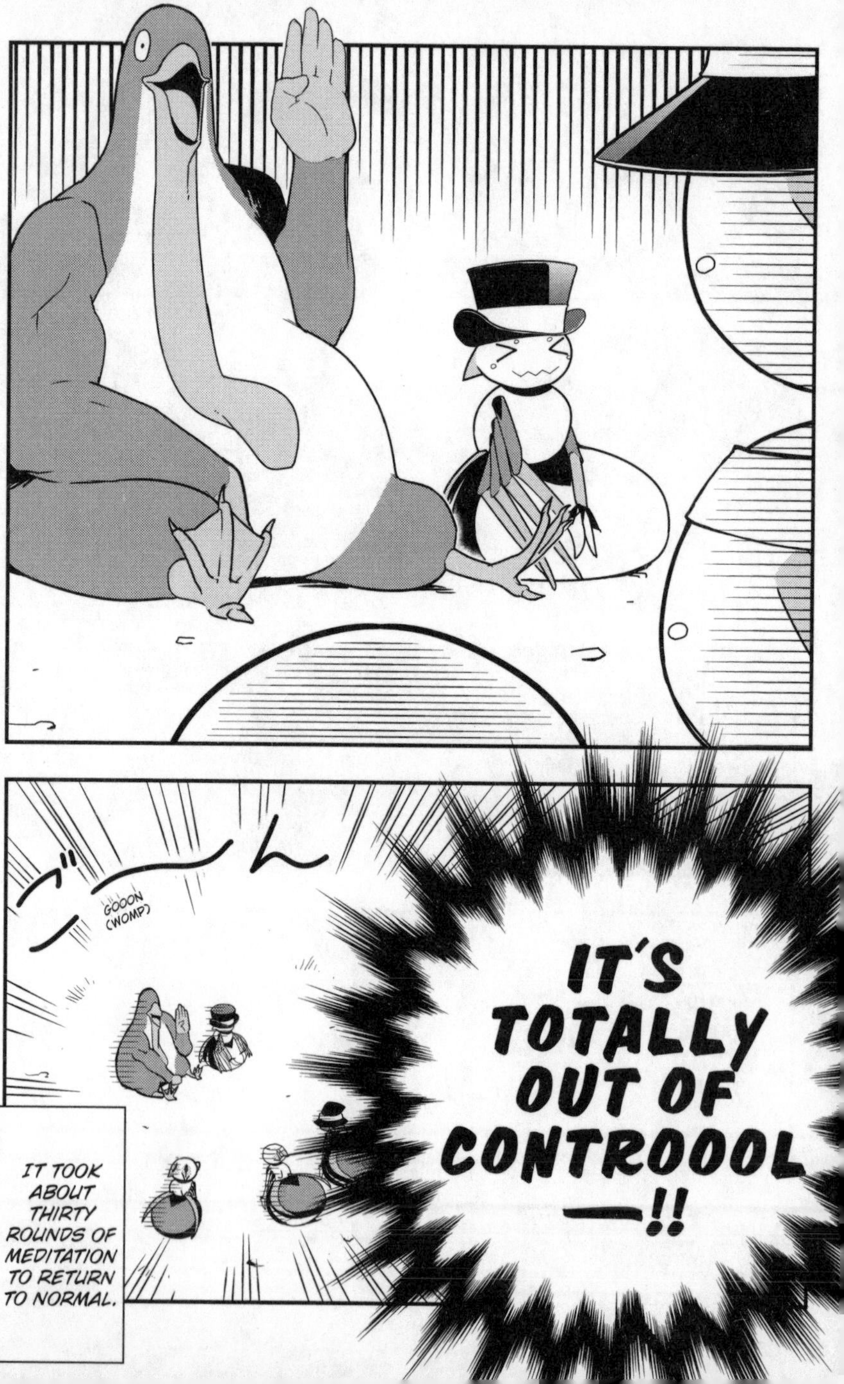
IT'S TOTALLY OUT OF CONTROOOL—!!
ゴーーーん
GOOON (WOMP)
IT TOOK ABOUT THIRTY ROUNDS OF MEDITATION TO RETURN TO NORMAL.

So I'm a Spider, So What?

THE DAILY LIVES OF THE KUMOKO SISTERS

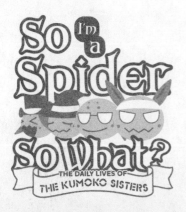

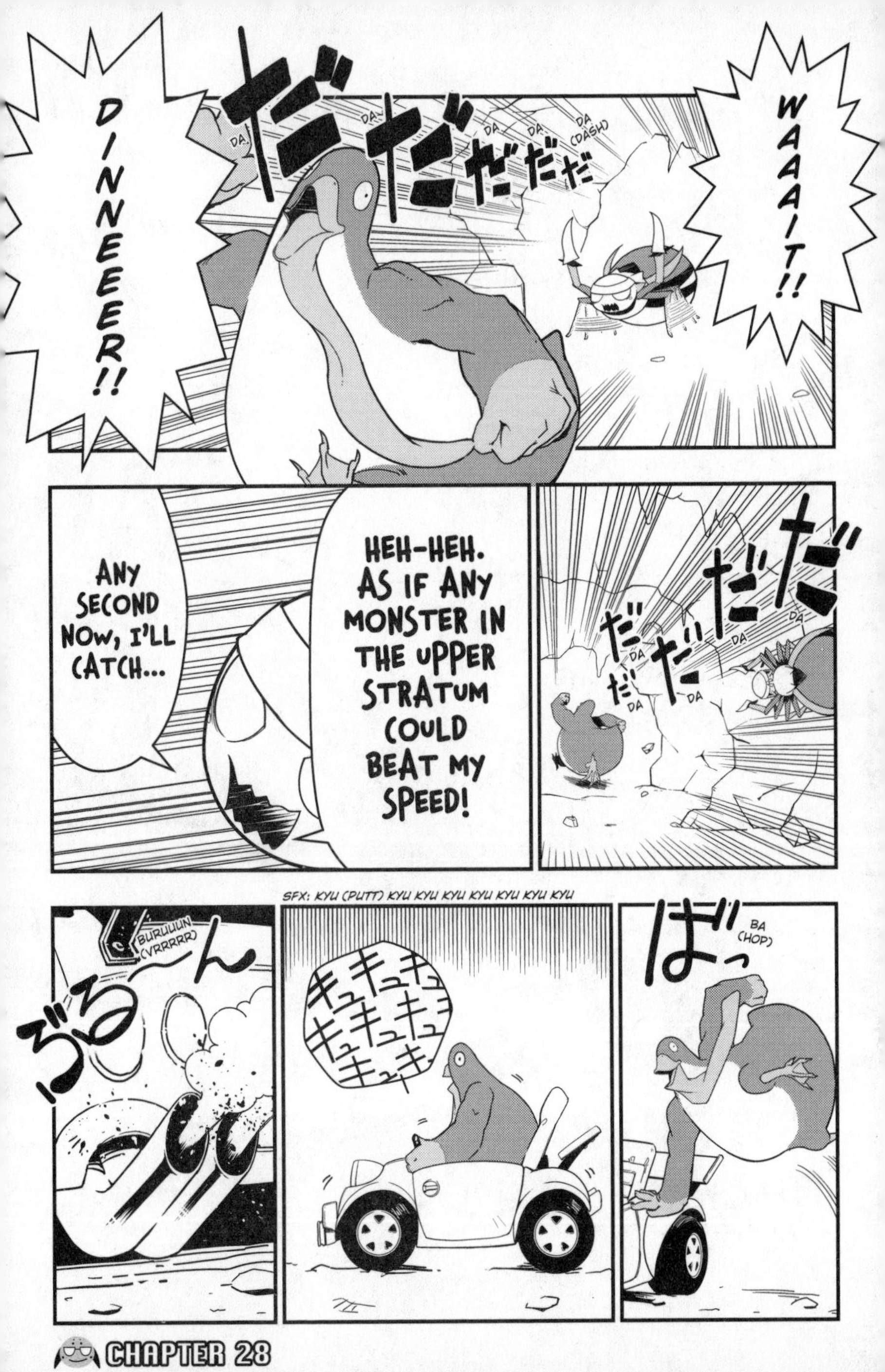
WAAAIT!!
DA DA DA DA DA (DASH)
DINNEEEER!!
DA DA DA DA DA
HEH-HEH. AS IF ANY MONSTER IN THE UPPER STRATUM COULD BEAT MY SPEED!
ANY SECOND NOW, I'LL CATCH...
BA (HOP)
SFX: KYU (PUTT) KYU KYU KYU KYU KYU KYU KYU
BURUUUN (VRRRRR)

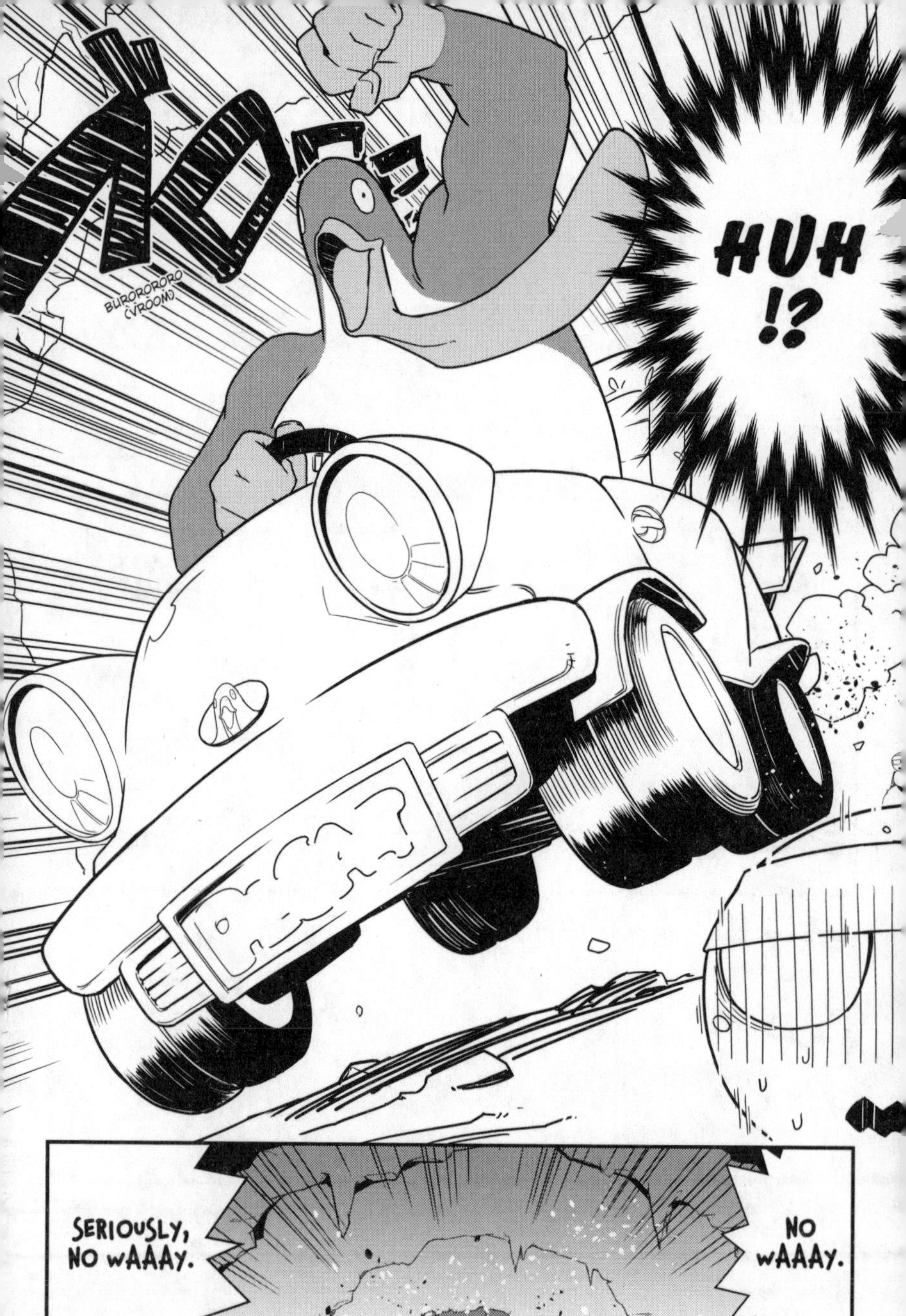
HUH !?
BURORORORO (VROOM)
NO wAAAY.
SERIOUSLY, NO wAAAY.

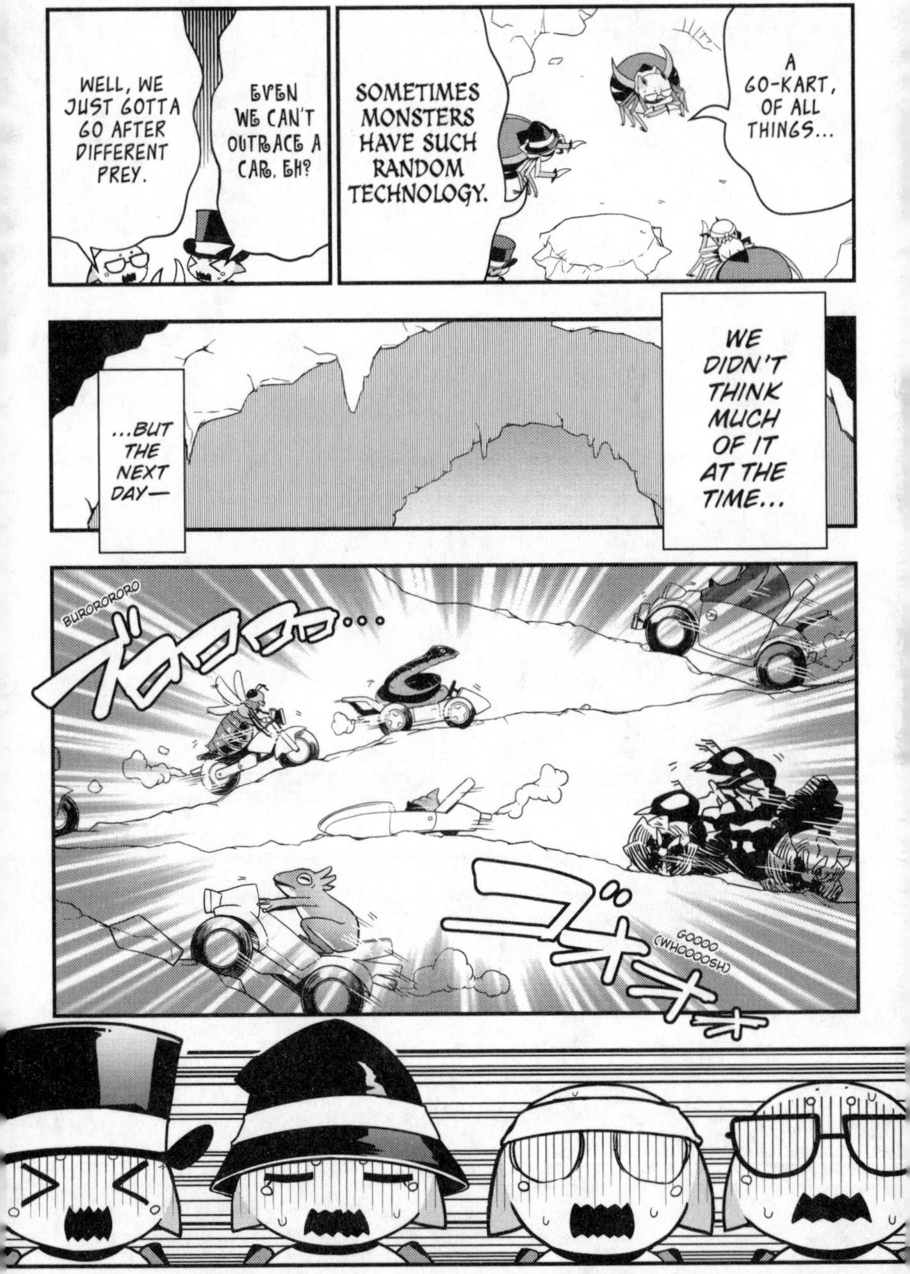

A GO-KART, OF ALL THINGS...
SOMETIMES MONSTERS HAVE SUCH RANDOM TECHNOLOGY.
EVEN WE CAN'T OUTRACE A CAR, EH?
WELL, WE JUST GOTTA GO AFTER DIFFERENT PREY.
WE DIDN'T THINK MUCH OF IT AT THE TIME...
...BUT THE NEXT DAY—
ブロロロロ…
BURORORORO
ゴオオオ
GOOOO (WHOOOOSH)

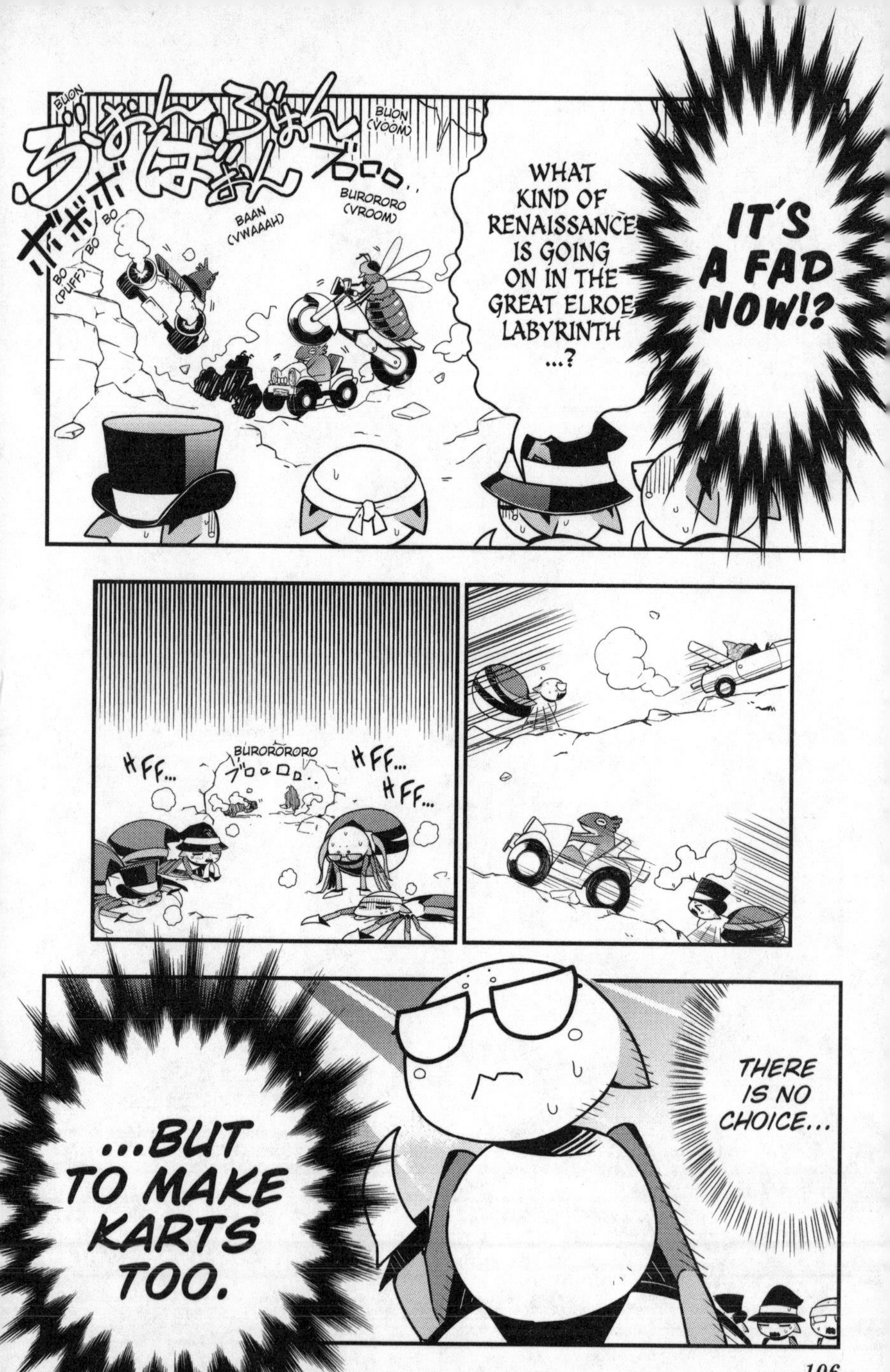
IT'S A FAD NOW!?
WHAT KIND OF RENAISSANCE IS GOING ON IN THE GREAT ELROE LABYRINTH ...?
BUON
BUON (VOOM)
BURORORO (VROOM)
BAAN (VWAAAH)
BO BO BO (PUFF)
HFF...
BURORORORO
HFF... HFF...
THERE IS NO CHOICE...
...BUT TO MAKE KARTS TOO.

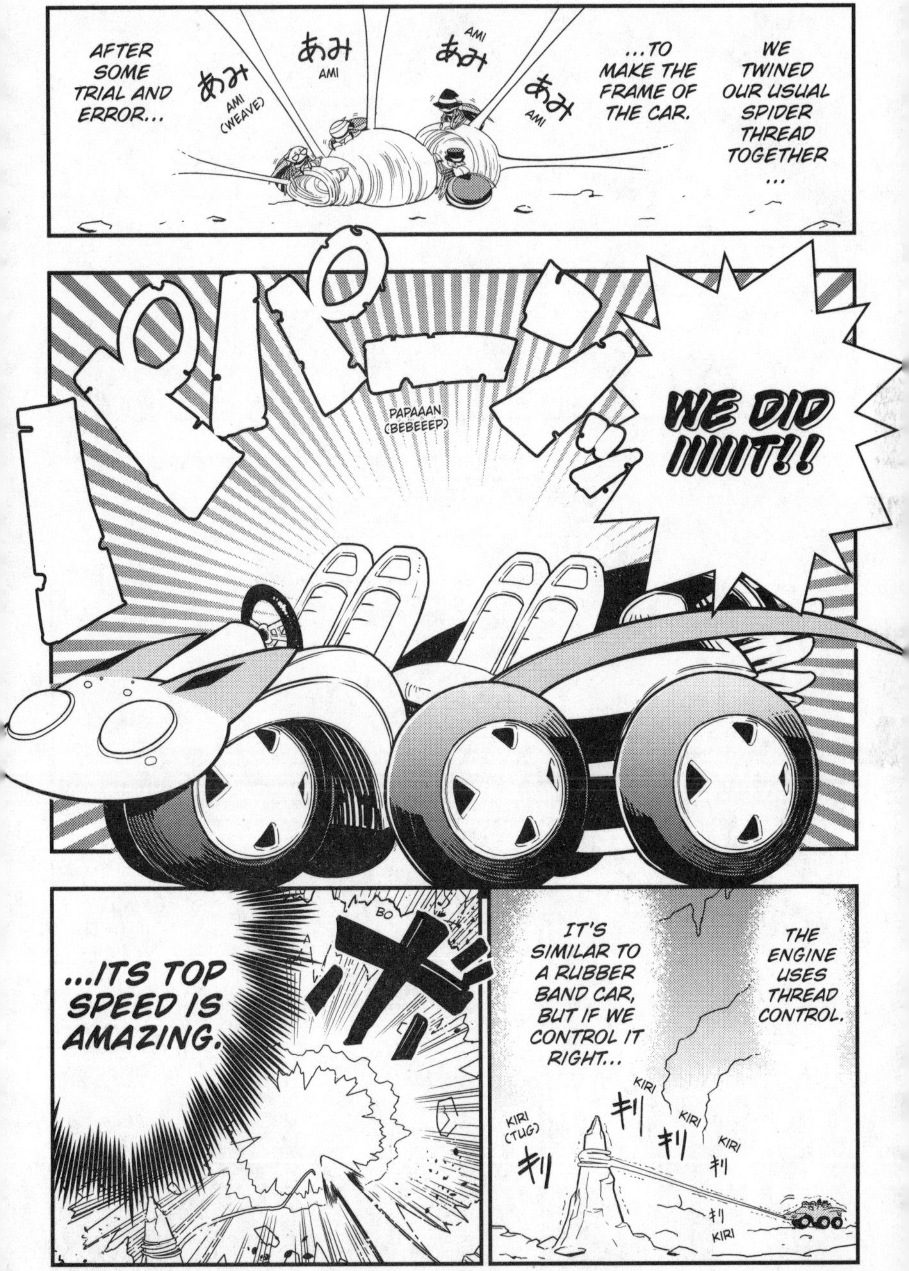
WE TWINED OUR USUAL SPIDER THREAD TOGETHER …
…TO MAKE THE FRAME OF THE CAR.
あみ
AMI
あみ
AMI
あみ
AMI
あみ
AMI (WEAVE)
AFTER SOME TRIAL AND ERROR…
WE DID IIIIIT!!
PAPAAAN (BEBEEEP)
THE ENGINE USES THREAD CONTROL.
IT'S SIMILAR TO A RUBBER BAND CAR, BUT IF WE CONTROL IT RIGHT…
KIRI
キリ
KIRI
キリ
KIRI
キリ
KIRI (TUG)
キリ
キリ
KIRI
BO
…ITS TOP SPEED IS AMAZING.

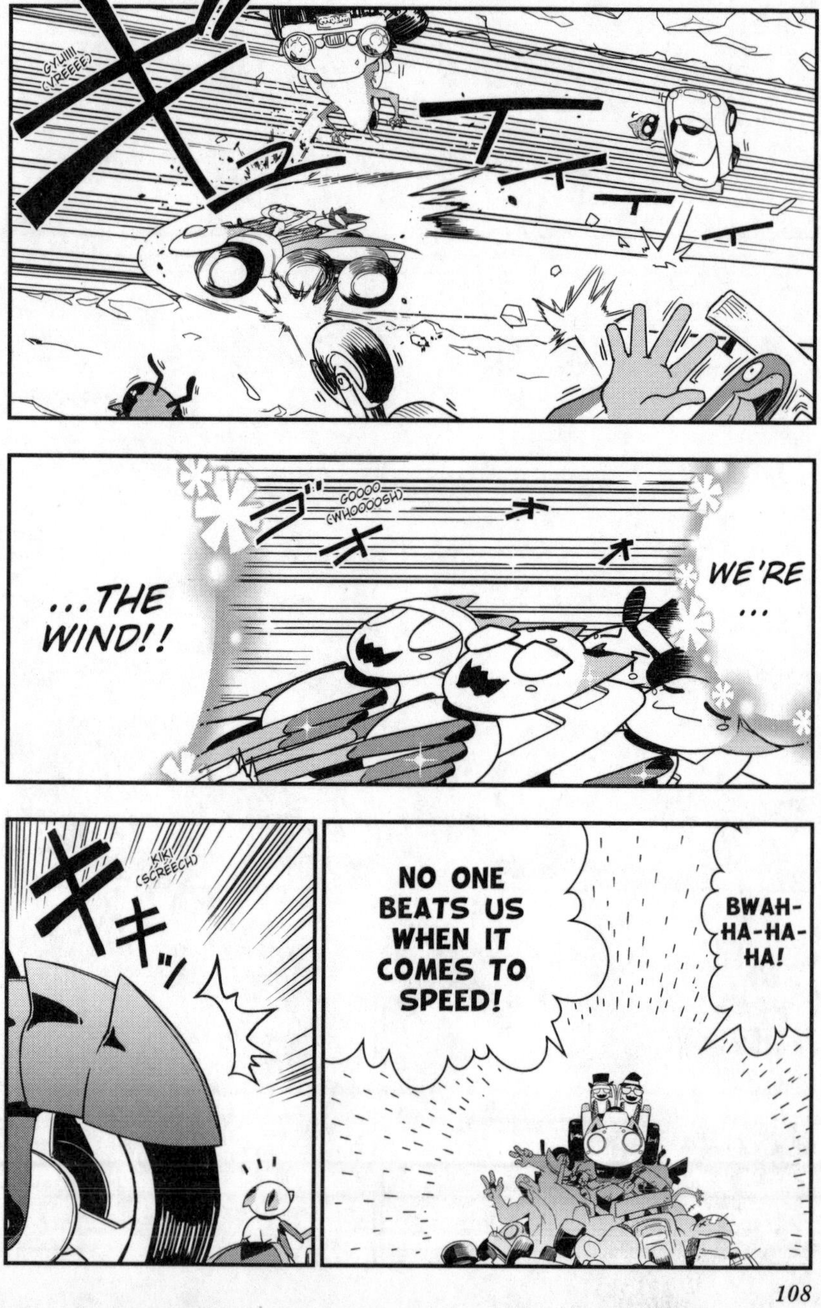
GYUIIIII (VREEEE)
GOOOO (WHOOOOSH)
WE'RE ...
...THE WIND!!
BWAH-HA-HA-HA!
NO ONE BEATS US WHEN IT COMES TO SPEED!
KIKI (SCREECH)

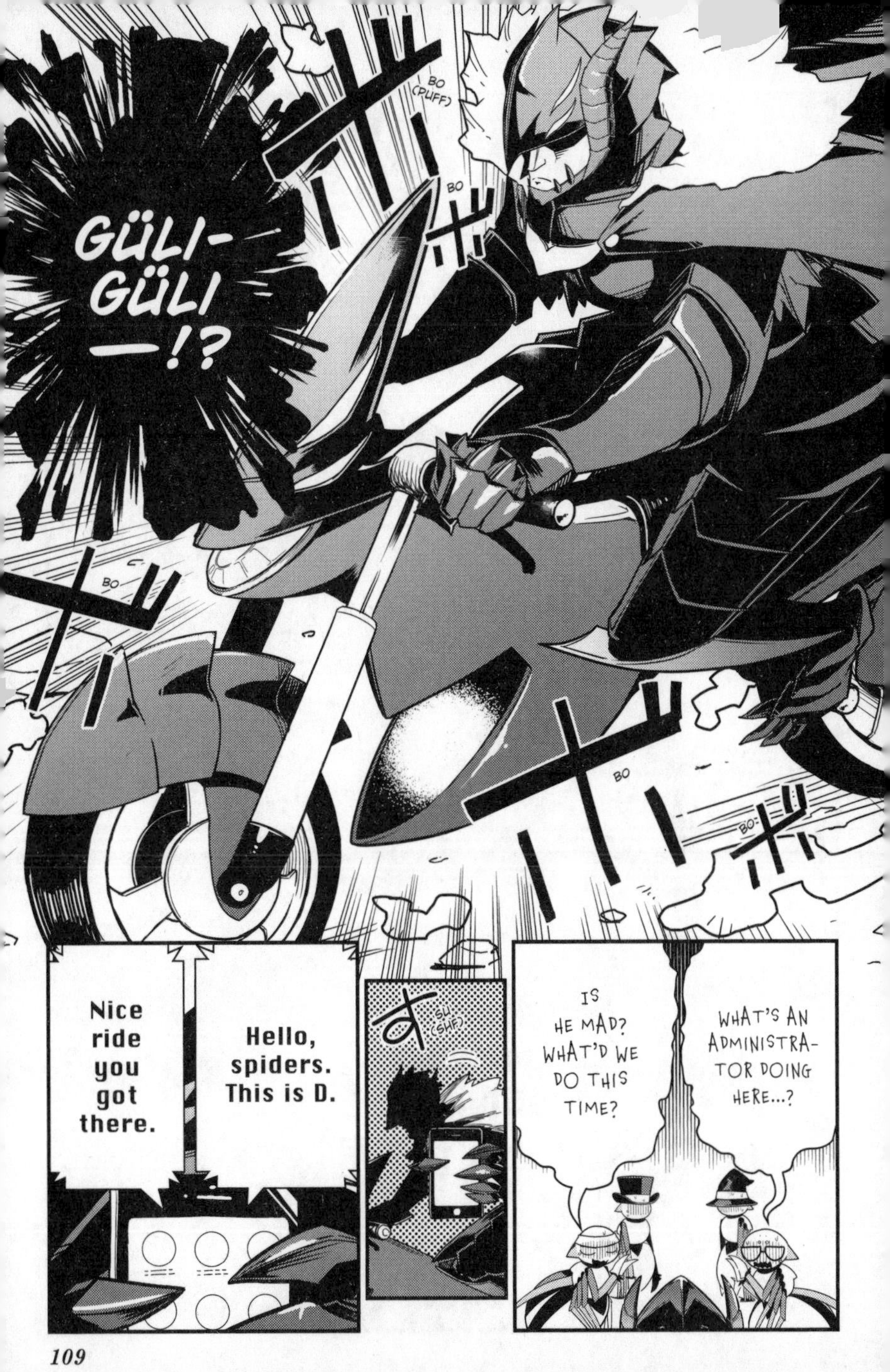
BO (PUFF)
BO
GÜLI-GÜLI—!?
BO
BO
BO
WHAT'S AN ADMINISTRATOR DOING HERE...?
IS HE MAD? WHAT'D WE DO THIS TIME?
SU (SHF)
Hello, spiders. This is D.
Nice ride you got there.

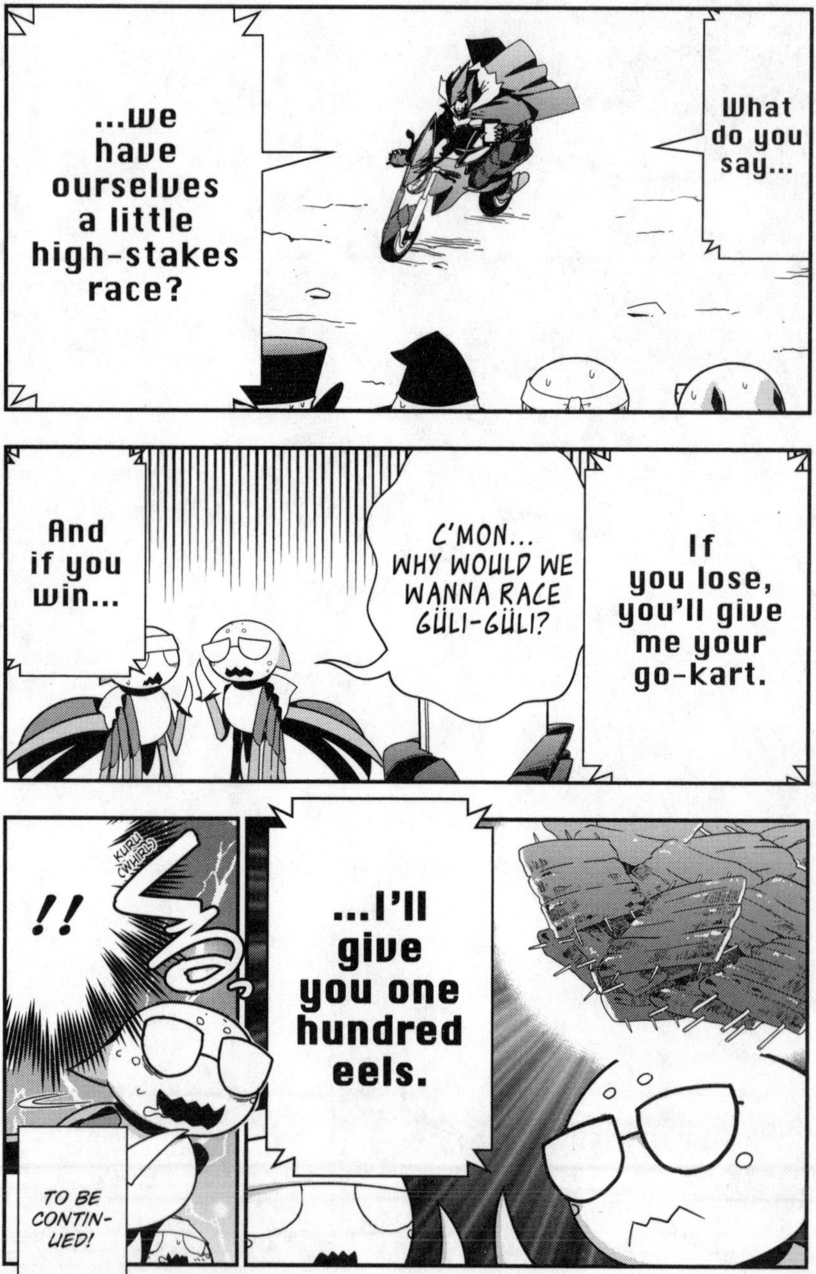
What do you say...
...we have ourselves a little high-stakes race?
If you lose, you'll give me your go-kart.
C'MON... WHY WOULD WE WANNA RACE GÜLI-GÜLI?
And if you win...
...I'll give you one hundred eels.
KURU (WHIRL)
!!
TO BE CONTIN-UED!

So I'm a Spider, So What?
THE DAILY LIVES OF
THE KUMOKO SISTERS

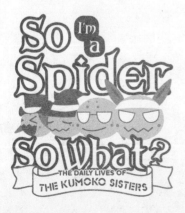

CHAPTER 29

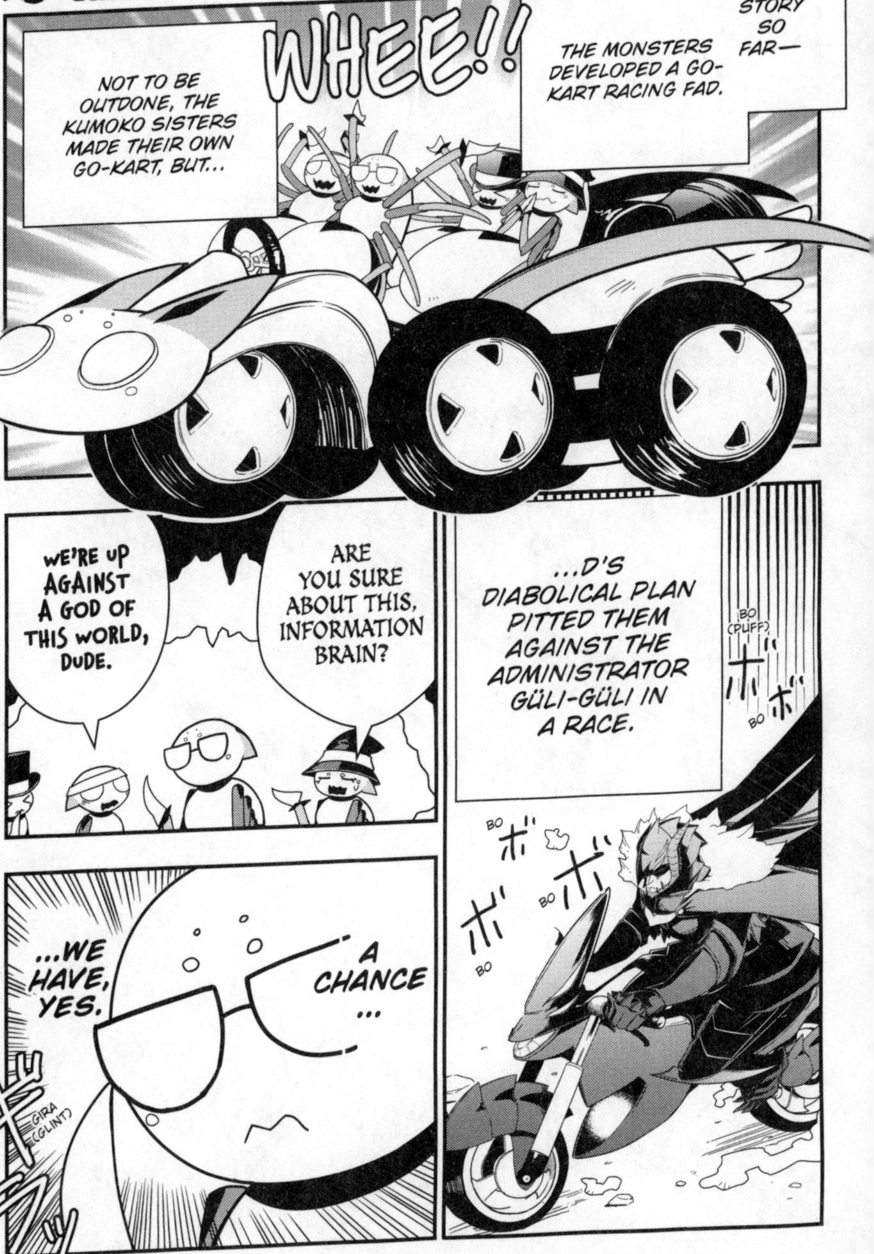
THE STORY SO FAR—
THE MONSTERS DEVELOPED A GO-KART RACING FAD.
WHEE!!
NOT TO BE OUTDONE, THE KUMOKO SISTERS MADE THEIR OWN GO-KART, BUT...
...D'S DIABOLICAL PLAN PITTED THEM AGAINST THE ADMINISTRATOR GÜLI-GÜLI IN A RACE.
BO (PUFF)
BO
BO
BO
BO
ARE YOU SURE ABOUT THIS, INFORMATION BRAIN?
WE'RE UP AGAINST A GOD OF THIS WORLD, DUDE.
A CHANCE ...
...WE HAVE, YES.
GIRA (GLINT)

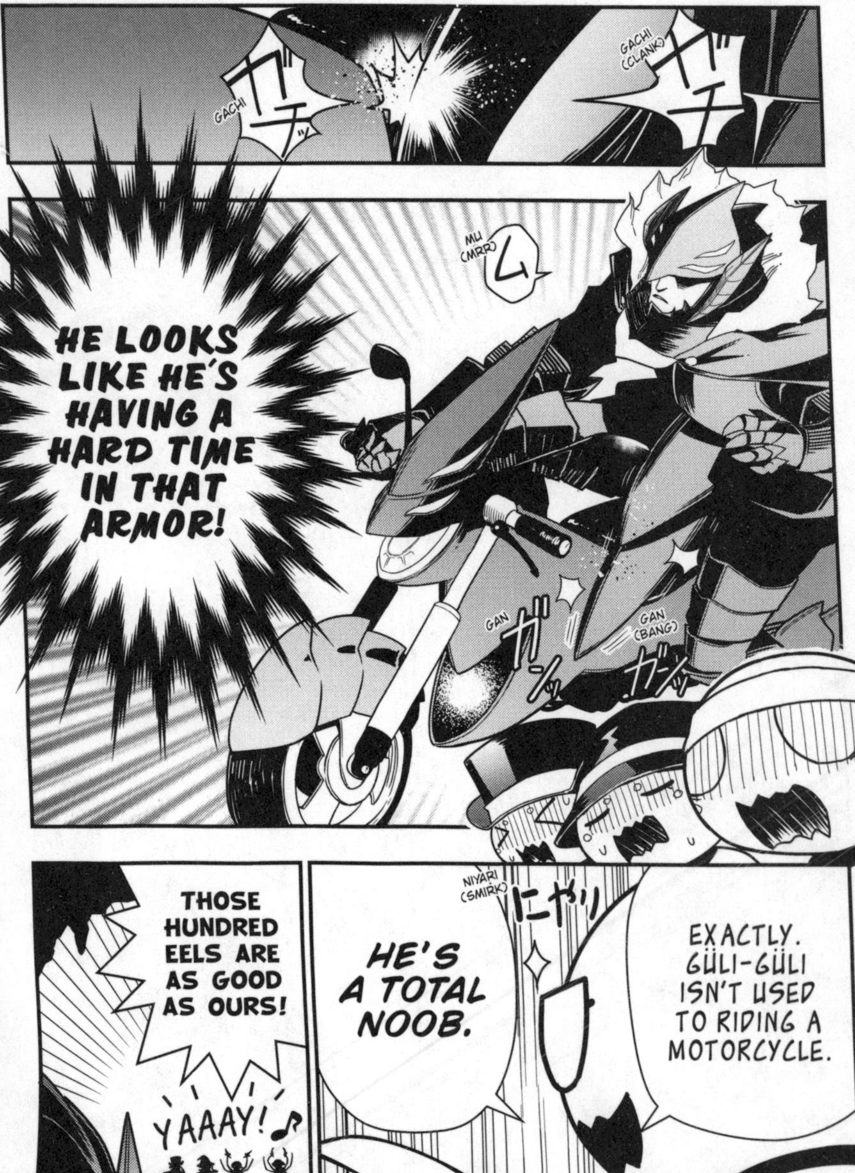
GACHI (CLANK)
ガチッ
GACHI
ガチッ
MU (MRR)
ム
HE LOOKS LIKE HE'S HAVING A HARD TIME IN THAT ARMOR!
GAN (BANG)
ガンッ
GAN
ガンッ
NIYARI (SMIRK)
にやり
EXACTLY. GÜLI-GÜLI ISN'T USED TO RIDING A MOTORCYCLE.
HE'S A TOTAL NOOB.
THOSE HUNDRED EELS ARE AS GOOD AS OURS!
YAAAY!♪

CHAPTER 29

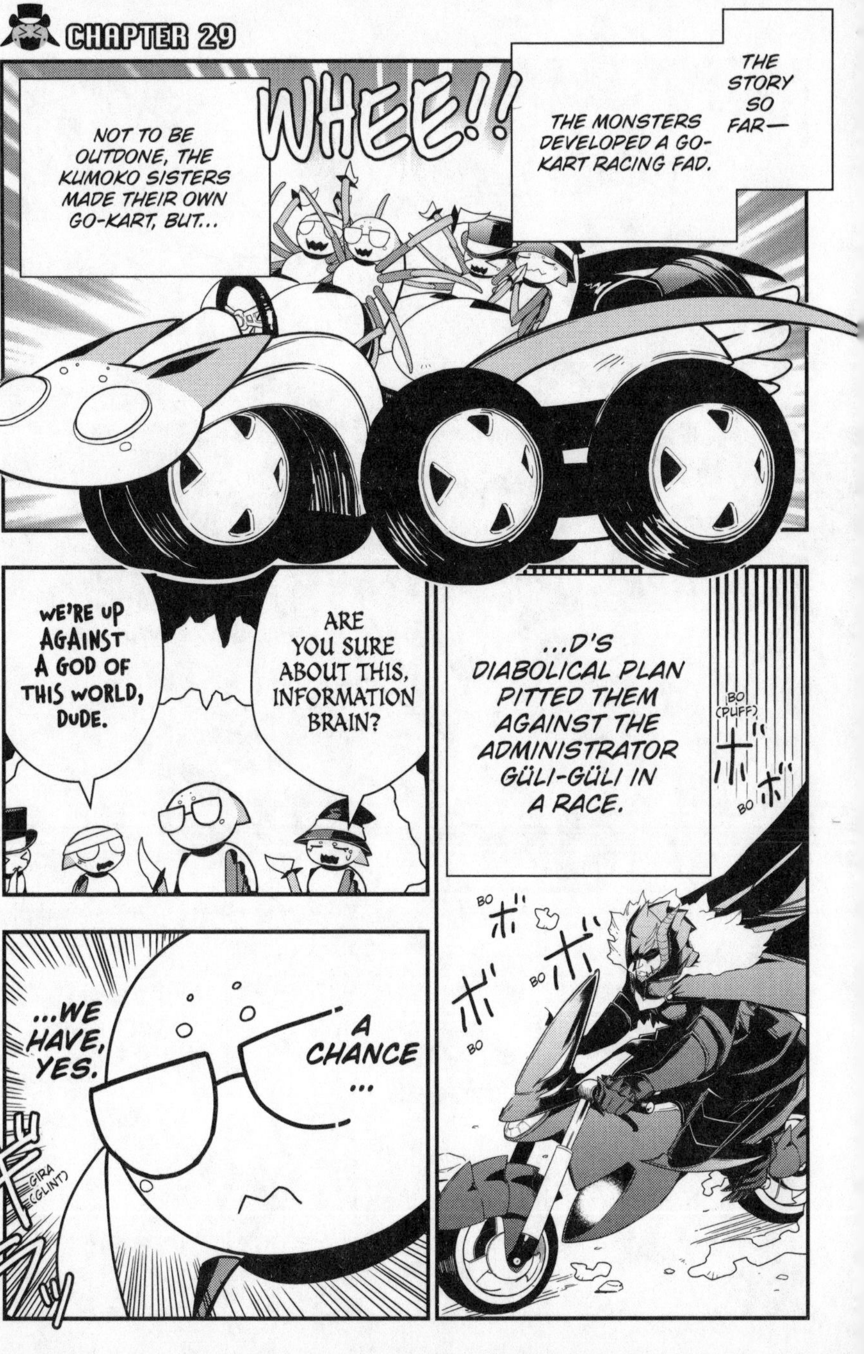
THE STORY SO FAR—
THE MONSTERS DEVELOPED A GO-KART RACING FAD.
WHEE!!
NOT TO BE OUTDONE, THE KUMOKO SISTERS MADE THEIR OWN GO-KART, BUT...
...D'S DIABOLICAL PLAN PITTED THEM AGAINST THE ADMINISTRATOR GÜLI-GÜLI IN A RACE.
BO (PUFF)
BO
ARE YOU SURE ABOUT THIS, INFORMATION BRAIN?
WE'RE UP AGAINST A GOD OF THIS WORLD, DUDE.
BO
BO
BO
A CHANCE ...
...WE HAVE, YES.
GIRA (GLINT)

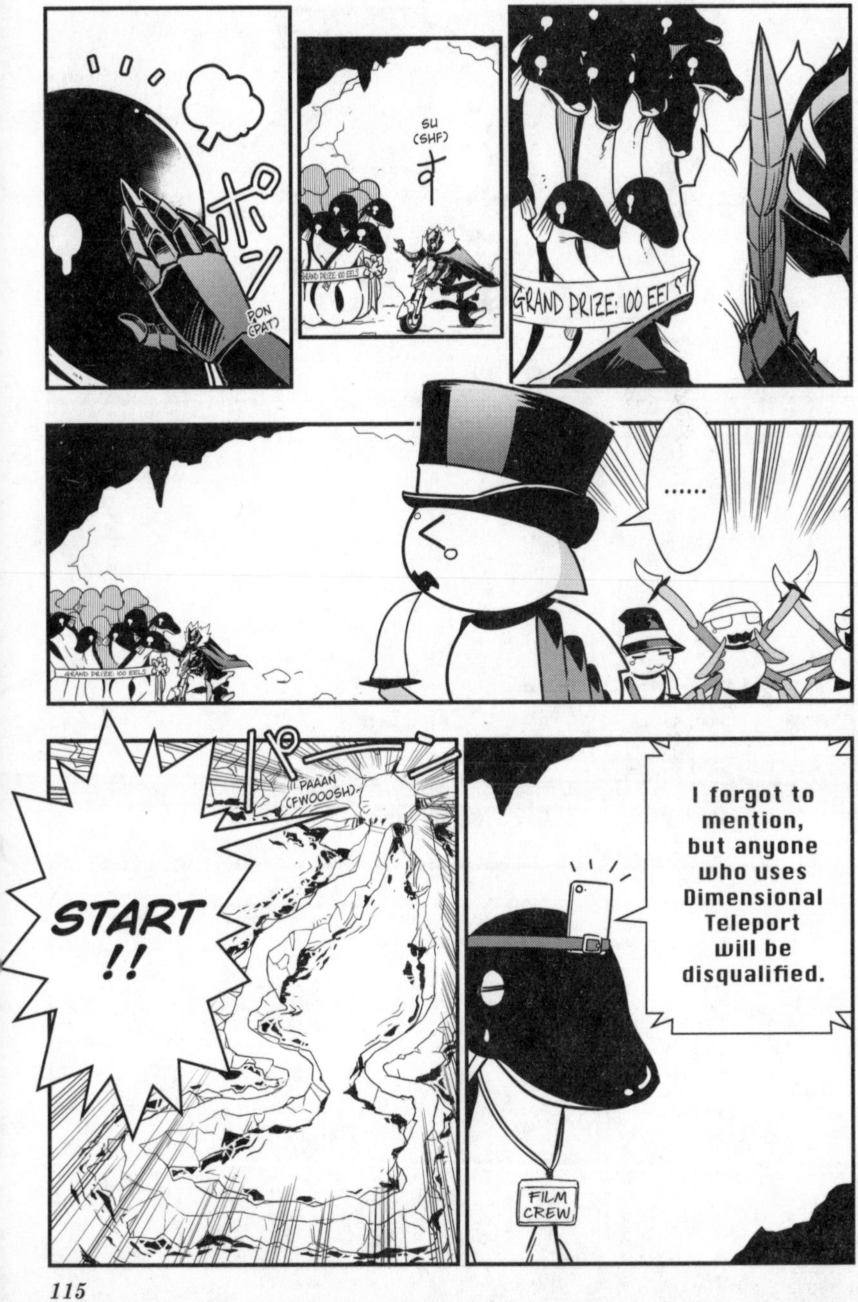
GRAND PRIZE: 100 EEL
SU (SHF)
す
GRAND PRIZE: 100 EELS
ポン
PON (PAT)
......
GRAND PRIZE: 100 EELS
I forgot to mention, but anyone who uses Dimensional Teleport will be disqualified.
FILM CREW
パーン
PAAAN (FWOOOSH)
START!!

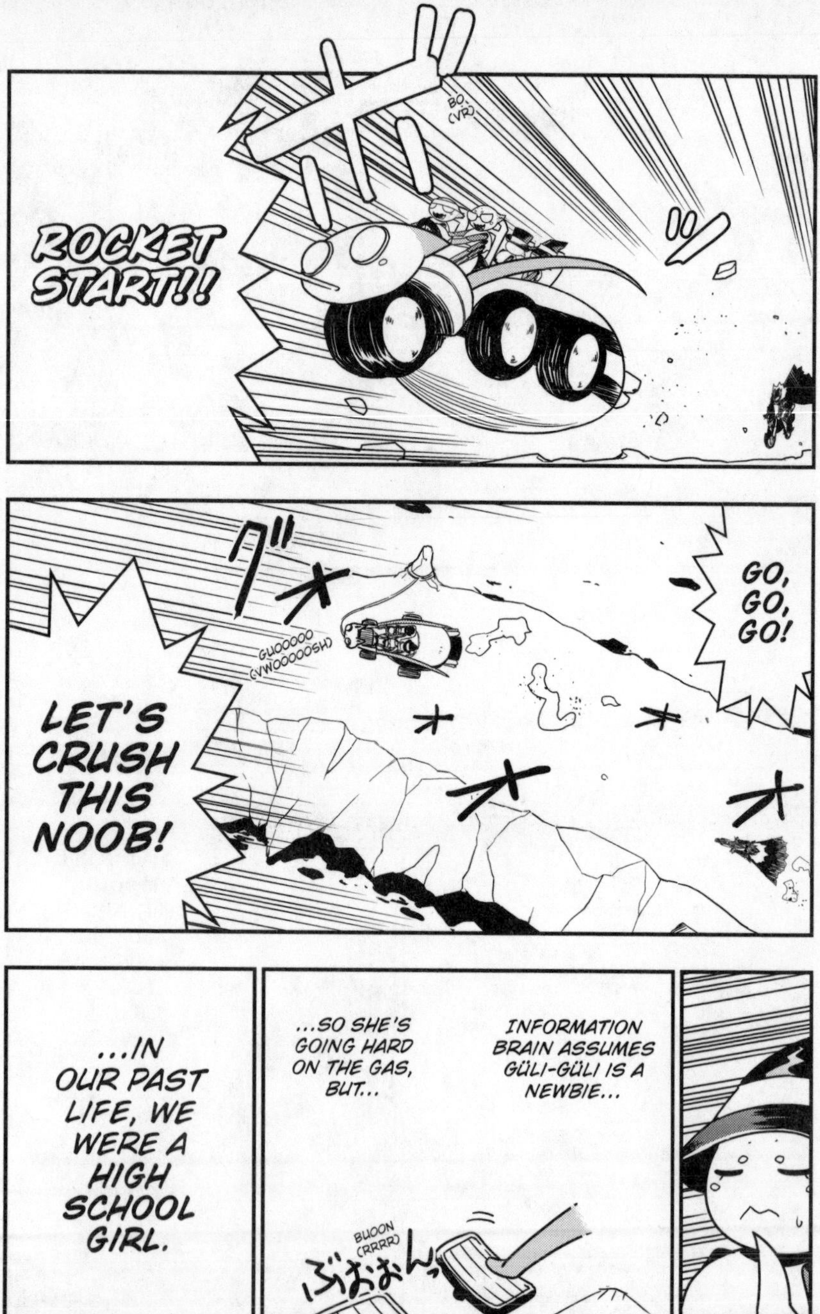
BO- (VR)
ROCKET START!!
GO, GO, GO!
GUOOOOO (VWOOOOOSH)
LET'S CRUSH THIS NOOB!
INFORMATION BRAIN ASSUMES GÜLI-GÜLI IS A NEWBIE...
...SO SHE'S GOING HARD ON THE GAS, BUT...
BUOON (RRRR)
ぶおおんっ
...IN OUR PAST LIFE, WE WERE A HIGH SCHOOL GIRL.

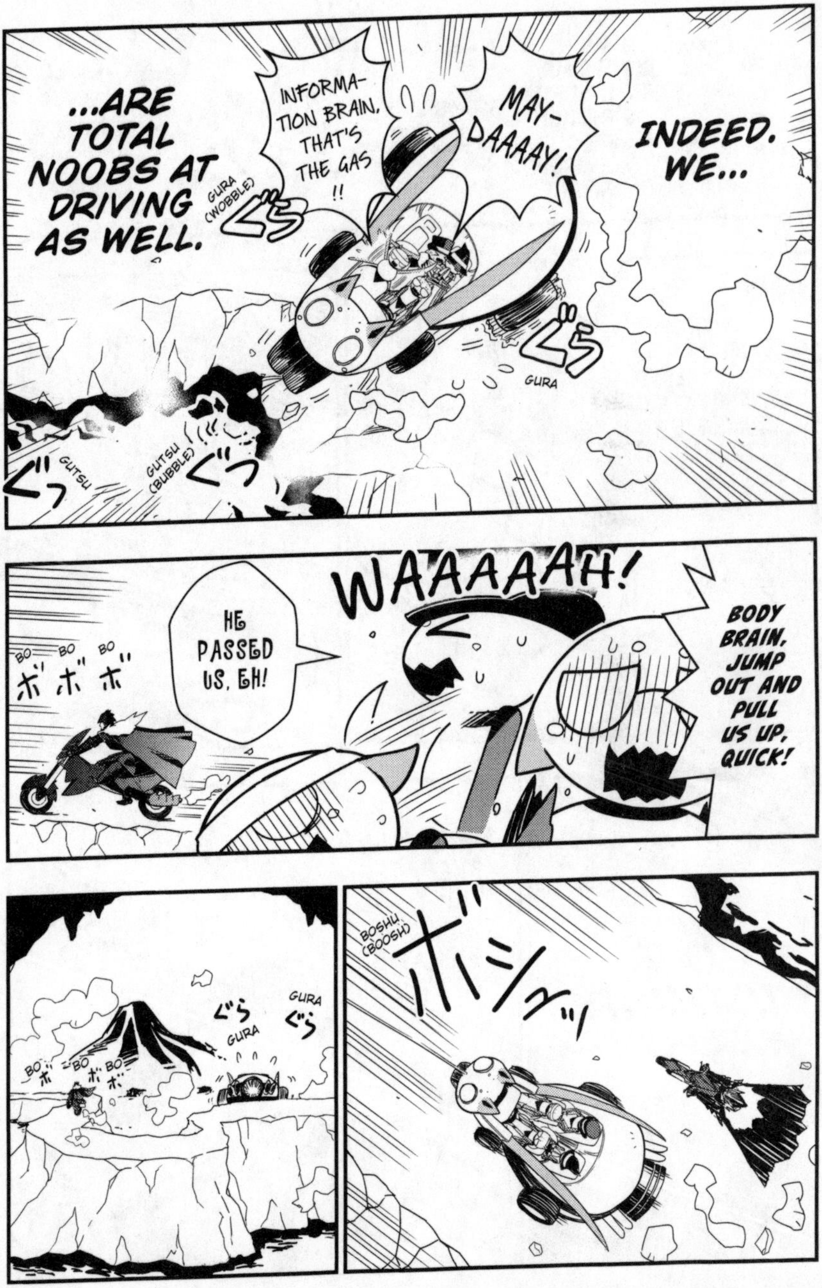
INDEED. WE...
MAY-DAAAAY!
INFORMATION BRAIN, THAT'S THE GAS!!
...ARE TOTAL NOOBS AT DRIVING AS WELL.
ぐら GURA
ぐら GURA (WOBBLE)
ぐつ GUTSU (BUBBLE)
ぐつ GUTSU
BODY BRAIN, JUMP OUT AND PULL US UP, QUICK!
WAAAAAH!
HE PASSED US, EH!
ボボボ BO BO BO
ボシュッ BOSHU (BOOSH)
ぐら GURA
ぐら GURA
ボボボ BO BO BO

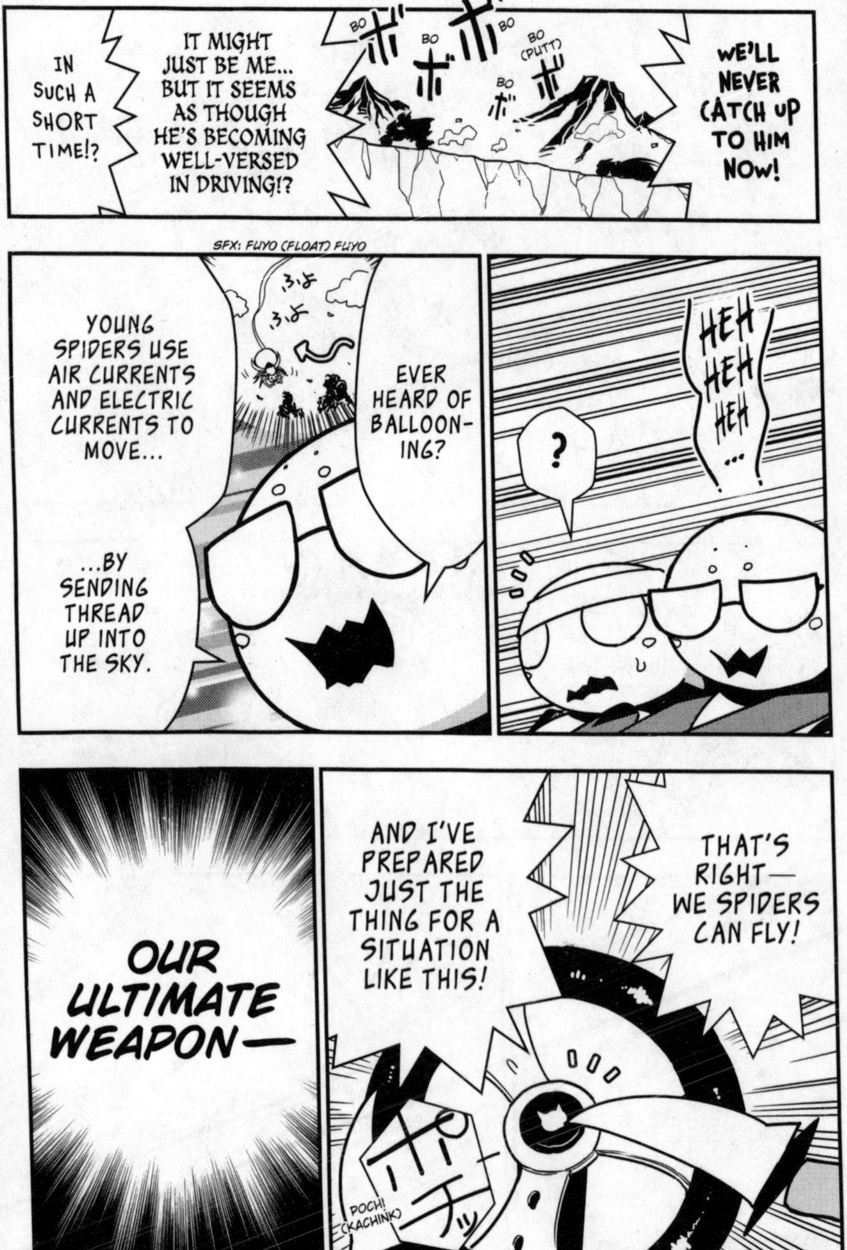
WE'LL NEVER CATCH UP TO HIM NOW!
BO BO BO BO BO (PUTT)
IT MIGHT JUST BE ME... BUT IT SEEMS AS THOUGH HE'S BECOMING WELL-VERSED IN DRIVING!?
IN SUCH A SHORT TIME!?
HEH HEH HEH...
?
SFX: FUYO (FLOAT) FUYO
EVER HEARD OF BALLOONING?
YOUNG SPIDERS USE AIR CURRENTS AND ELECTRIC CURRENTS TO MOVE...
...BY SENDING THREAD UP INTO THE SKY.
THAT'S RIGHT— WE SPIDERS CAN FLY!
AND I'VE PREPARED JUST THE THING FOR A SITUATION LIKE THIS!
POCHI! (KACHINK)
OUR ULTIMATE WEAPON—

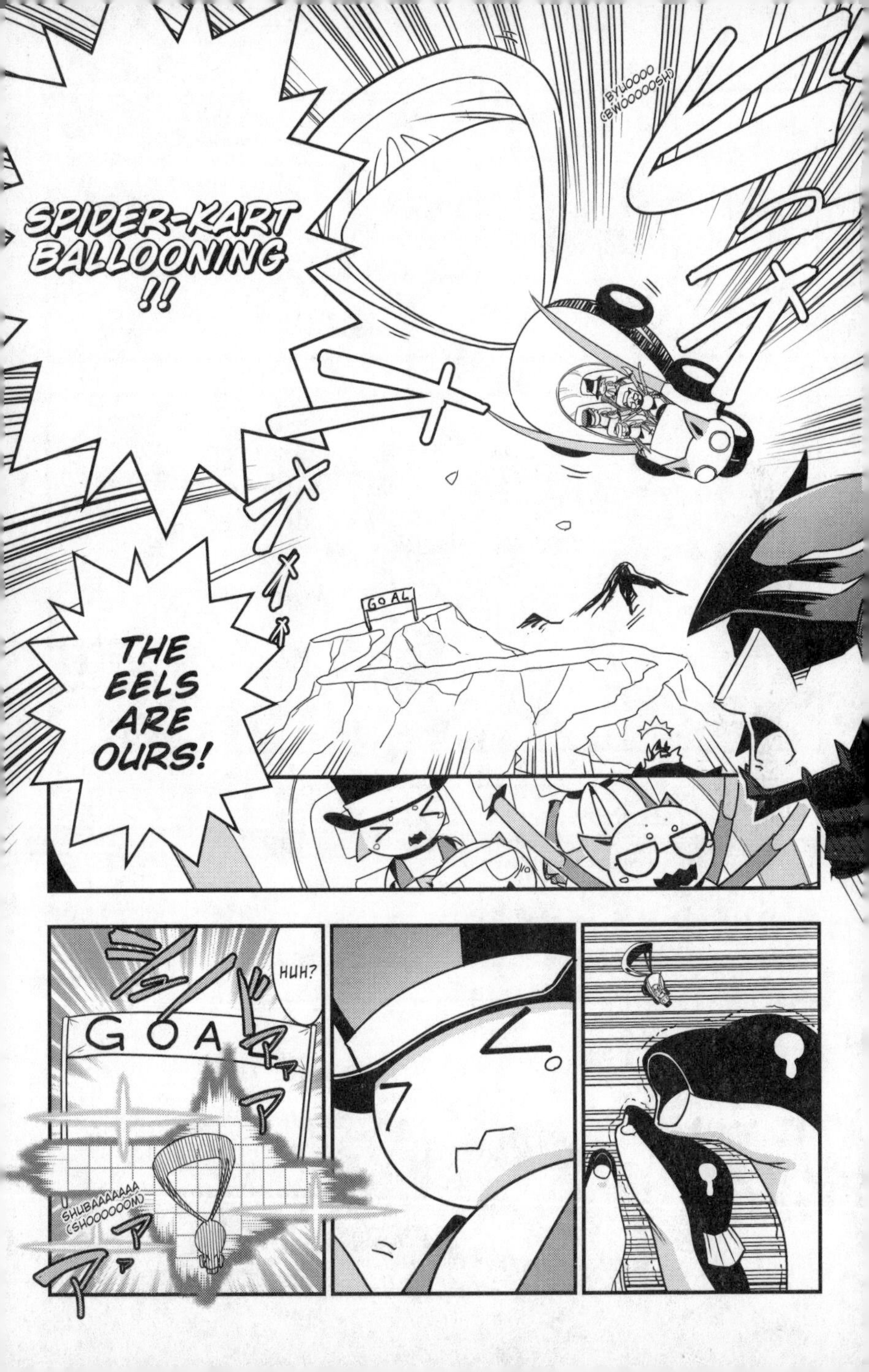
BYUOOOO
(BWOOOOOSH)
SPIDER-KART BALLOONING!!
THE EELS ARE OURS!
GOAL
HUH?
GOA
SHUBAAAAAAA
(SHOOOOOOM)

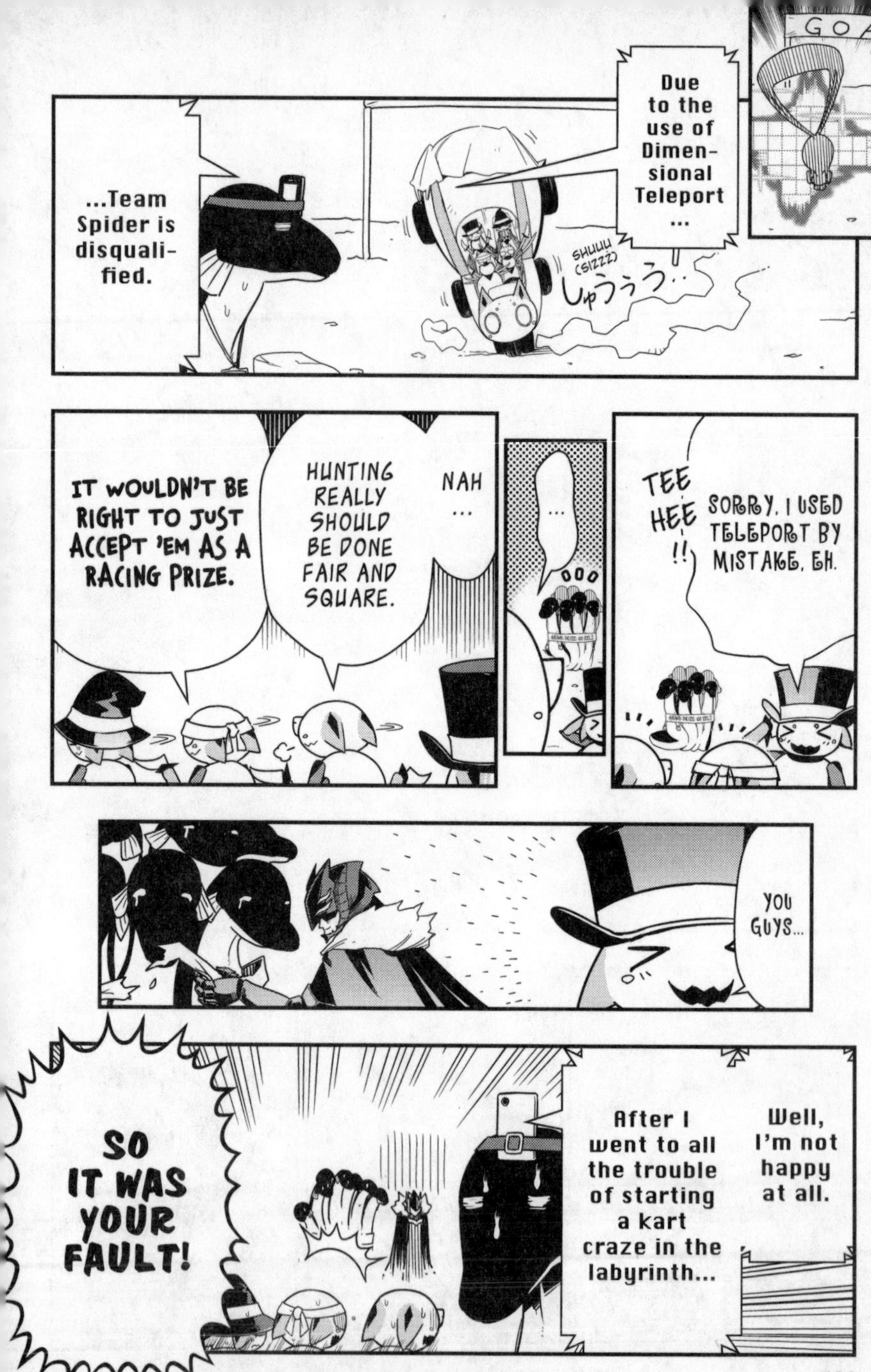
Due to the use of Dimensional Teleport ...
SHUUU (SIZZZ)
しゅううう…
...Team Spider is disqualified.
TEE HEE !!
SORRY, I USED TELEPORT BY MISTAKE, EH.
...
NAH ...
HUNTING REALLY SHOULD BE DONE FAIR AND SQUARE.
IT WOULDN'T BE RIGHT TO JUST ACCEPT 'EM AS A RACING PRIZE.
YOU GUYS...
Well, I'm not happy at all.
After I went to all the trouble of starting a kart craze in the labyrinth...
SO IT WAS YOUR FAULT!

So I'm a Spider, So What?

THE DAILY LIVES OF THE KUMOKO SISTERS

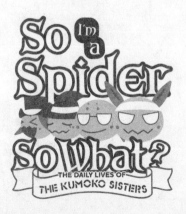

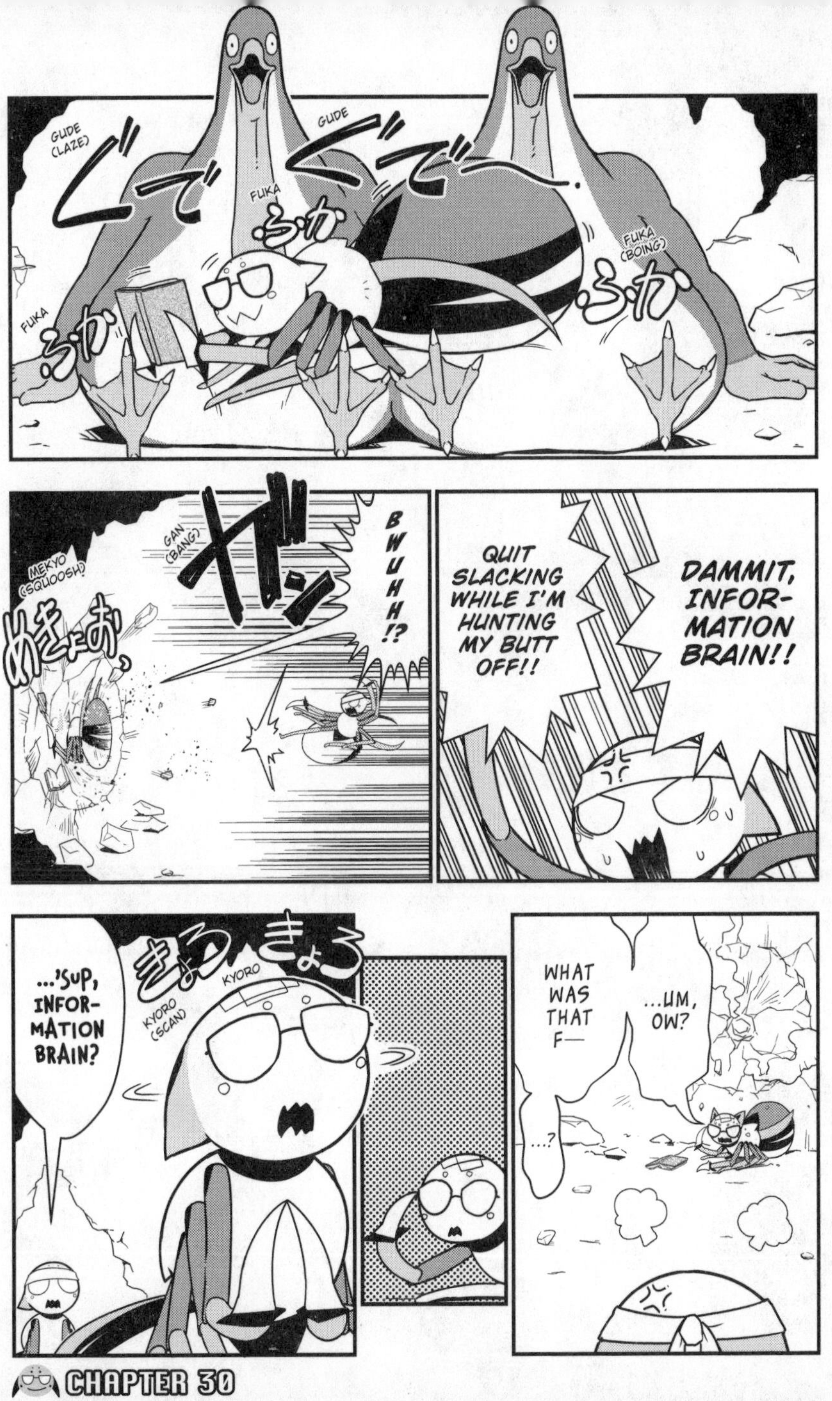
GUDE
GUDE (LAZE)
ぐでぐでー
FUKA
ふか
FUKA (BOING)
ふか
FUKA
ふか
DAMMIT, INFORMATION BRAIN!!
QUIT SLACKING WHILE I'M HUNTING MY BUTT OFF!!
BWUHHH!?
GAN (BANG)
MEKYO (SQUOOSH)
めきょ
...UM, OW?
WHAT WAS THAT F—
...?
KYORO
きょろ きょろ
KYORO (SCAN)
...'SUP, INFORMATION BRAIN?

CHAPTER 30

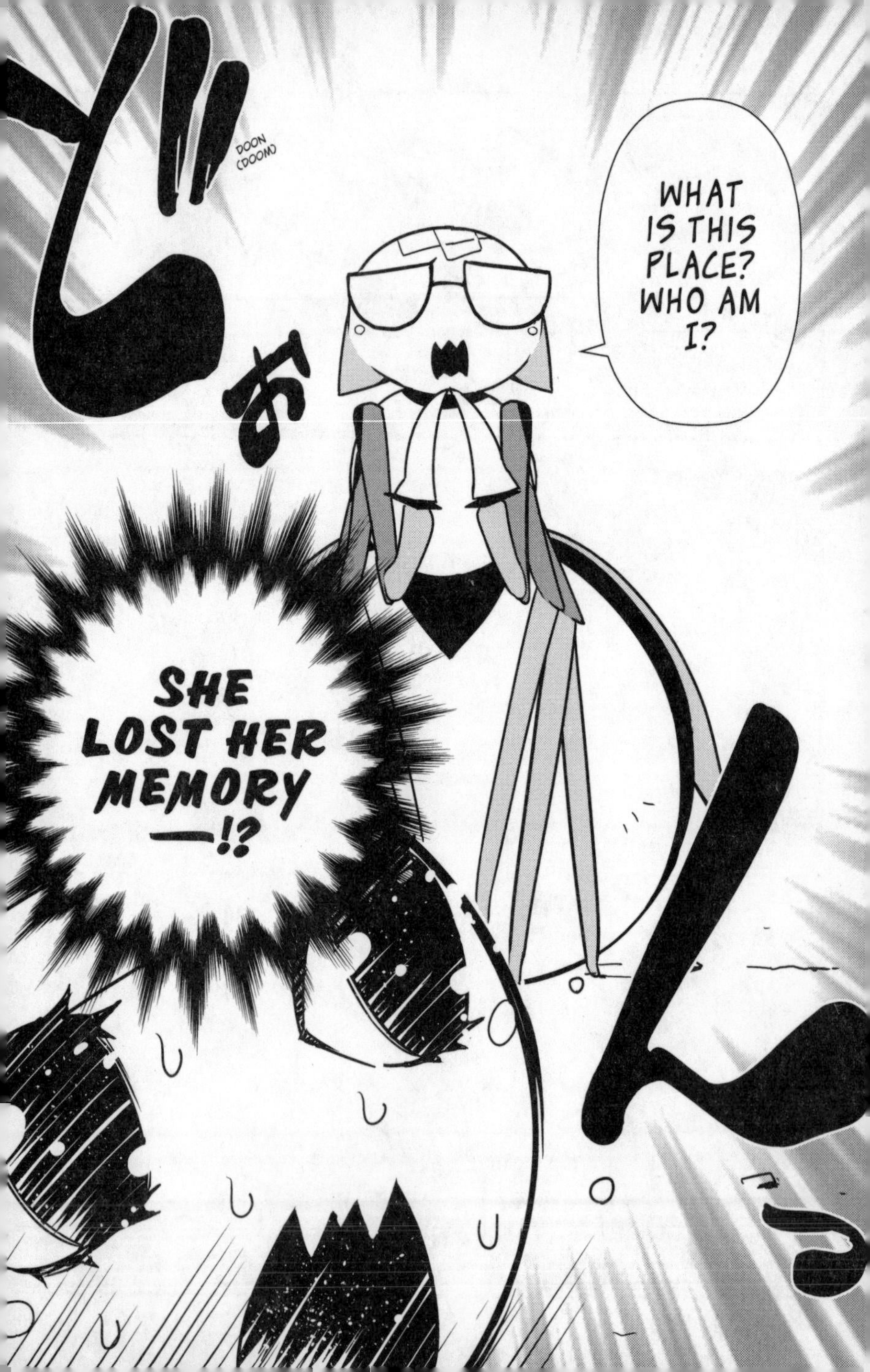
WHAT IS THIS PLACE? WHO AM I?
どおん
DOON (DOOM)
SHE LOST HER MEMORY —!?

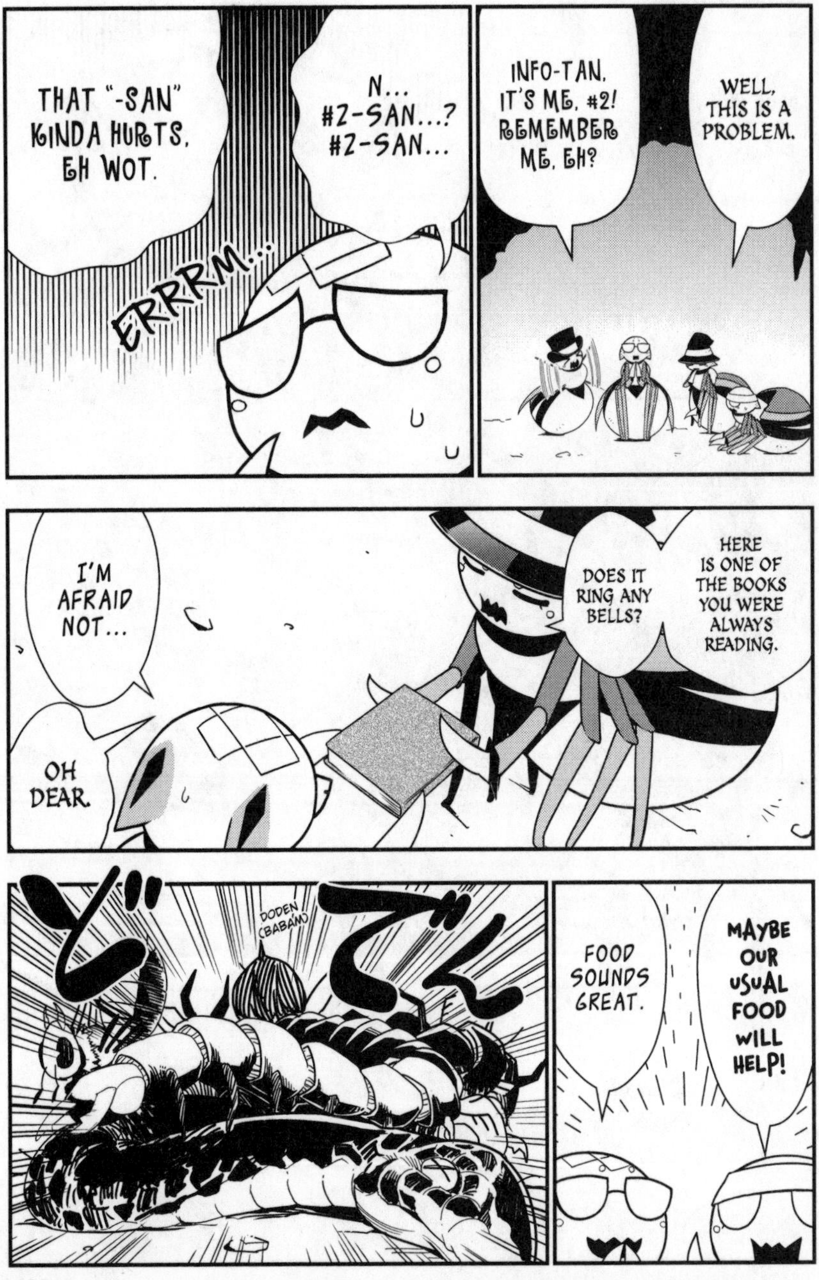
WELL, THIS IS A PROBLEM.
INFO-TAN, IT'S ME, #2! REMEMBER ME, EH?
N... #2-SAN...? #2-SAN...
ERRRM...
THAT "-SAN" KINDA HURTS, EH WOT.
HERE IS ONE OF THE BOOKS YOU WERE ALWAYS READING.
DOES IT RING ANY BELLS?
I'M AFRAID NOT...
OH DEAR.
MAYBE OUR USUAL FOOD WILL HELP!
FOOD SOUNDS GREAT.
どでん
DODEN (BABAM)

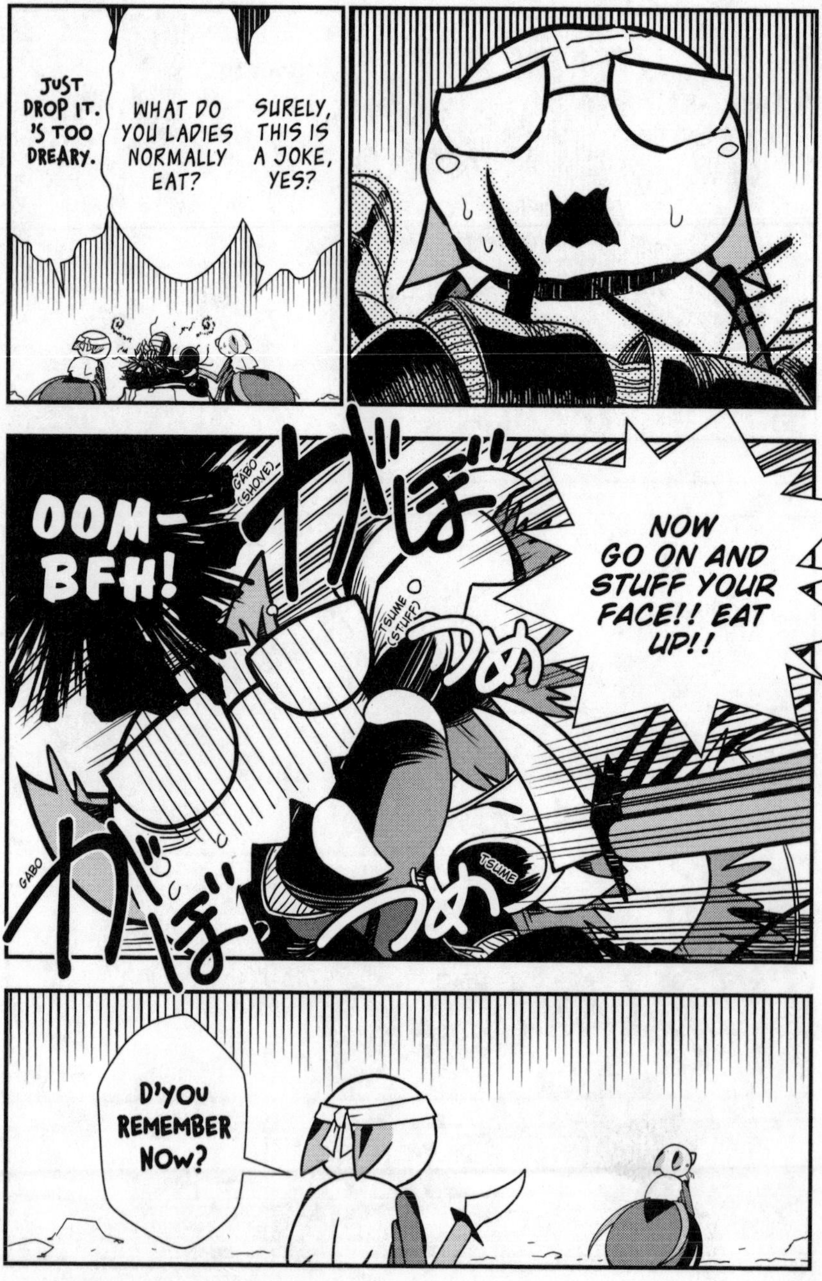
SURELY, THIS IS A JOKE, YES?
WHAT DO YOU LADIES NORMALLY EAT?
JUST DROP IT. 'S TOO DREARY.
NOW GO ON AND STUFF YOUR FACE!! EAT UP!!
がぼ
GABO (SHOVE)
つめ
TSLIME (STUFF)
OOM-BFH!
がぼ
GABO
つめ
TSLIME
D'YOU REMEMBER NOW?

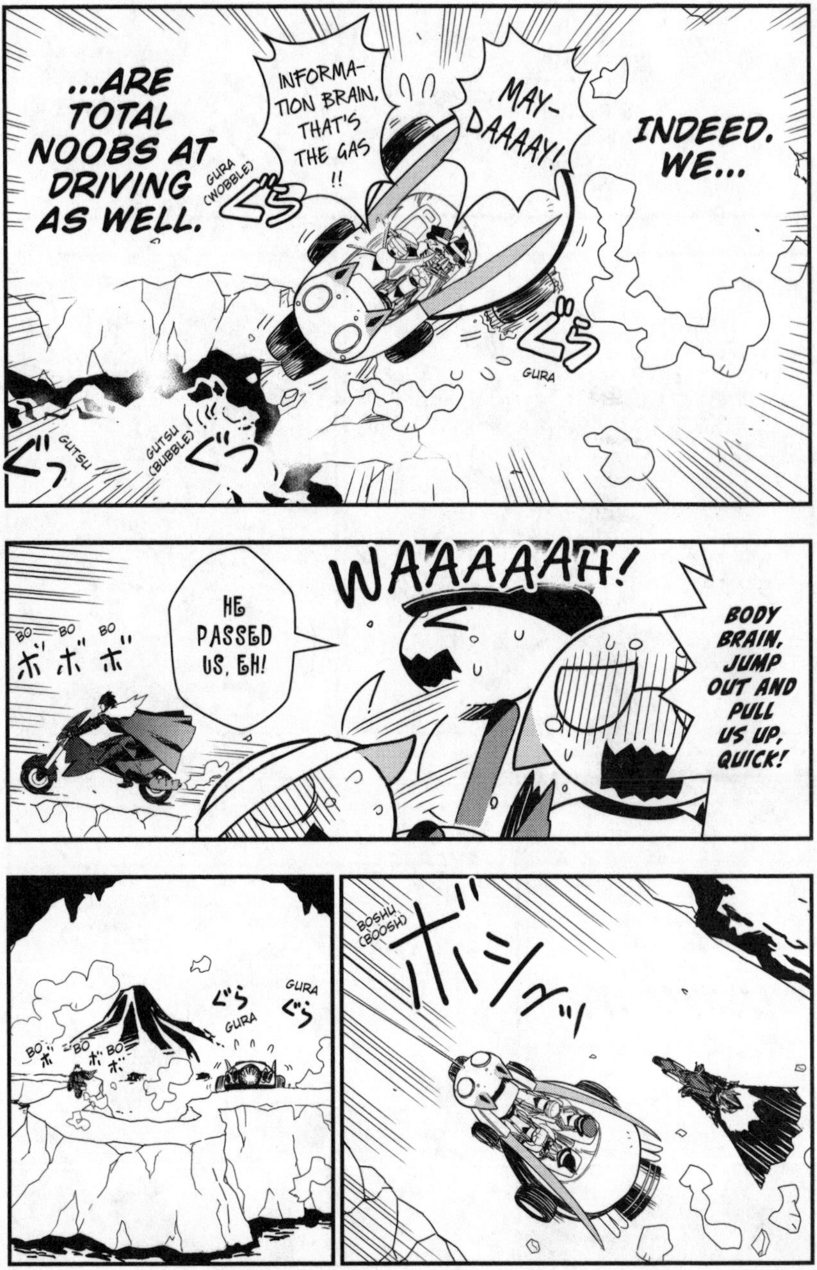
INDEED. WE...
MAY-DAAAAY!!
INFORMATION BRAIN, THAT'S THE GAS!!
...ARE TOTAL NOOBS AT DRIVING AS WELL.
GURA (WOBBLE) ぐら
ぐら GURA
GUTSU (BUBBLE) ぐつ
GUTSU ぐつ
BODY BRAIN, JUMP OUT AND PULL US UP, QUICK!
WAAAAAH!
HE PASSED US, EH!
BO BO BO ボボボ
BOSHU (BOOSH) ボシュッ
GURA ぐら
GURA ぐら
BO BO BO ボボボ

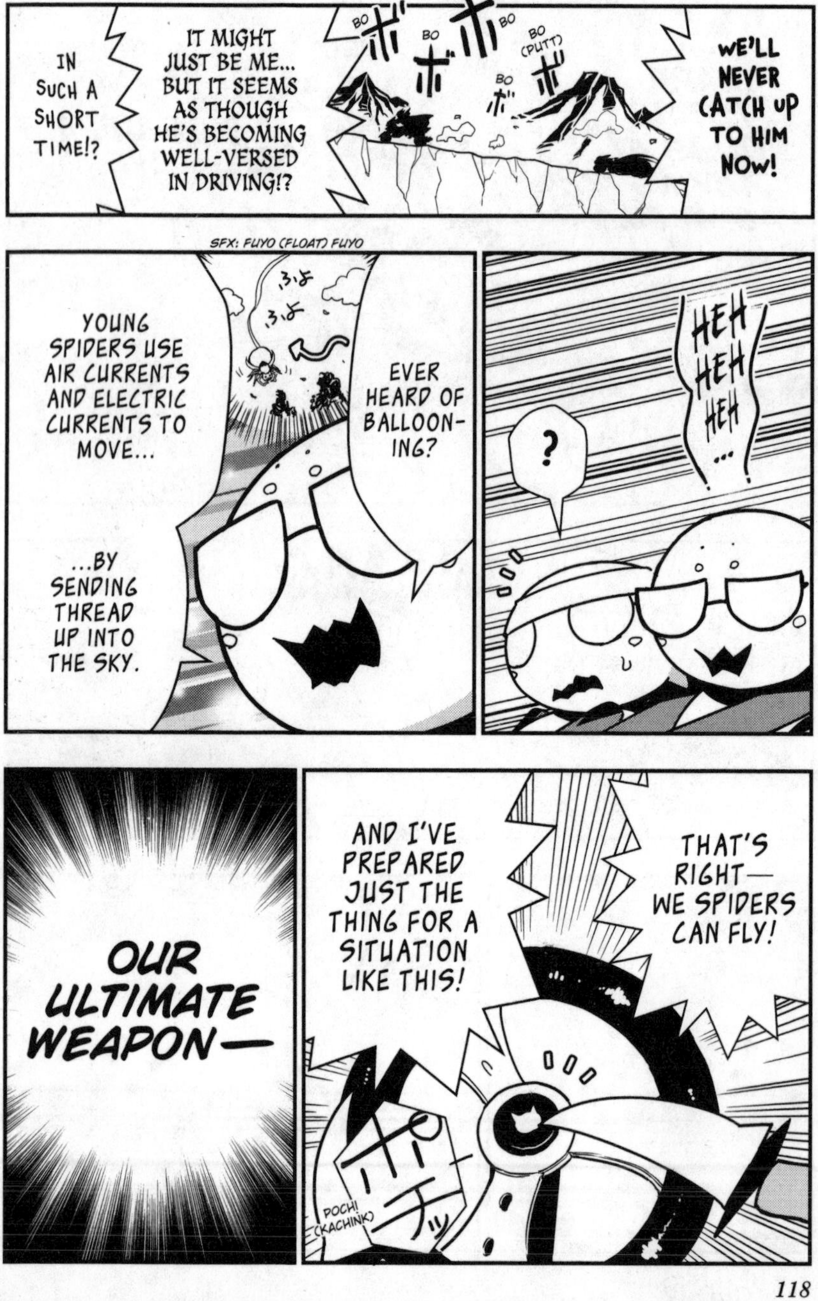
WE'LL NEVER CATCH UP TO HIM NOW!
BO BO BO BO BO (PUTT)
IT MIGHT JUST BE ME... BUT IT SEEMS AS THOUGH HE'S BECOMING WELL-VERSED IN DRIVING!?
IN SUCH A SHORT TIME!?
SFX: FUYO (FLOAT) FUYO
HEH HEH HEH ...
?
EVER HEARD OF BALLOON-ING?
YOUNG SPIDERS USE AIR CURRENTS AND ELECTRIC CURRENTS TO MOVE...
...BY SENDING THREAD UP INTO THE SKY.
THAT'S RIGHT— WE SPIDERS CAN FLY!
AND I'VE PREPARED JUST THE THING FOR A SITUATION LIKE THIS!
POCHI (KACHINK)
OUR ULTIMATE WEAPON—

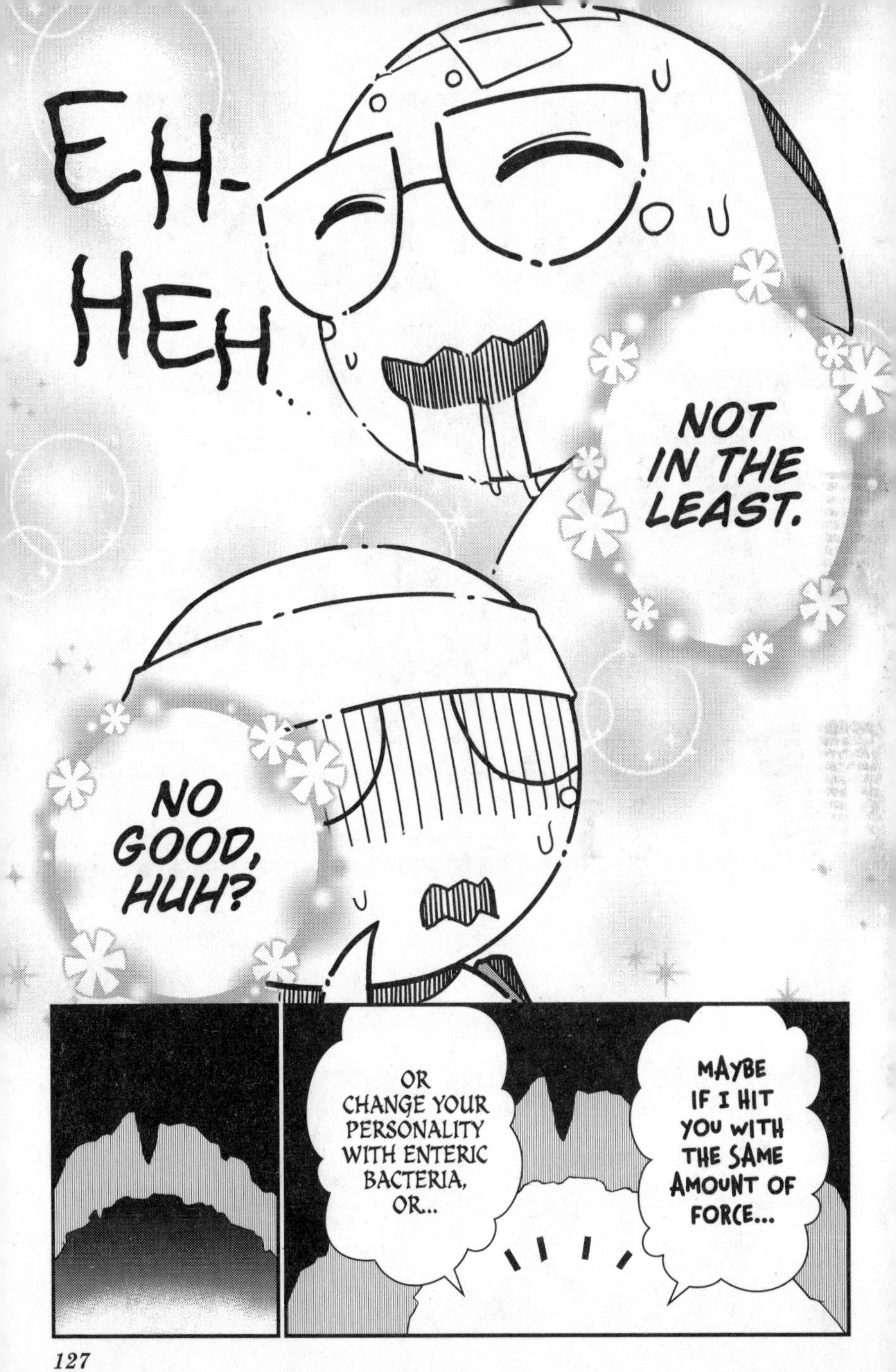
EH-HEH...
NOT IN THE LEAST.
NO GOOD, HUH?
MAYBE IF I HIT YOU WITH THE SAME AMOUNT OF FORCE...
OR CHANGE YOUR PERSONALITY WITH ENTERIC BACTERIA, OR...

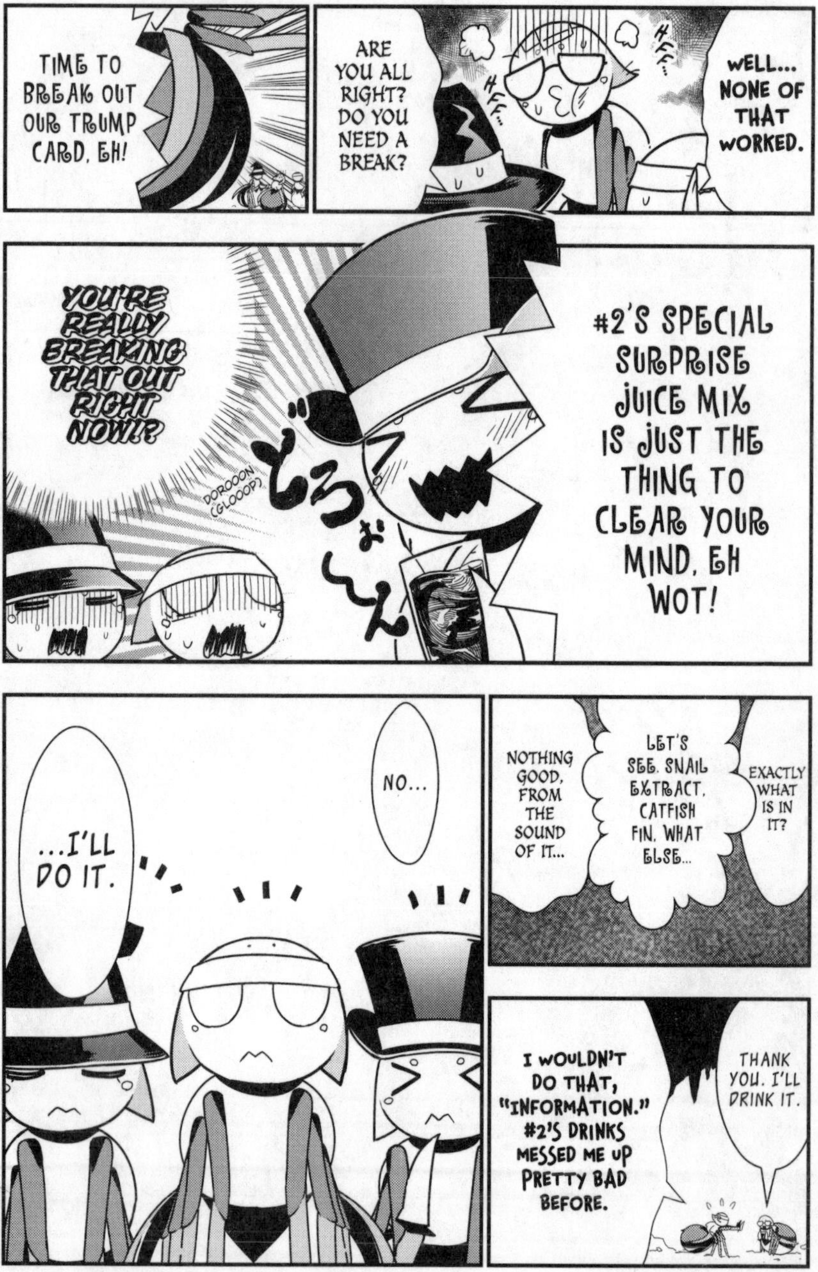
WELL... NONE OF THAT WORKED.
HFF...
HFF...
ARE YOU ALL RIGHT? DO YOU NEED A BREAK?
TIME TO BREAK OUT OUR TRUMP CARD, EH!
#2'S SPECIAL SURPRISE JUICE MIX IS JUST THE THING TO CLEAR YOUR MIND, EH WOT!
YOU'RE REALLY BREAKING THAT OUT RIGHT NOW!?
どろぉ〜ん
DOROOON (GLOOOP)
EXACTLY WHAT IS IN IT?
LET'S SEE. SNAIL EXTRACT, CATFISH FIN, WHAT ELSE...
NOTHING GOOD, FROM THE SOUND OF IT...
THANK YOU. I'LL DRINK IT.
I WOULDN'T DO THAT, "INFORMATION." #2'S DRINKS MESSED ME UP PRETTY BAD BEFORE.
NO...
...I'LL DO IT.

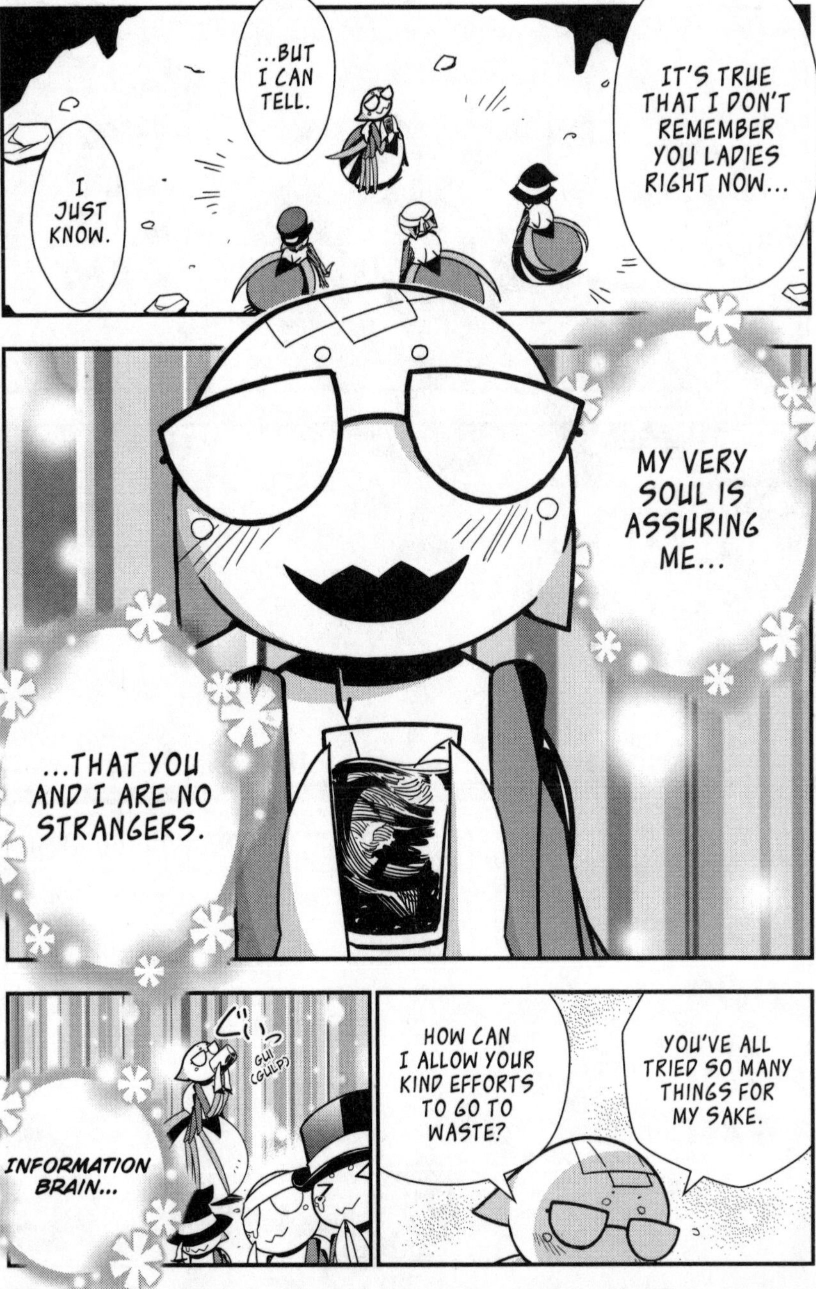
IT'S TRUE THAT I DON'T REMEMBER YOU LADIES RIGHT NOW...
...BUT I CAN TELL.
I JUST KNOW.
MY VERY SOUL IS ASSURING ME...
...THAT YOU AND I ARE NO STRANGERS.
YOU'VE ALL TRIED SO MANY THINGS FOR MY SAKE.
HOW CAN I ALLOW YOUR KIND EFFORTS TO GO TO WASTE?
ぐいっ
GUI (GULP)
INFORMATION BRAIN...

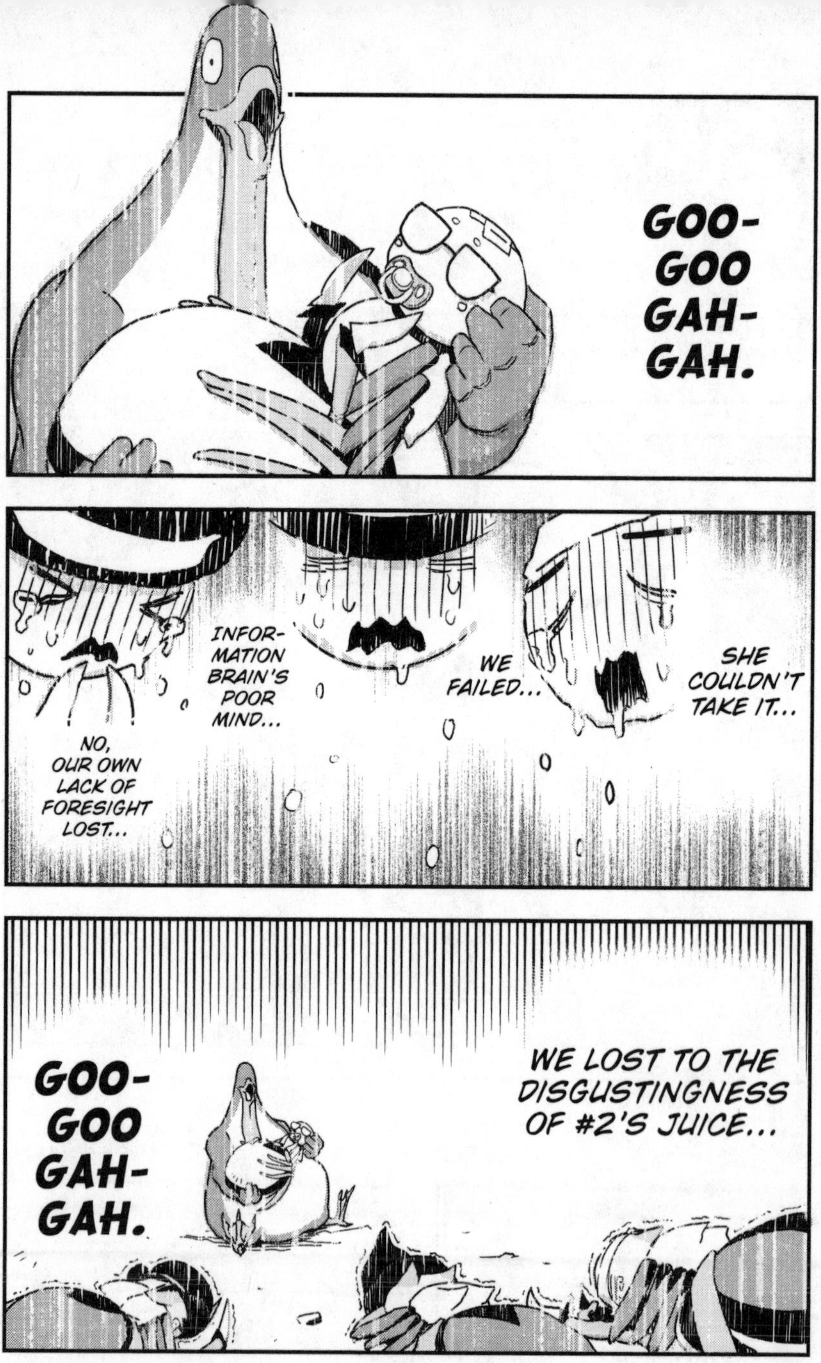
GOO-GOO GAH-GAH.
SHE COULDN'T TAKE IT...
WE FAILED...
INFORMATION BRAIN'S POOR MIND...
NO, OUR OWN LACK OF FORESIGHT LOST...
WE LOST TO THE DISGUSTINGNESS OF #2'S JUICE...
GOO-GOO GAH-GAH.

So I'm a Spider, so What?

THE DAILY LIVES OF THE KUMOKO SISTERS

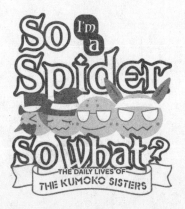

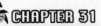

CHAPTER 31

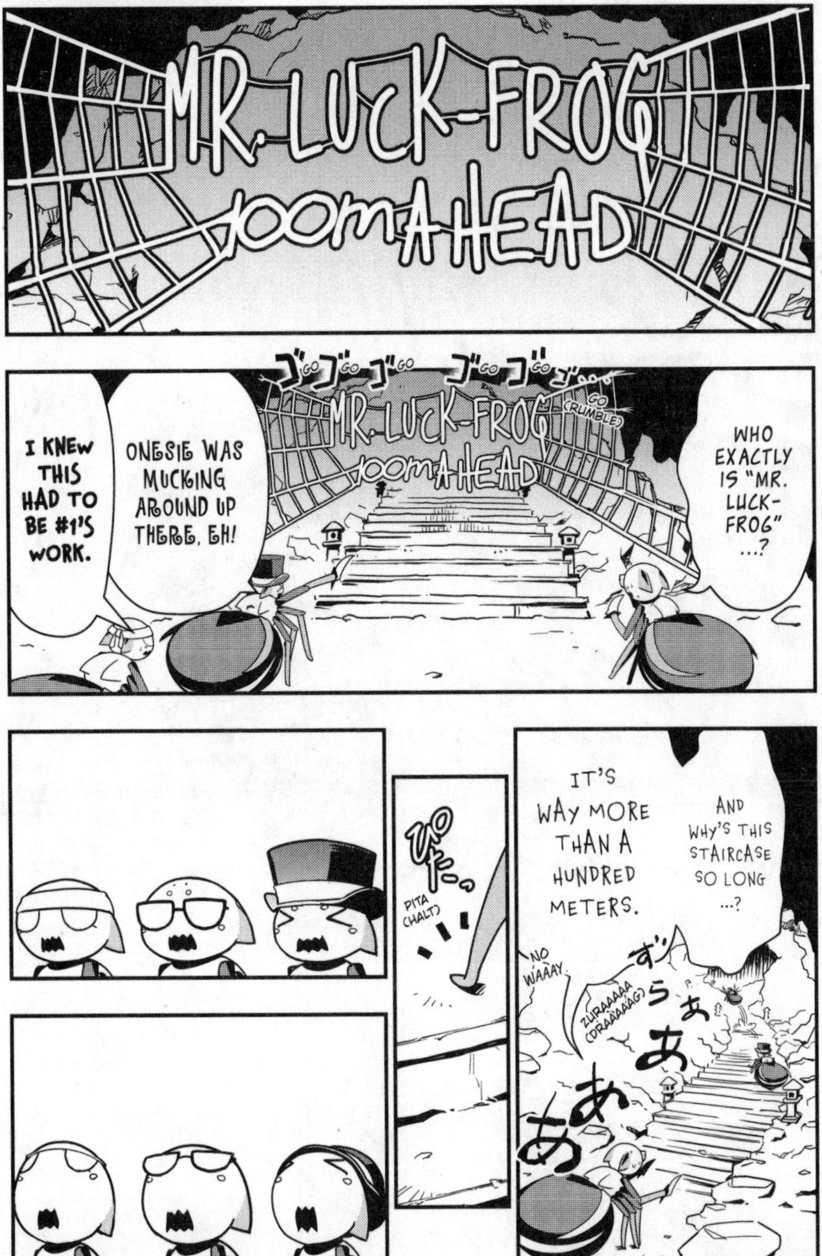
MR. LUCK-FROG 100M AHEAD
ゴゴゴゴゴ… GO (RUMBLE)
MR. LUCK-FROG 100M AHEAD
WHO EXACTLY IS "MR. LUCK-FROG"...?
ONESIE WAS MUCKING AROUND UP THERE, EH!
I KNEW THIS HAD TO BE #1'S WORK.
AND WHY'S THIS STAIRCASE SO LONG...?
IT'S WAY MORE THAN A HUNDRED METERS.
ずらあああ
ZURAAAAA (DRAAAAAG)
NO WAAAY.
ぴたーっ
PITA (HALT)

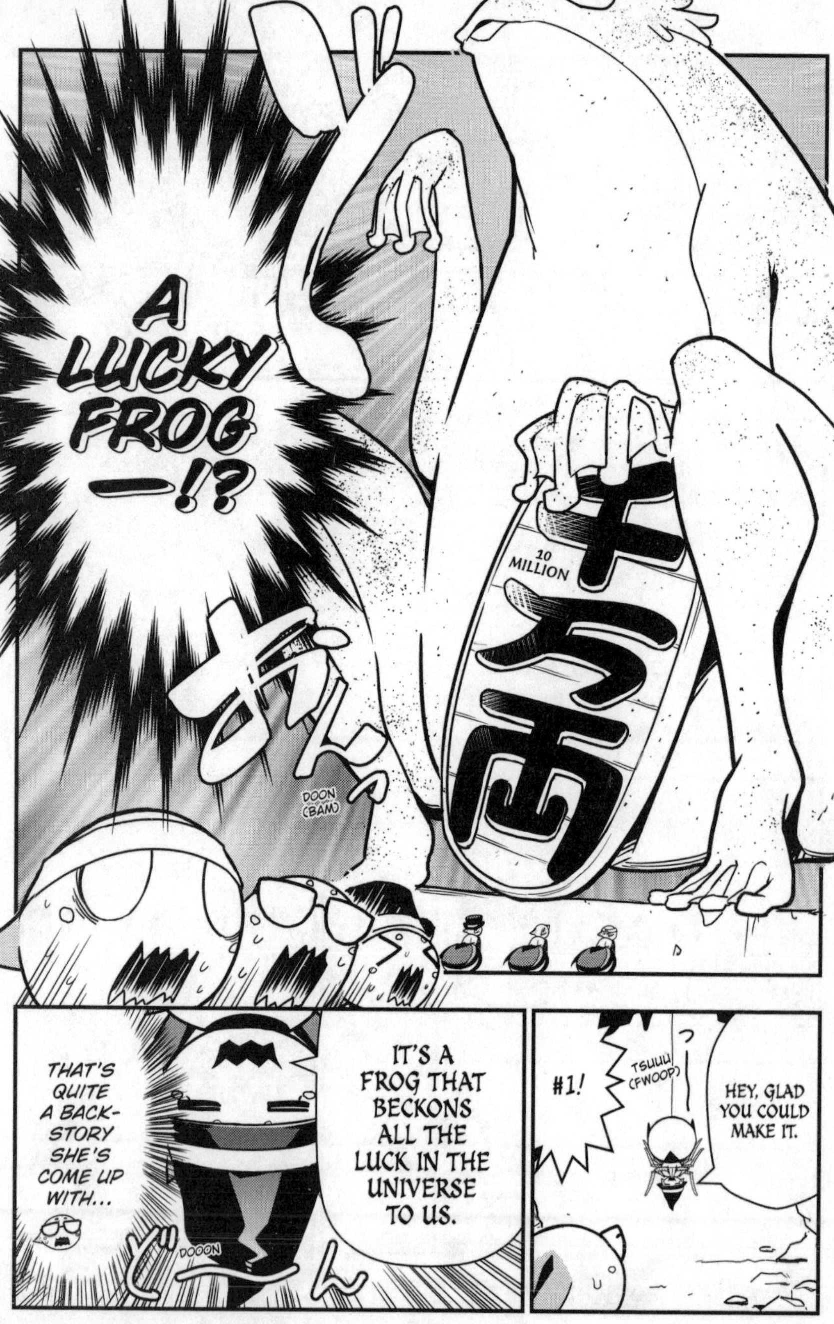
A LUCKY FROG—!?
10 MILLION
DOON (BAM)
HEY, GLAD YOU COULD MAKE IT.
TSUUU (FWOOP)
#1!
IT'S A FROG THAT BECKONS ALL THE LUCK IN THE UNIVERSE TO US.
DOOON
THAT'S QUITE A BACK-STORY SHE'S COME UP WITH...

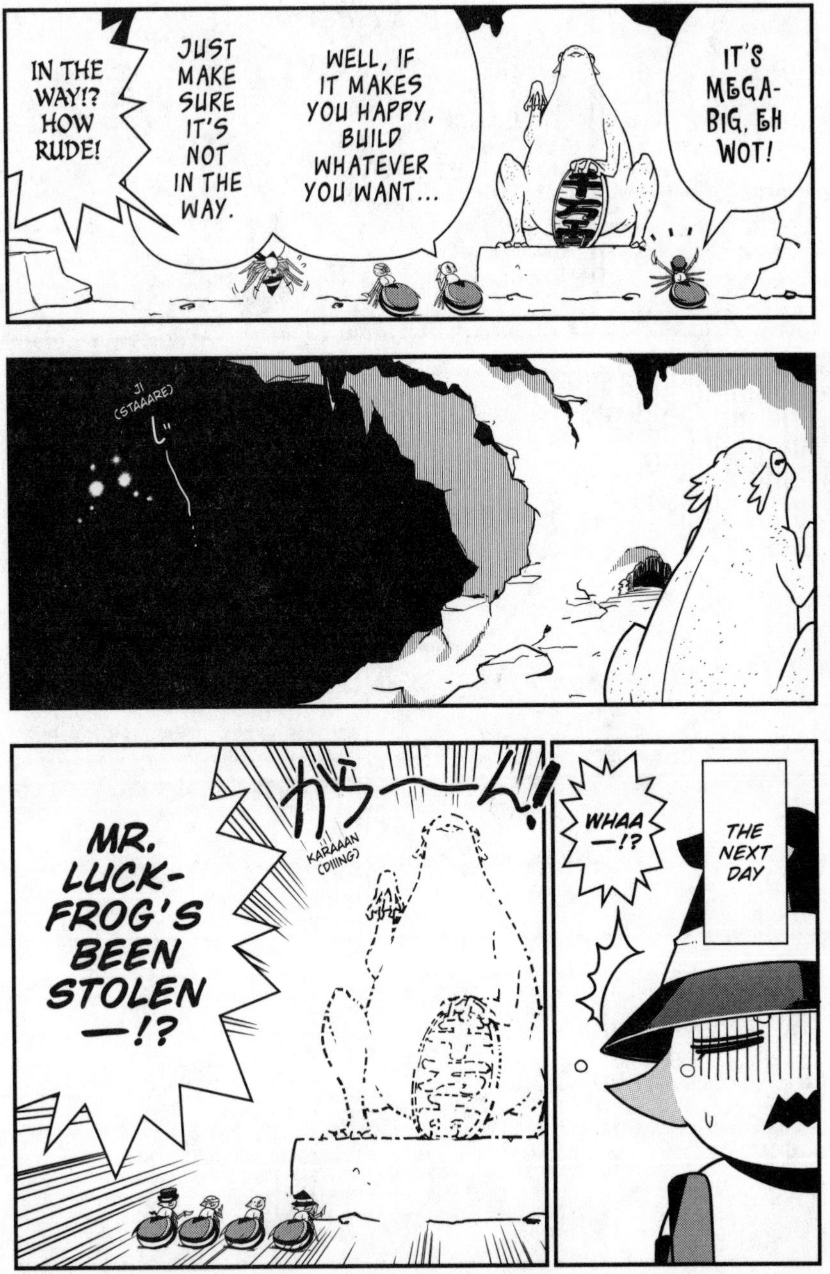
IT'S MEGA-BIG, EH WOT!
WELL, IF IT MAKES YOU HAPPY, BUILD WHATEVER YOU WANT...
JUST MAKE SURE IT'S NOT IN THE WAY.
IN THE WAY!? HOW RUDE!
JI (STAAARE)
THE NEXT DAY
WHAA—!?
から〜ん!
KARAAAN (DIIING)
MR. LUCK-FROG'S BEEN STOLEN—!?

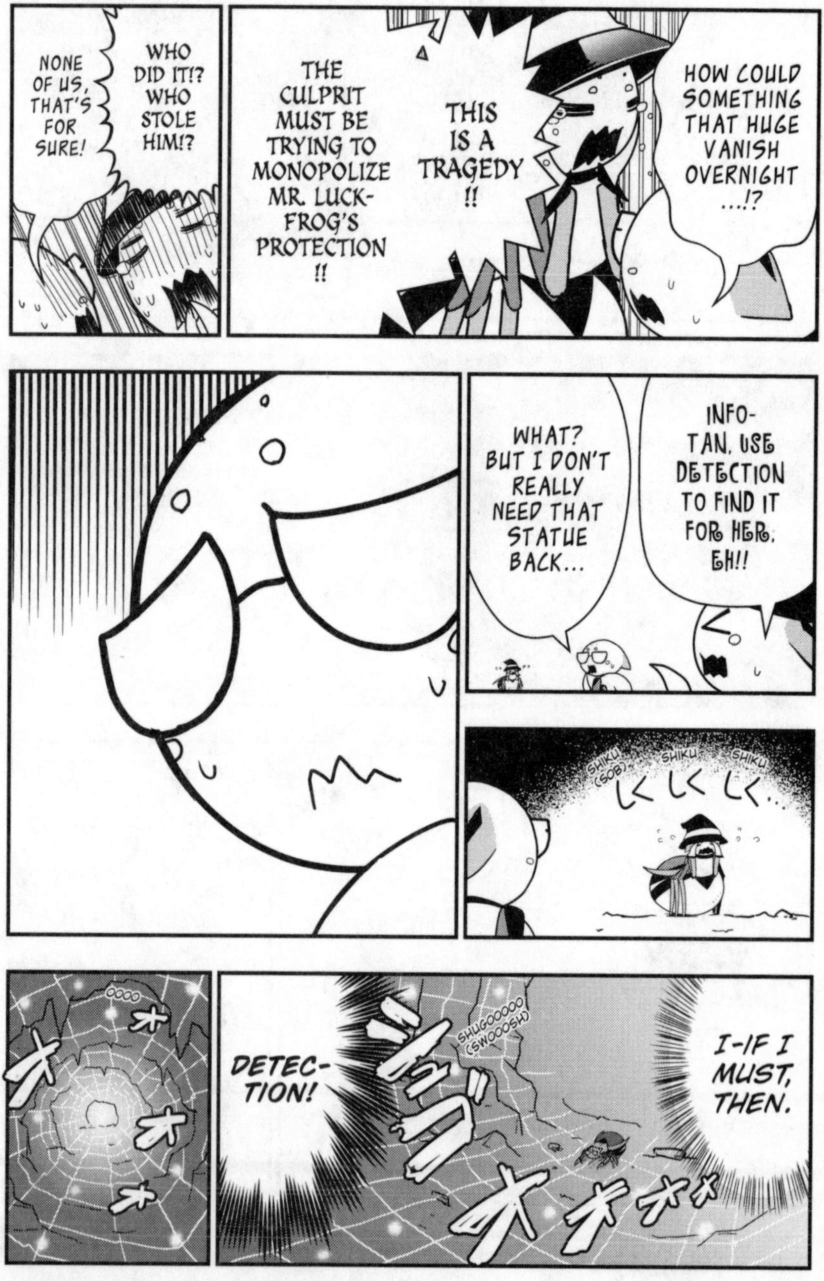
HOW COULD SOMETHING THAT HUGE VANISH OVERNIGHT ....!?
THIS IS A TRAGEDY !!
THE CULPRIT MUST BE TRYING TO MONOPOLIZE MR. LUCK-FROG'S PROTECTION !!
WHO DID IT!? WHO STOLE HIM!?
NONE OF US, THAT'S FOR SURE!
INFO-TAN, USE DETECTION TO FIND IT FOR HER, EH!!
WHAT? BUT I DON'T REALLY NEED THAT STATUE BACK...
SHIKU (SOB) SHIKU SHIKU
しくしく...
I-IF I MUST, THEN.
SHUGOOOOO (SWOOOSH)
DETECTION!
OOOO

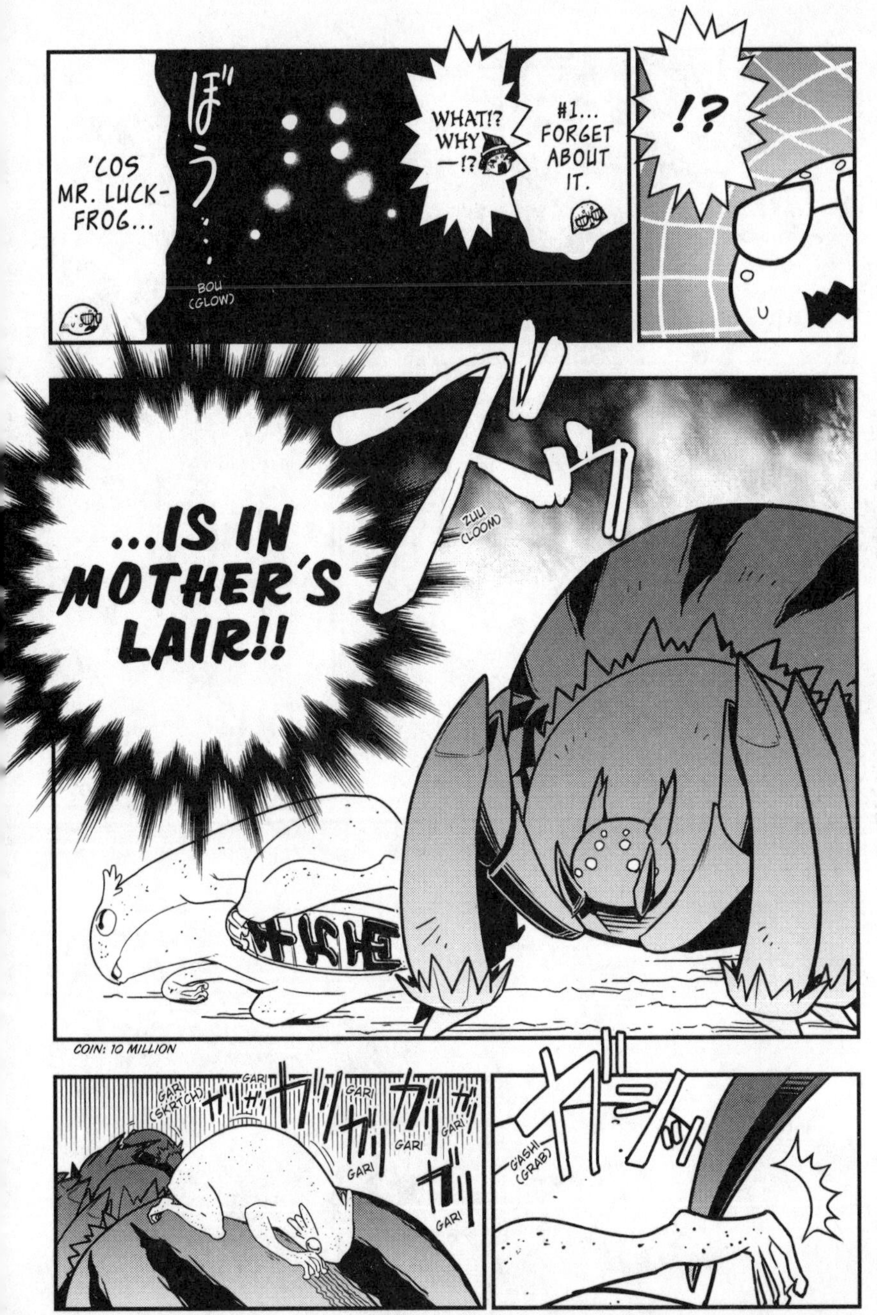
!?
WHAT!? WHY—!?
#1... FORGET ABOUT IT.
ぼう
BOU (GLOW)
'COS MR. LUCK-FROG...
ズッ
ZUU (LOOM)
...IS IN MOTHER'S LAIR!!
ガシッ
GASHI (GRAB)
ガリガリガリガリガリガリ
GARI (SKRTCH)
GARI
GARI
GARI
GARI
GARI
GARI
COIN: 10 MILLION

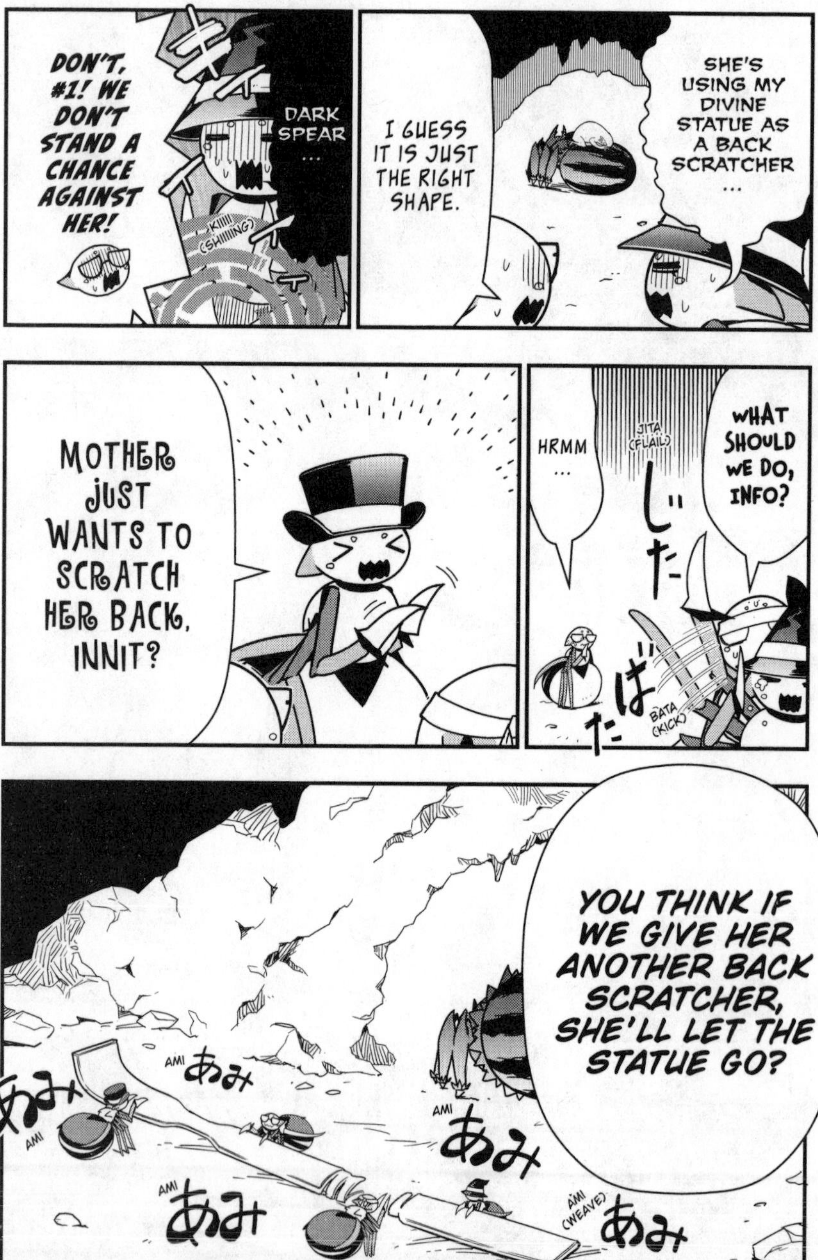
SHE'S USING MY DIVINE STATUE AS A BACK SCRATCHER ...
I GUESS IT IS JUST THE RIGHT SHAPE.
DARK SPEAR ...
KIIIII (SHIIIING)
DON'T, #1! WE DON'T STAND A CHANCE AGAINST HER!
WHAT SHOULD WE DO, INFO?
JITA (FLAIL)
じた
HRMM ...
ばた
BATA (KICK)
MOTHER JUST WANTS TO SCRATCH HER BACK, INNIT?
YOU THINK IF WE GIVE HER ANOTHER BACK SCRATCHER, SHE'LL LET THE STATUE GO?
AMI あみ
AMI あみ
AMI あみ
AMI (WEAVE) あみ
AMI あみ

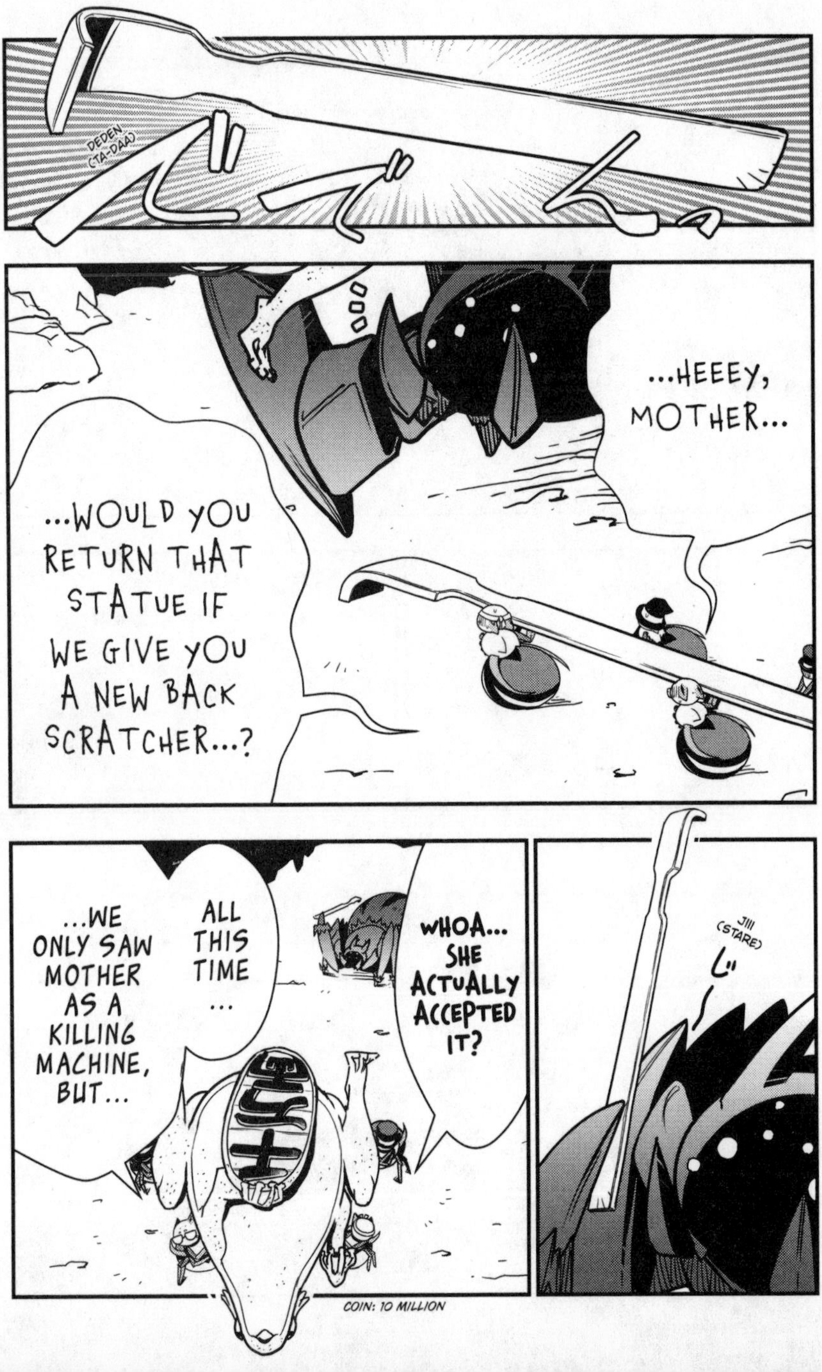
DEDEN (TA-DAA)
...HEEEY, MOTHER...
...WOULD YOU RETURN THAT STATUE IF WE GIVE YOU A NEW BACK SCRATCHER...?
JIII (STARE)
WHOA... SHE ACTUALLY ACCEPTED IT?
ALL THIS TIME...
...WE ONLY SAW MOTHER AS A KILLING MACHINE, BUT...
COIN: 10 MILLION

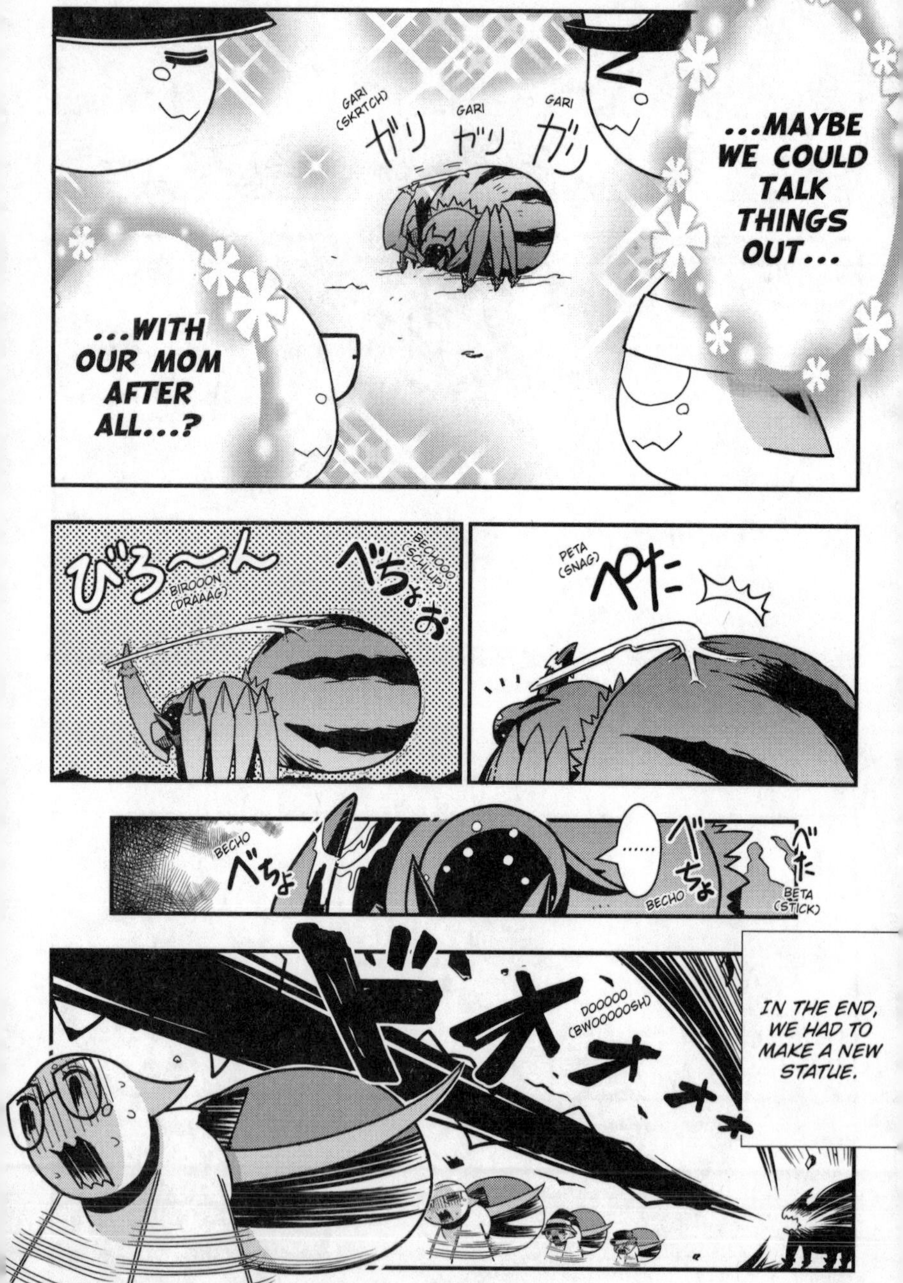
...MAYBE WE COULD TALK THINGS OUT...
GARI
GARI
GARI (SKRTCH)
...WITH OUR MOM AFTER ALL...?
PETA (SNAG)
BECHOOO (SCHLUP)
BIROOON (DRAAAG)
BETA (STICK)
BECHO
......
BECHO
IN THE END, WE HAD TO MAKE A NEW STATUE.
DOOOOO (BWOOOOOSH)

So I'm a Spider, so What?

THE DAILY LIVES OF

THE KUMOKO SISTERS

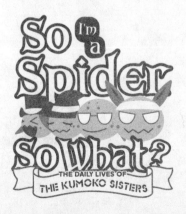

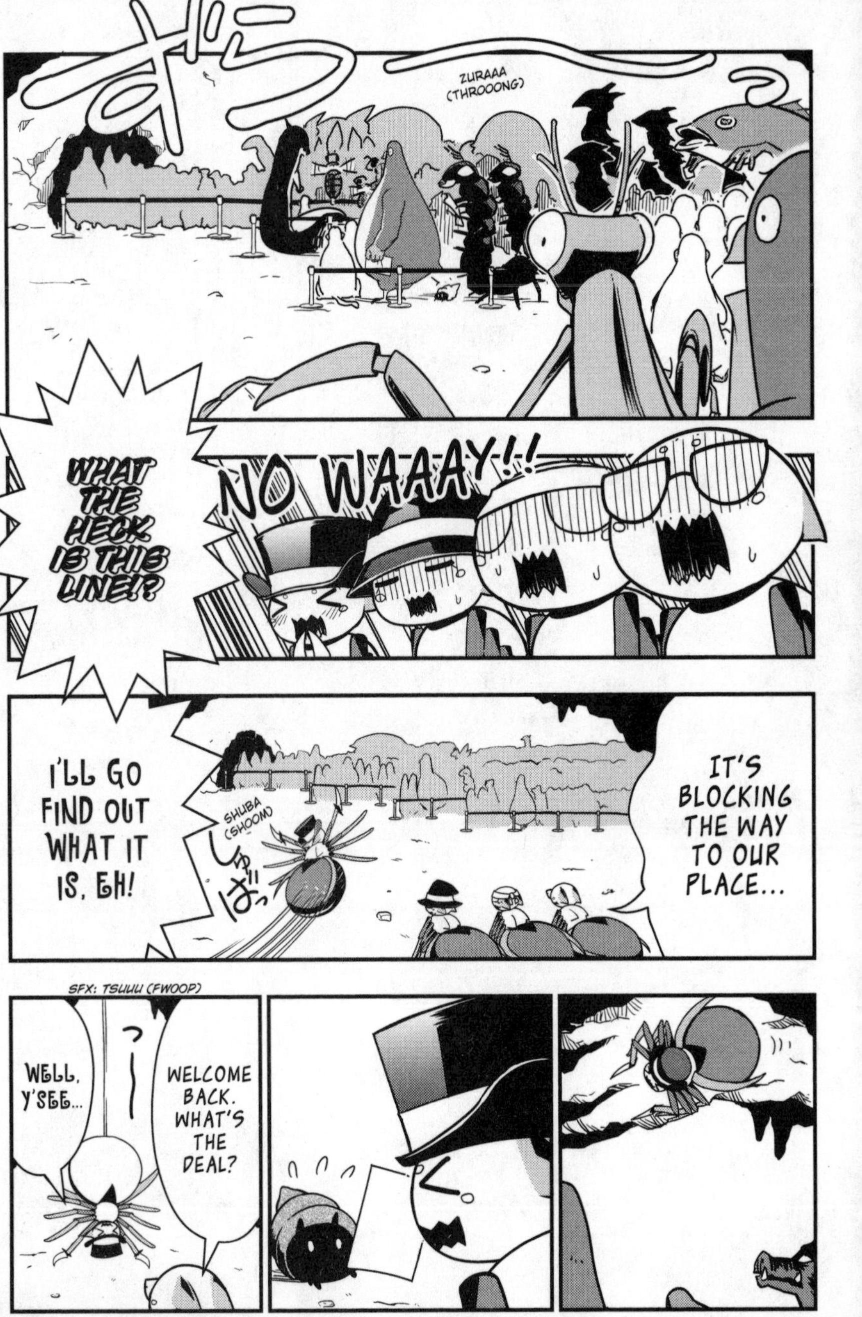
ZURAAA (THROOONG)
NO WAAAY!!
WHAT THE HECK IS THIS LINE!?
IT'S BLOCKING THE WAY TO OUR PLACE...
SHUBA (SHOOM)
I'LL GO FIND OUT WHAT IT IS, EH!
SFX: TSUUU (FWOOP)
WELCOME BACK. WHAT'S THE DEAL?
WELL, Y'SEE...

CHAPTER 32

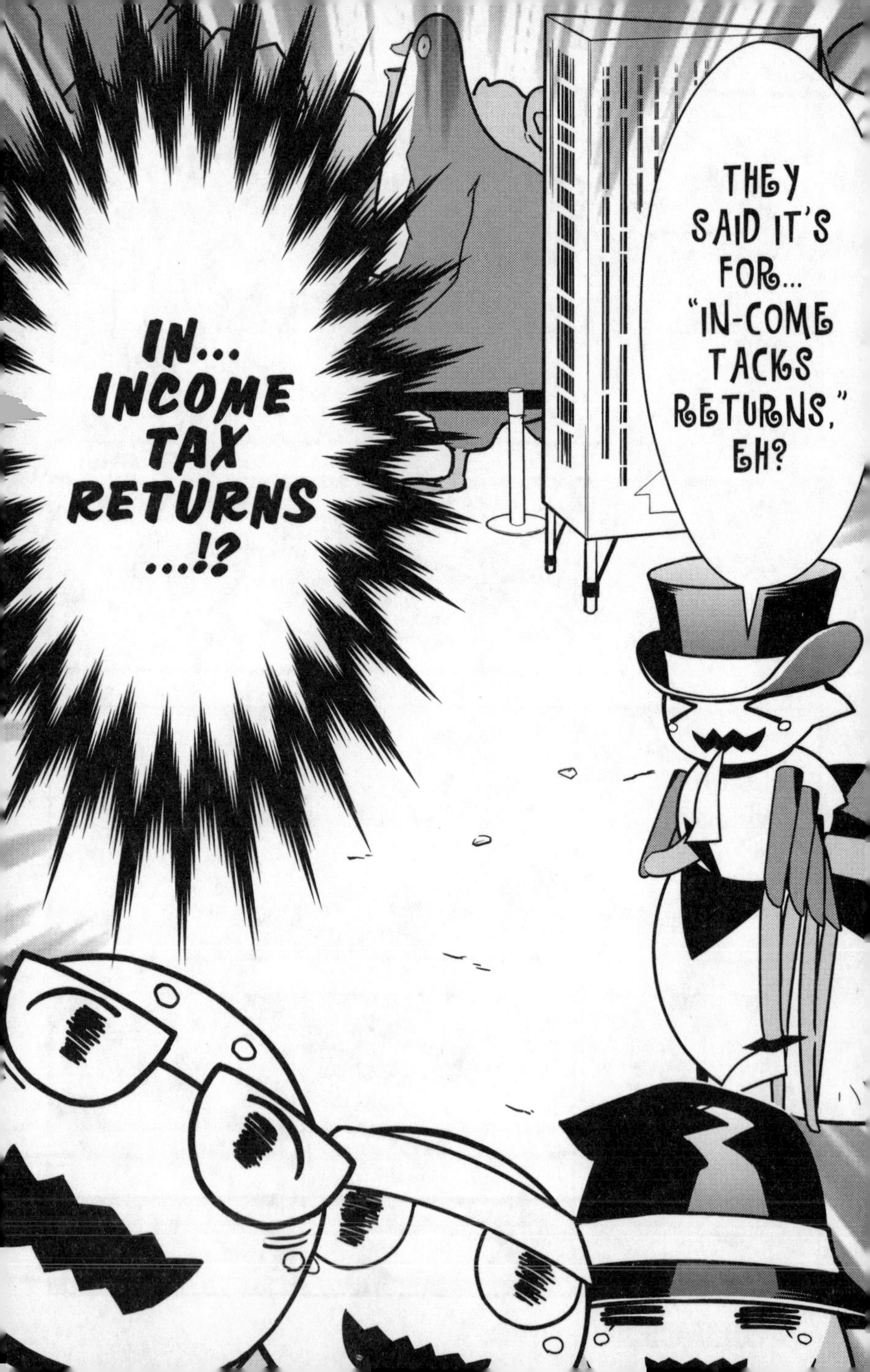
THEY SAID IT'S FOR... "IN-COME TACKS RETURNS," EH?
IN... INCOME TAX RETURNS ...!?

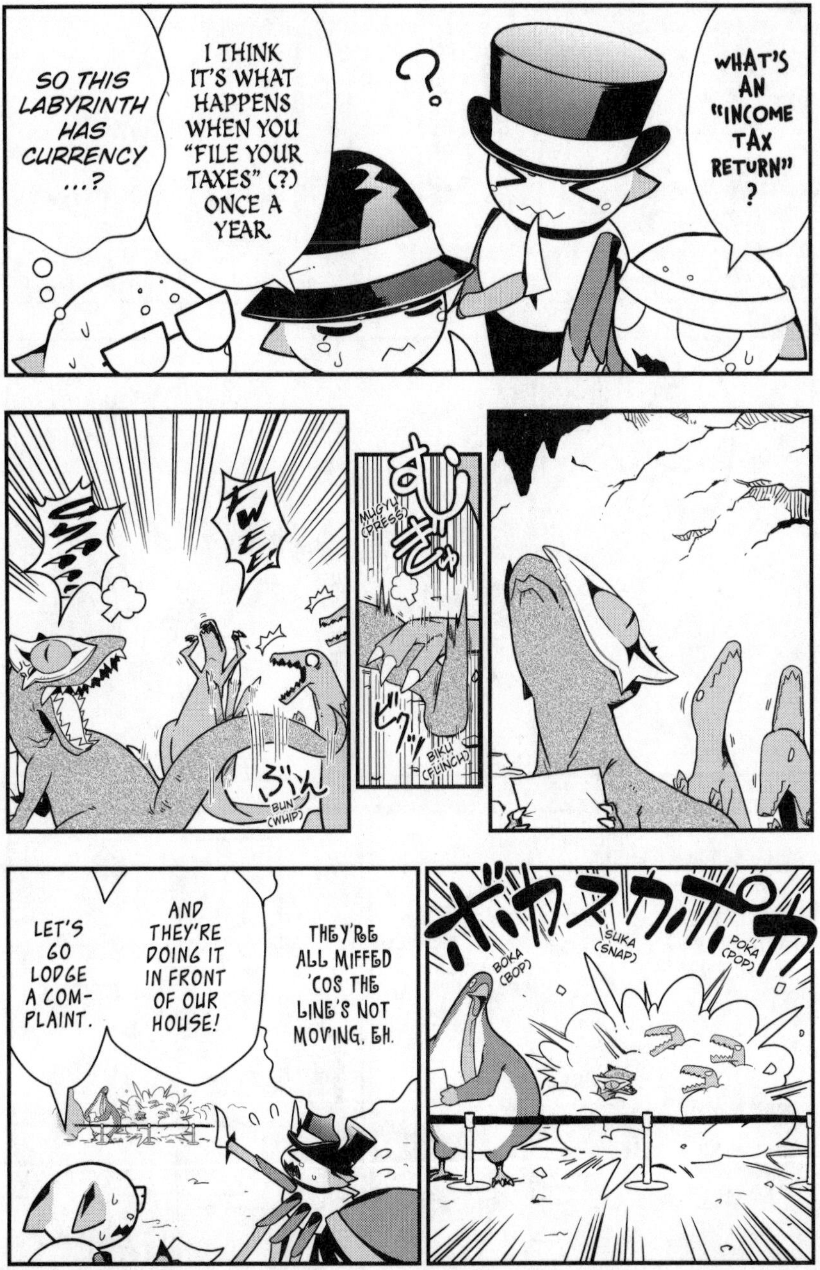
WHAT'S AN "INCOME TAX RETURN"?
?
I THINK IT'S WHAT HAPPENS WHEN YOU "FILE YOUR TAXES" (?) ONCE A YEAR.
SO THIS LABYRINTH HAS CURRENCY...?
むぎゅ
MUGYU (PRESS)
ビクッ
BIKU (FLINCH)
FWEE!
ぶぅん
BUN (WHIP)
ボカスカポカ
BOKA (BOP)
SUKA (SNAP)
POKA (POP)
THEY'RE ALL MIFFED 'COS THE LINE'S NOT MOVING, EH.
AND THEY'RE DOING IT IN FRONT OF OUR HOUSE!
LET'S GO LODGE A COM-PLAINT.

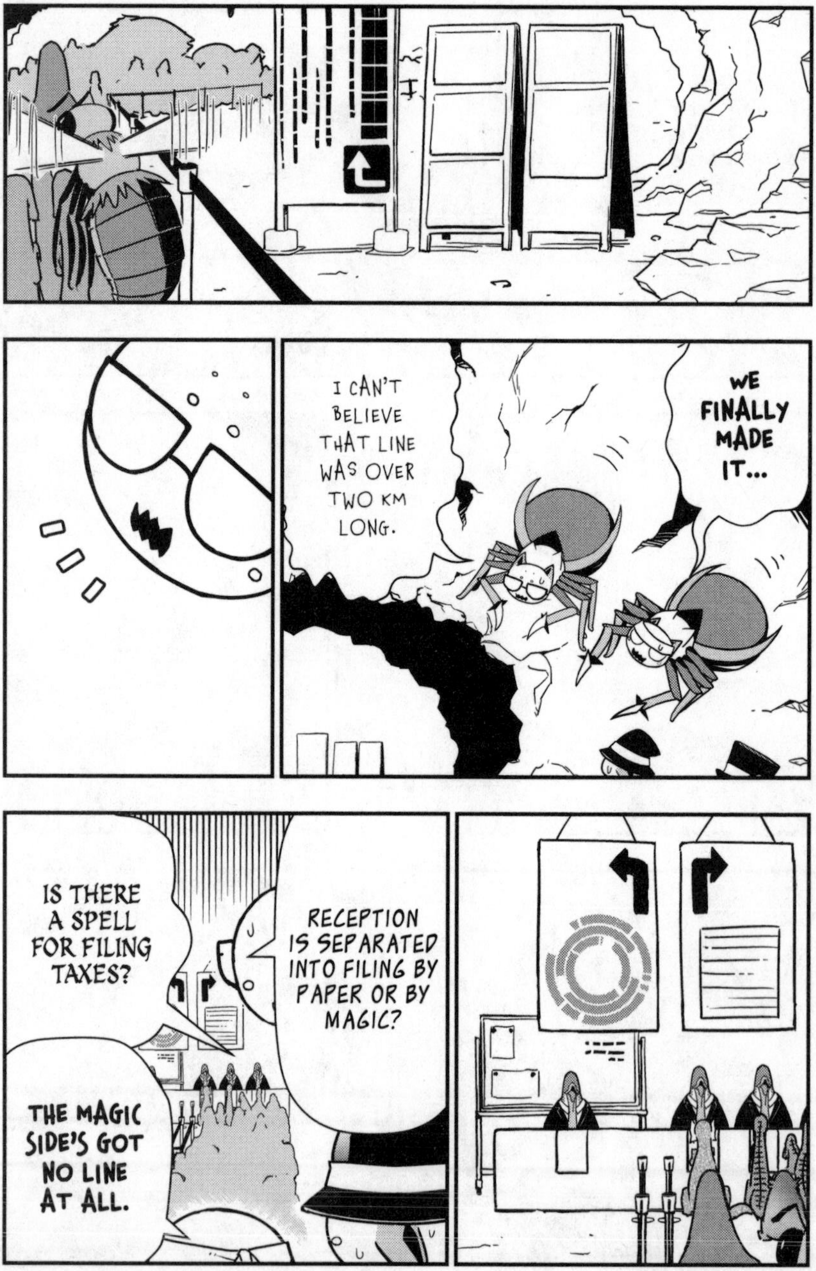
WE FINALLY MADE IT...
I CAN'T BELIEVE THAT LINE WAS OVER TWO KM LONG.
RECEPTION IS SEPARATED INTO FILING BY PAPER OR BY MAGIC?
IS THERE A SPELL FOR FILING TAXES?
THE MAGIC SIDE'S GOT NO LINE AT ALL.

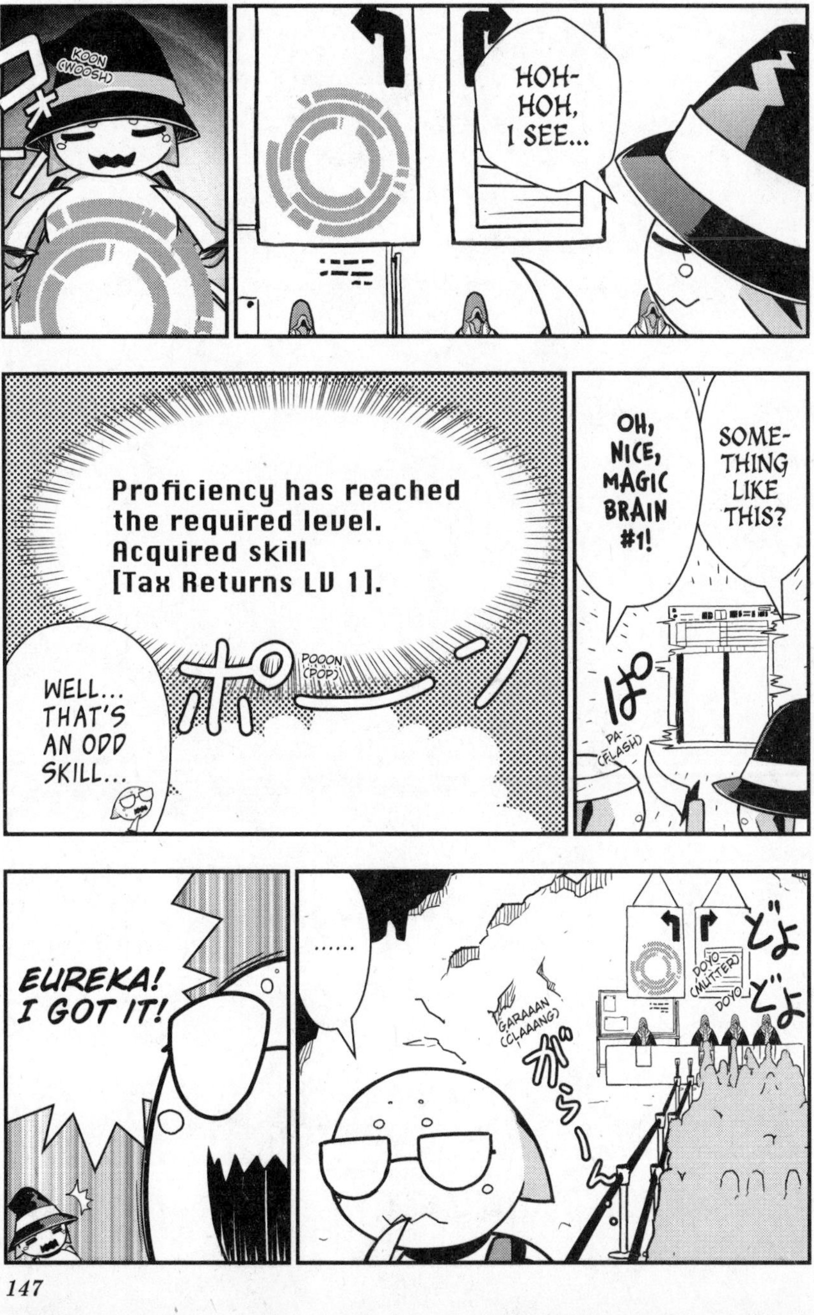
HOH-HOH, I SEE...
KOON (WOOSH)
SOME-THING LIKE THIS?
OH, NICE, MAGIC BRAIN #1!
PA- (FLASH)
Proficiency has reached the required level. Acquired skill [Tax Returns LV 1].
POOON (POP)
WELL... THAT'S AN ODD SKILL...
DOYO (MUTTER) DOYO
......
GARAAAN (CLAAANG)
EUREKA! I GOT IT!

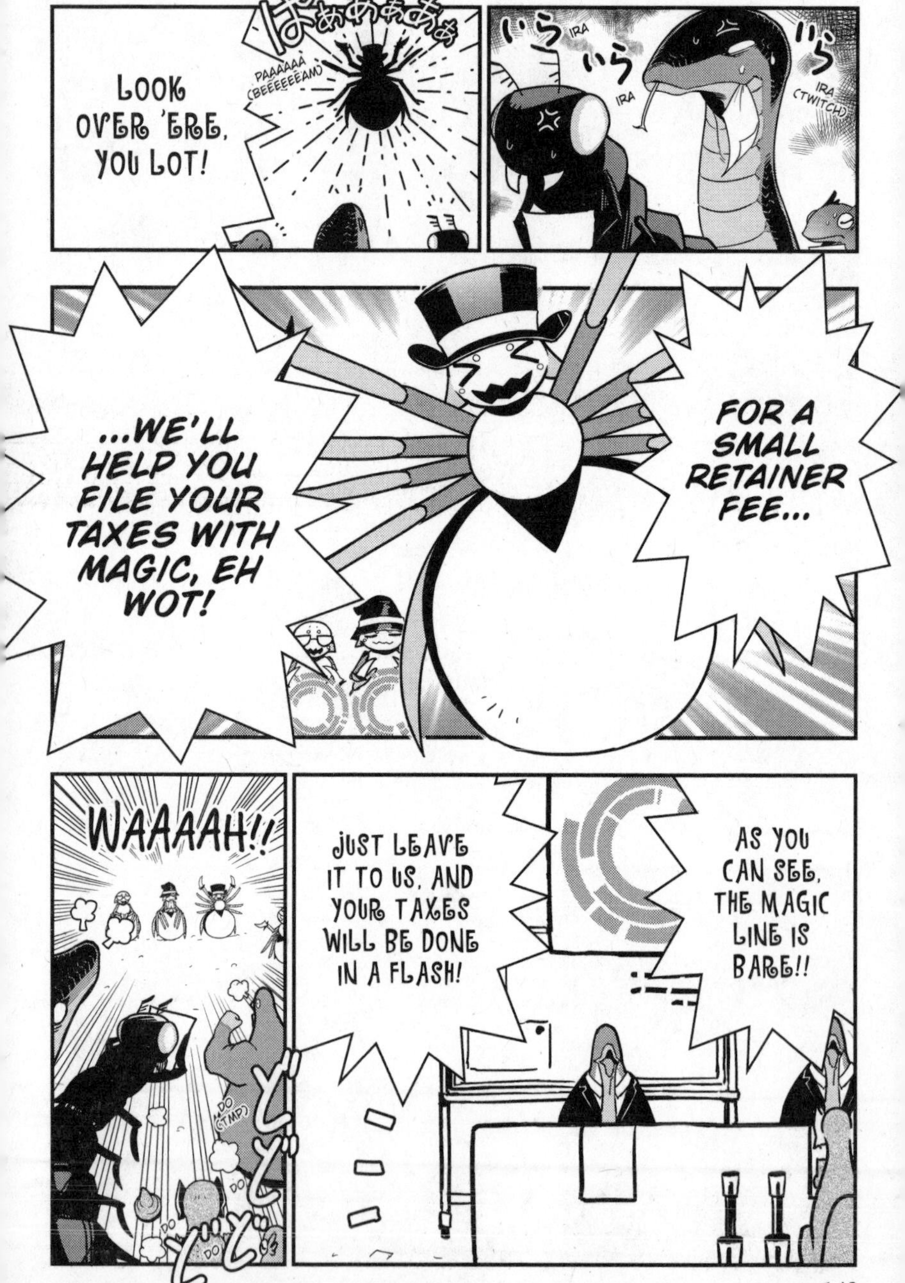
いら
IRA
いら
IRA
いら
IRA (TWITCH)
ぱぁぁぁぁぁ
PAAAAAA (BEEEEEEAM)
LOOK OVER 'ERE, YOU LOT!
FOR A SMALL RETAINER FEE...
...WE'LL HELP YOU FILE YOUR TAXES WITH MAGIC, EH WOT!
AS YOU CAN SEE, THE MAGIC LINE IS BARE!!
JUST LEAVE IT TO US, AND YOUR TAXES WILL BE DONE IN A FLASH!
WAAAAH!!
DO (TMP)
DO
DO
DO

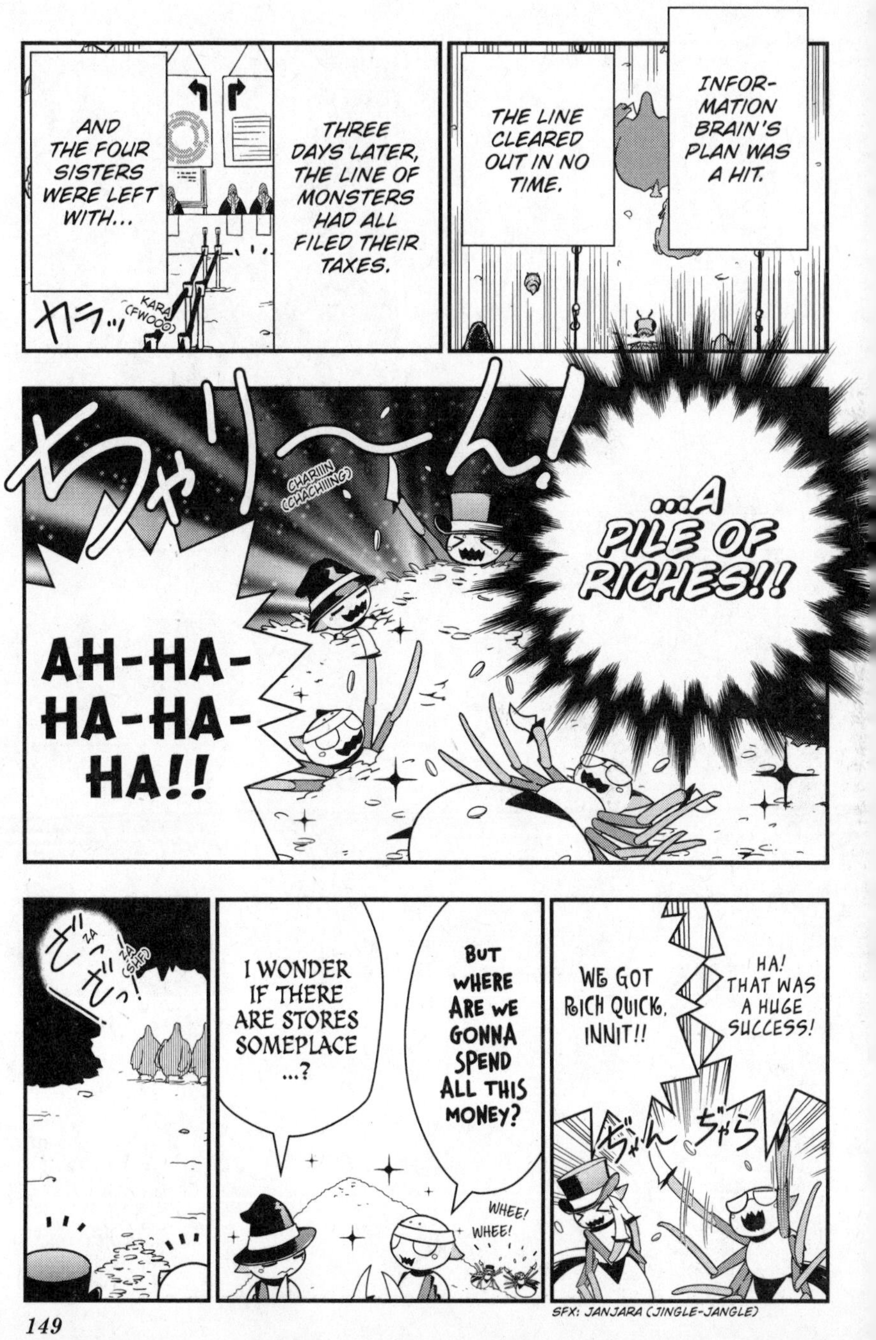
INFORMATION BRAIN'S PLAN WAS A HIT.
THE LINE CLEARED OUT IN NO TIME.
THREE DAYS LATER, THE LINE OF MONSTERS HAD ALL FILED THEIR TAXES.
AND THE FOUR SISTERS WERE LEFT WITH...
KARA (FWOOO)
...A PILE OF RICHES!!
CHARIIIN (CHACHIIING)
AH-HA-HA-HA-HA!!
HA! THAT WAS A HUGE SUCCESS!
WE GOT RICH QUICK, INNIT!!
BUT WHERE ARE WE GONNA SPEND ALL THIS MONEY?
I WONDER IF THERE ARE STORES SOMEPLACE ...?
WHEE! WHEE!
ZA ZA (SHF)

SFX: JANJARA (JINGLE-JANGLE)

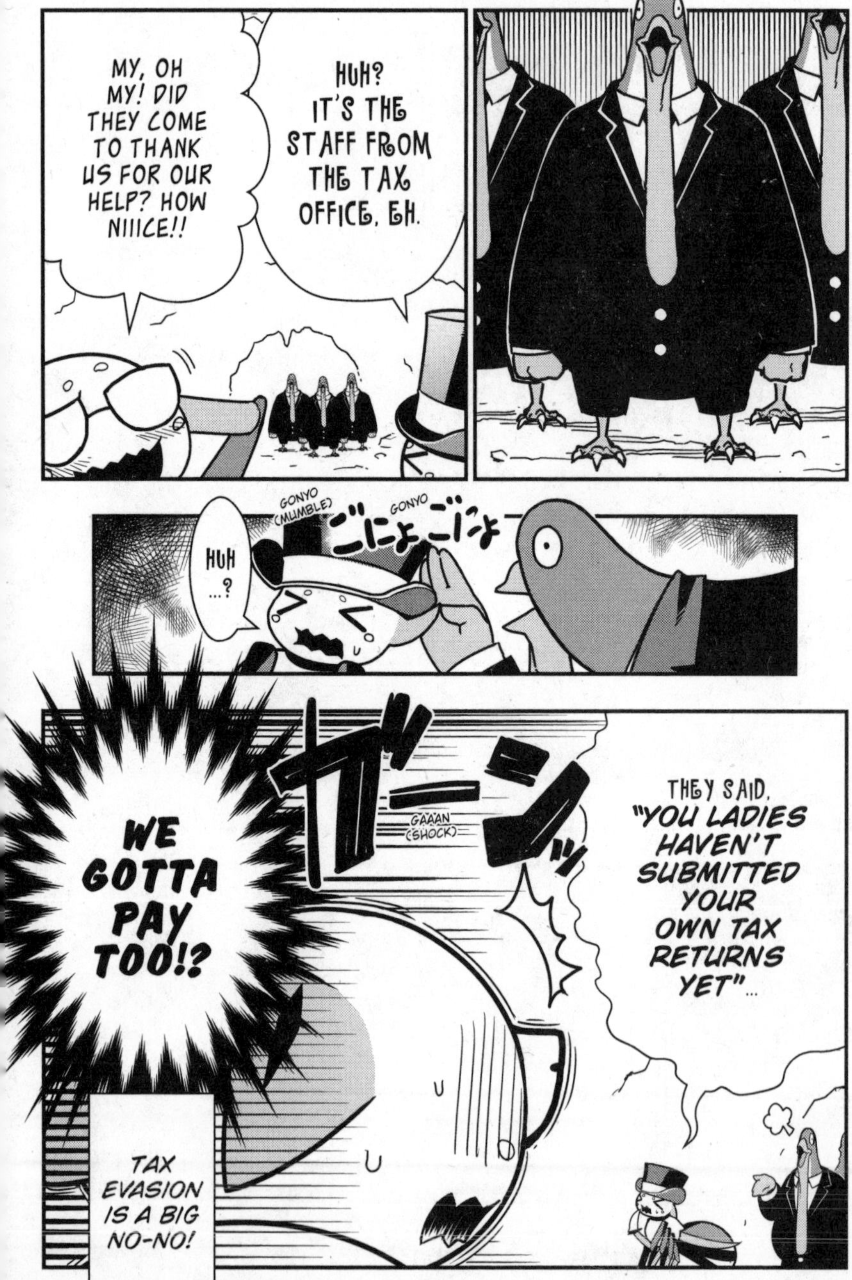
HUH? IT'S THE STAFF FROM THE TAX OFFICE, EH.
MY, OH MY! DID THEY COME TO THANK US FOR OUR HELP? HOW NIIICE!!
ごにょごにょ
GONYO GONYO (MUMBLE)
HUH ...?
THEY SAID, "YOU LADIES HAVEN'T SUBMITTED YOUR OWN TAX RETURNS YET"...
ガーン
GAAAN (SHOCK)
WE GOTTA PAY TOO!?
TAX EVASION IS A BIG NO-NO!

So I'm a Spider, so What?

THE DAILY LIVES OF THE KUMOKO SISTERS

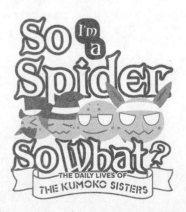

CHAPTER 33

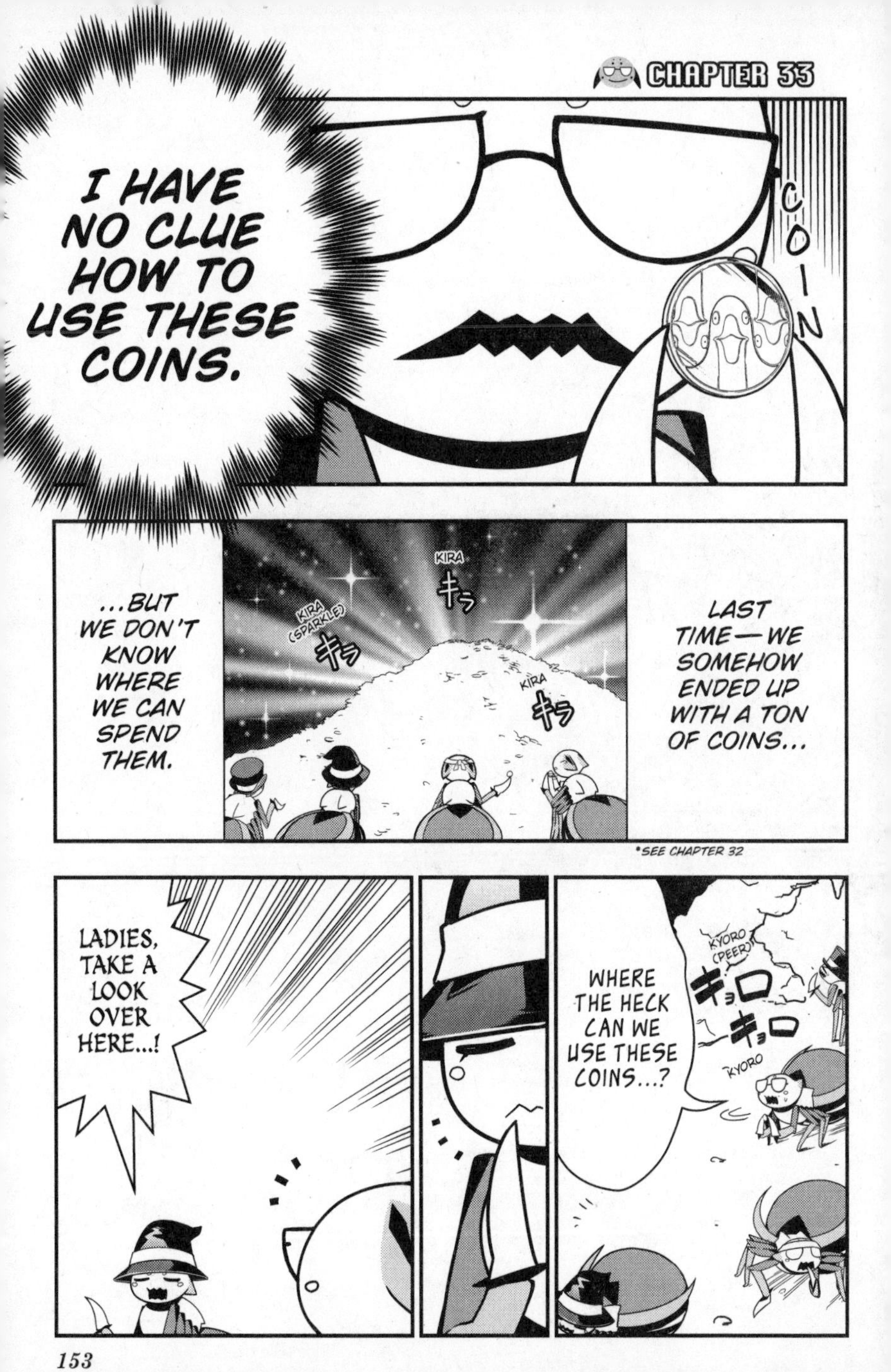
COIN
I HAVE NO CLUE HOW TO USE THESE COINS.
LAST TIME—WE SOMEHOW ENDED UP WITH A TON OF COINS...
KIRA
KIRA (SPARKLE)
KIRA
...BUT WE DON'T KNOW WHERE WE CAN SPEND THEM.
*SEE CHAPTER 32
KYORO (PEER)
WHERE THE HECK CAN WE USE THESE COINS...?
KYORO
LADIES, TAKE A LOOK OVER HERE...!

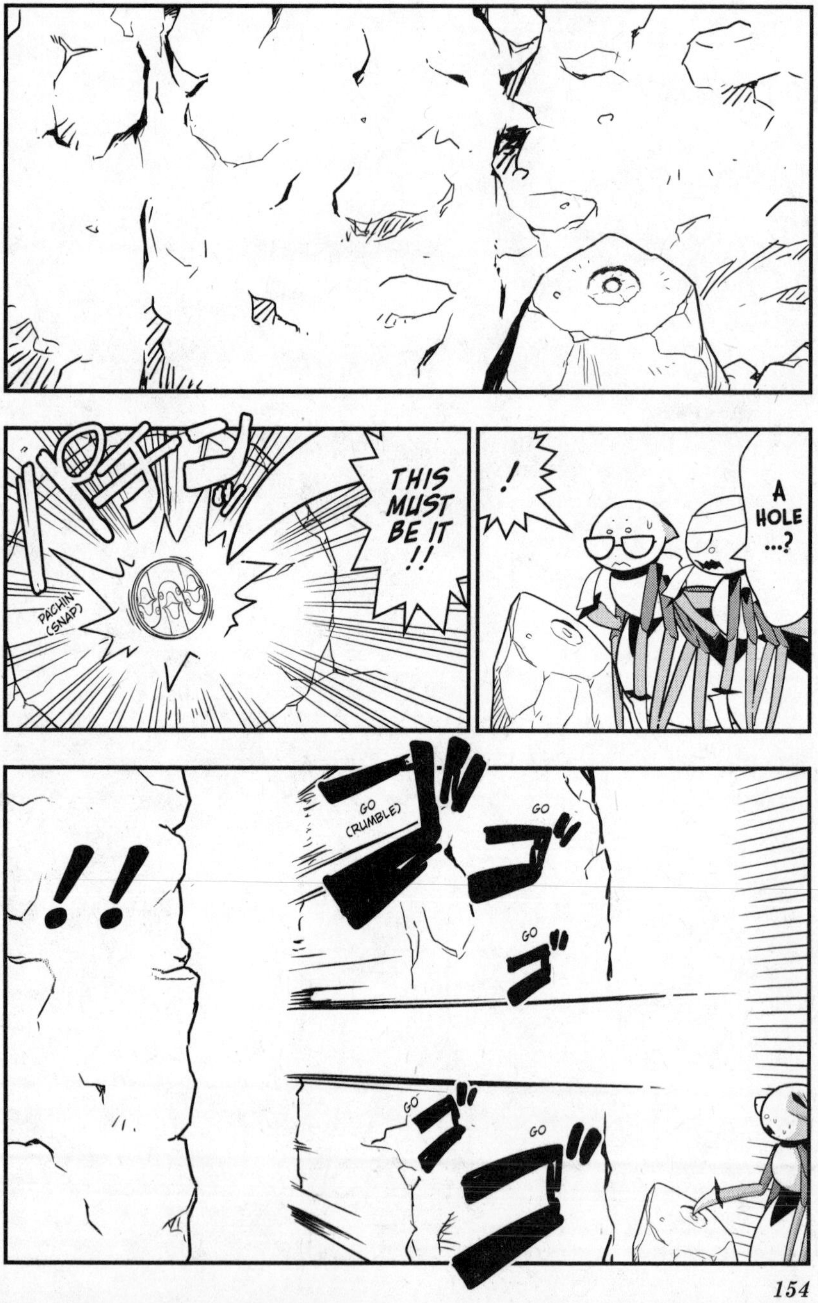
A HOLE ...?
!
THIS MUST BE IT !!
PACHIN (SNAP)
GO
GO (RUMBLE)
GO
GO
GO
!!

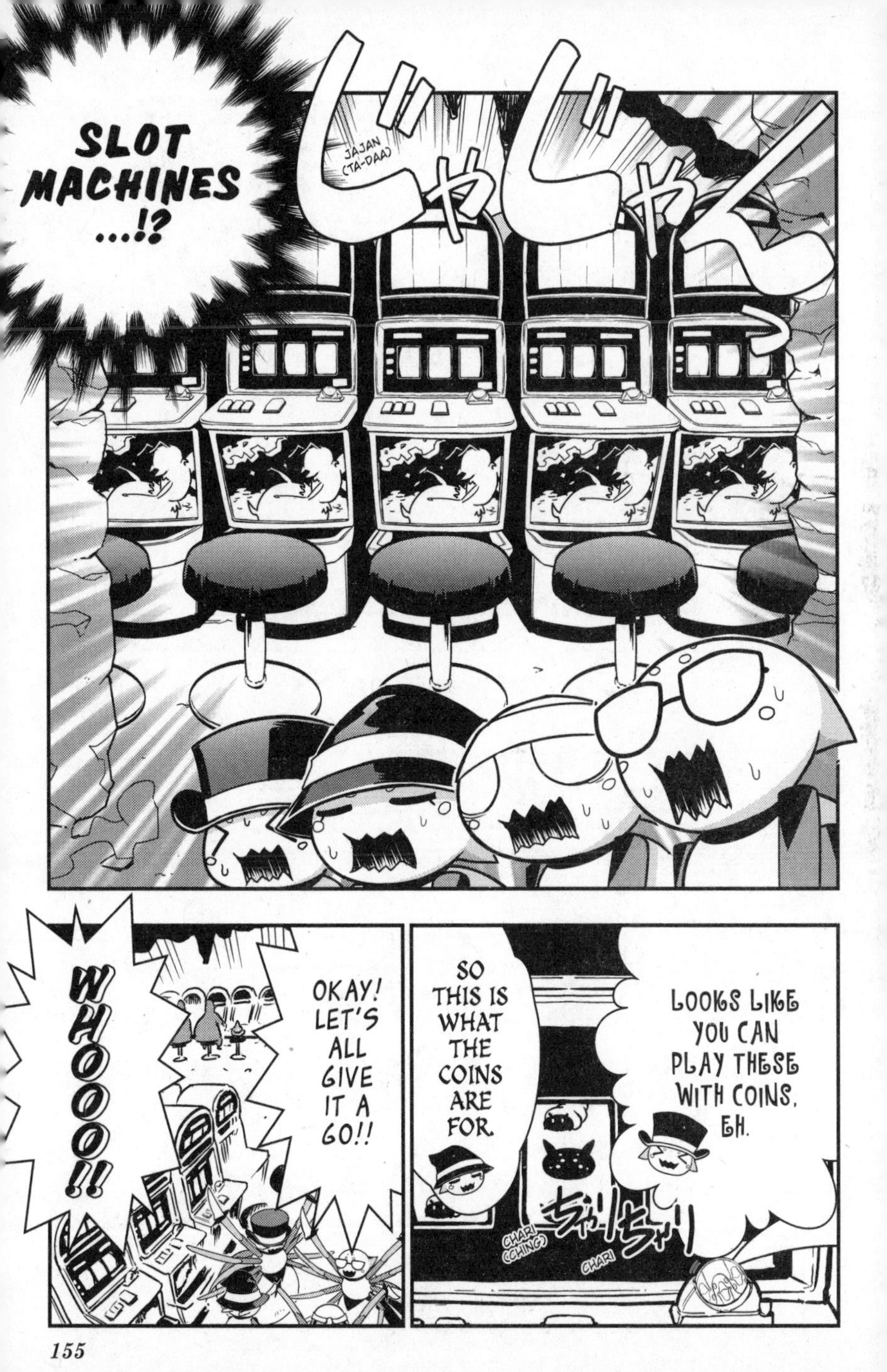
JAJAN (TA-DAA)
SLOT MACHINES ...!?
LOOKS LIKE YOU CAN PLAY THESE WITH COINS, EH.
SO THIS IS WHAT THE COINS ARE FOR.
CHARI (CHING)
CHARI
OKAY! LET'S ALL GIVE IT A GO!!
WHOOOOO!!

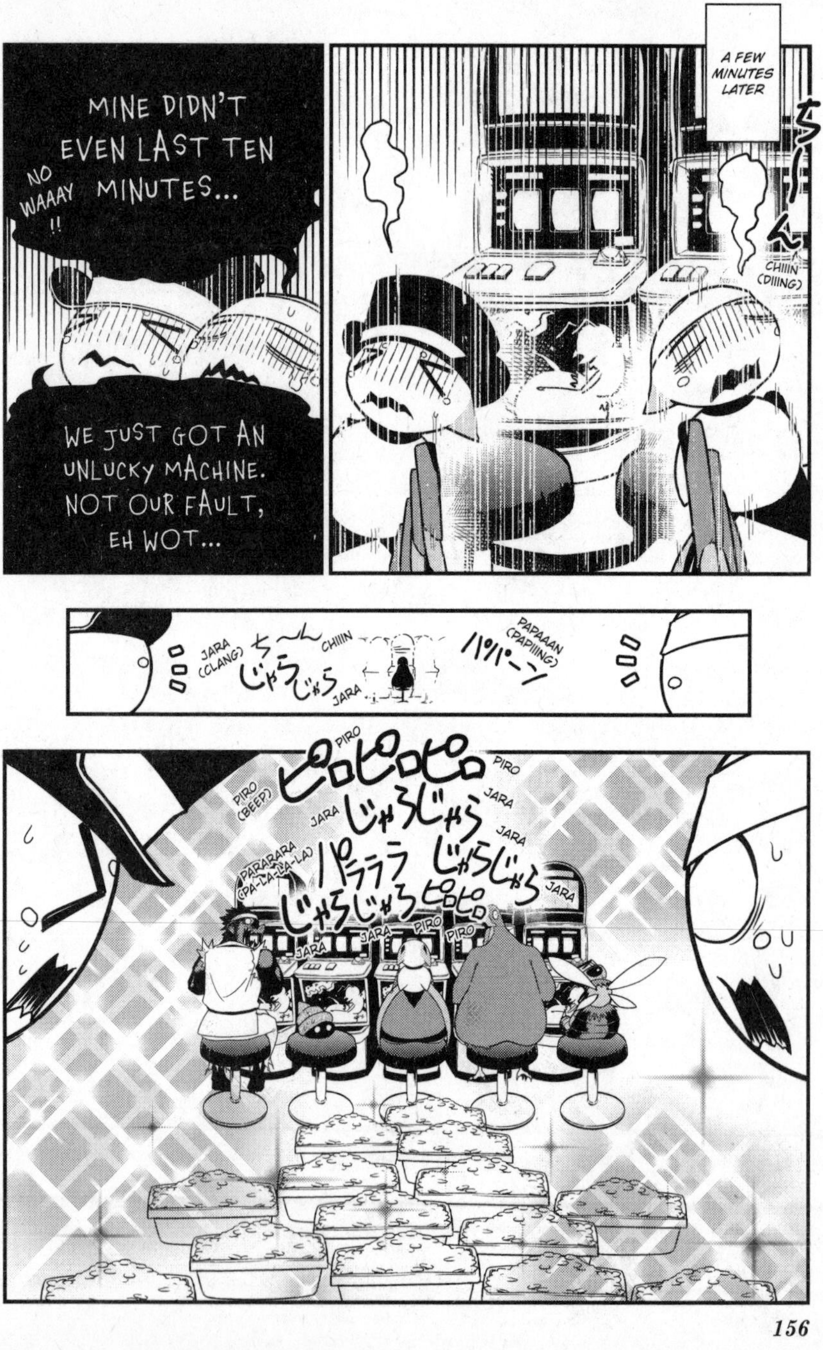
A FEW MINUTES LATER
ちーん
CHIIIN (DIIING)
MINE DIDN'T EVEN LAST TEN MINUTES...
NO WAAAY !!
WE JUST GOT AN UNLUCKY MACHINE. NOT OUR FAULT, EH WOT...
パパーン
PAPAAAN (PAPIIING)
ちーん
CHIIIN
じゃらじゃら
JARA (CLANG) JARA
ピロピロピロ
PIRO (BEEP) PIRO PIRO
じゃらじゃら
JARA JARA
パラララ
PARARARA (PA-LA-LA-LA)
じゃらじゃら
JARA JARA
じゃらじゃら
JARA JARA
ピロピロ
PIRO PIRO

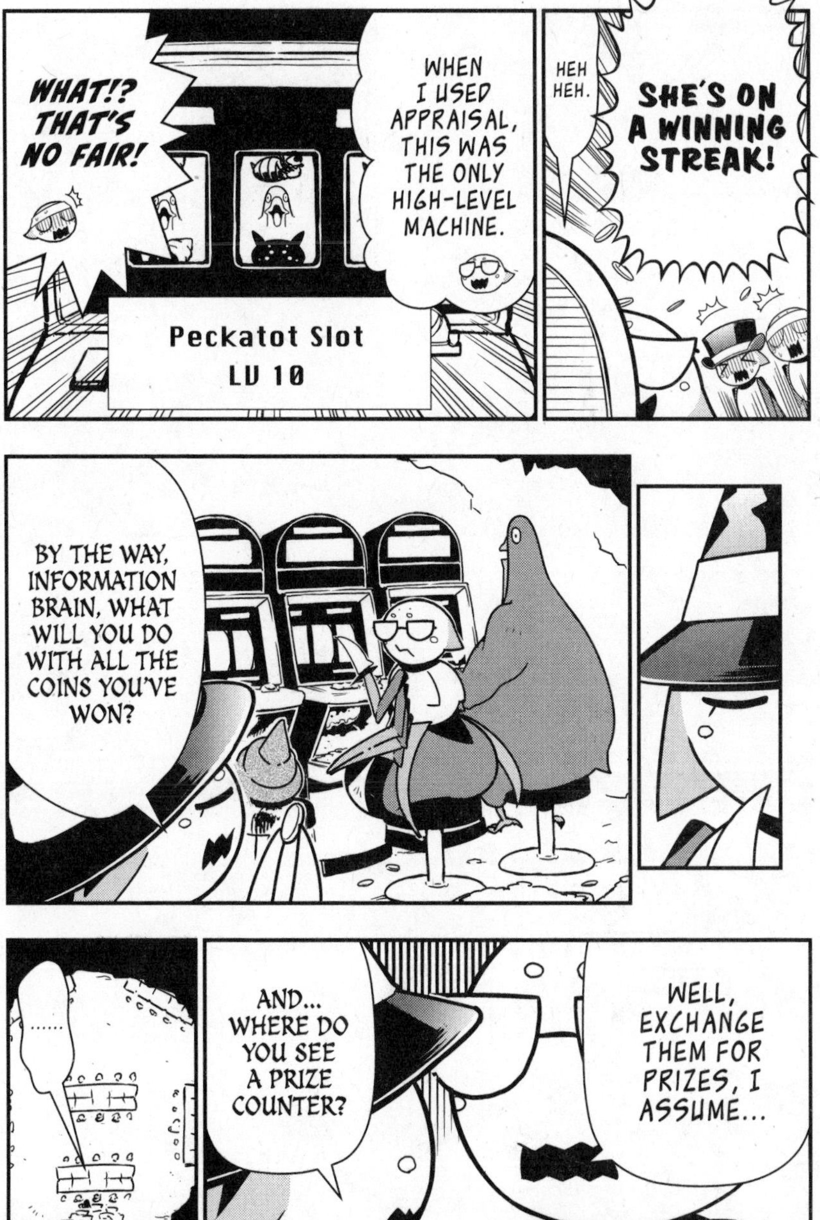
SHE'S ON A WINNING STREAK!
HEH HEH.
WHEN I USED APPRAISAL, THIS WAS THE ONLY HIGH-LEVEL MACHINE.
WHAT!? THAT'S NO FAIR!
Peckatot Slot
LV 10
BY THE WAY, INFORMATION BRAIN, WHAT WILL YOU DO WITH ALL THE COINS YOU'VE WON?
WELL, EXCHANGE THEM FOR PRIZES, I ASSUME...
AND... WHERE DO YOU SEE A PRIZE COUNTER?
......

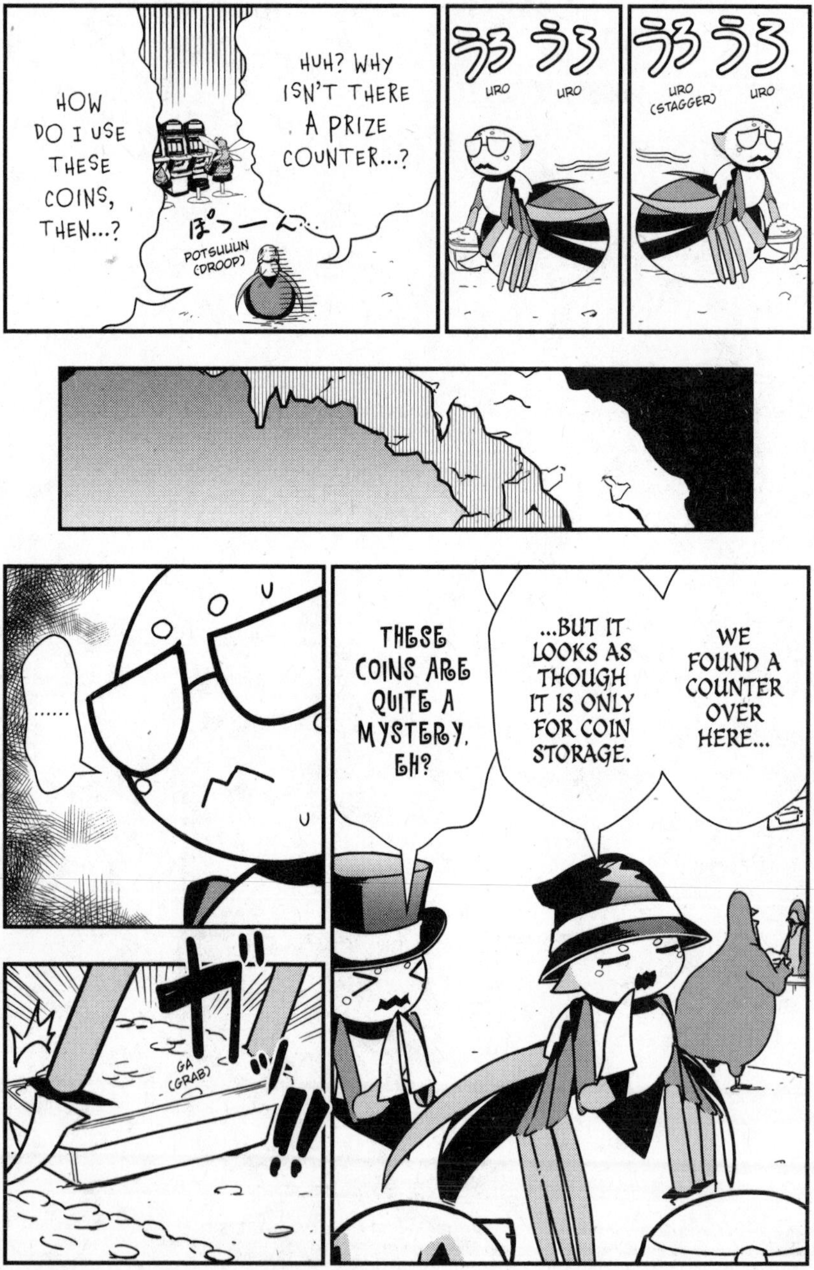
うろうろ
URO (STAGGER)
URO
うろうろ
URO
URO
HUH? WHY ISN'T THERE A PRIZE COUNTER...?
HOW DO I USE THESE COINS, THEN...?
ぽつーん…
POTSUUUN (DROOP)
WE FOUND A COUNTER OVER HERE...
...BUT IT LOOKS AS THOUGH IT IS ONLY FOR COIN STORAGE.
THESE COINS ARE QUITE A MYSTERY, EH?
......
GA (GRAB)
!!

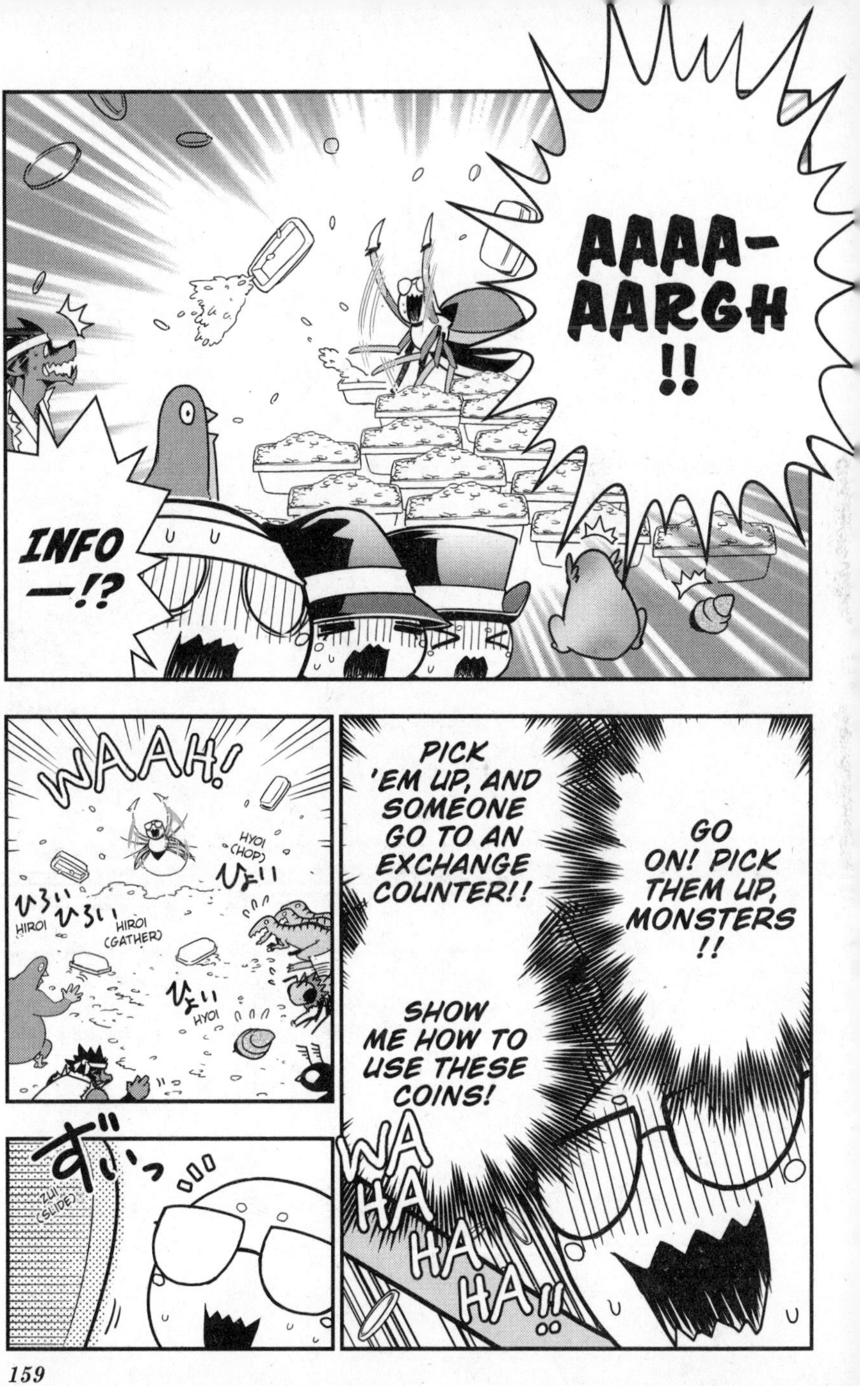
AAAA-AARGH!!
INFO—!?
GO ON! PICK THEM UP, MONSTERS!!
PICK 'EM UP, AND SOMEONE GO TO AN EXCHANGE COUNTER!!
SHOW ME HOW TO USE THESE COINS!
WA HA HA HA!!
WAAH!
ひょい
HYOI (HOP)
ひろい
HIROI (GATHER)
ひろい
HIROI
ひょい
HYOI
ずいっ
ZUI (SLIDE)

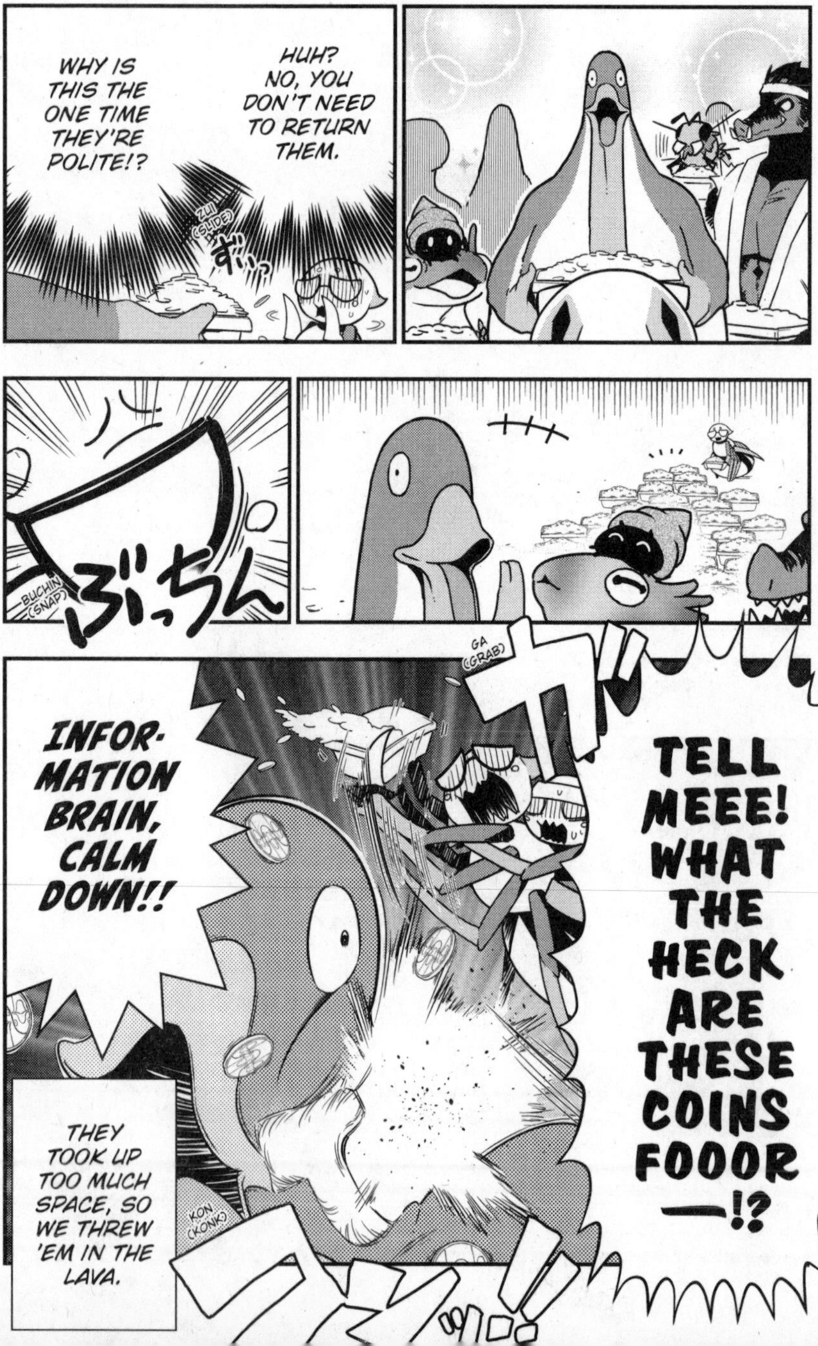
HUH? NO, YOU DON'T NEED TO RETURN THEM.
WHY IS THIS THE ONE TIME THEY'RE POLITE!?
ZUI (SLIDE)
ずいっ
BUCHIN (SNAP)
ぶっちん
GA (GRAB)
TELL MEEE! WHAT THE HECK ARE THESE COINS FOOOR—!?
INFORMATION BRAIN, CALM DOWN!!
THEY TOOK UP TOO MUCH SPACE, SO WE THREW 'EM IN THE LAVA.
KON (KONK)

So I'm a Spider, so What?

THE DAILY LIVES OF

THE KUMOKO SISTERS

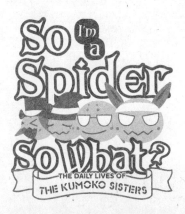

CHAPTER 34

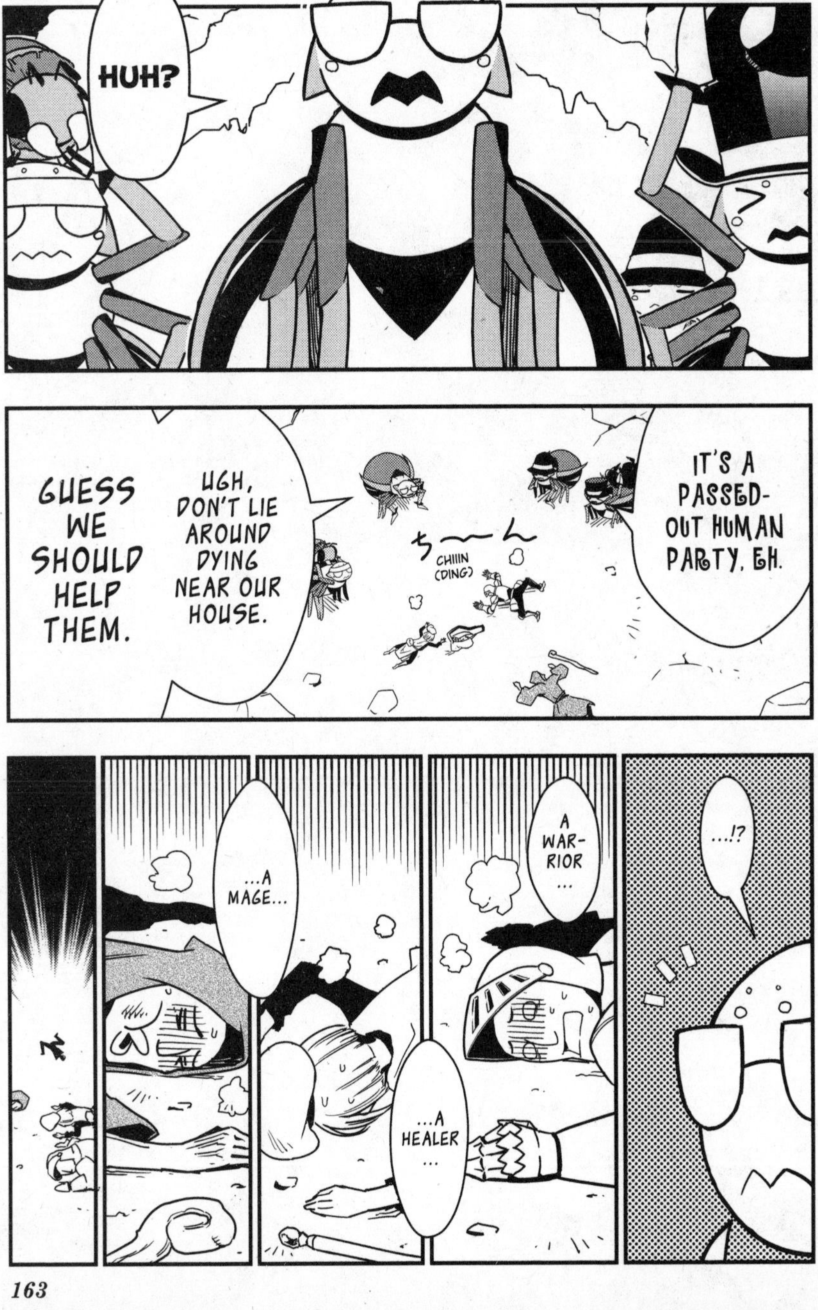
HUH?
IT'S A PASSED-OUT HUMAN PARTY, EH.
ちーん
CHIIIN (DING)
UGH, DON'T LIE AROUND DYING NEAR OUR HOUSE.
GUESS WE SHOULD HELP THEM.
....!?
A WARRIOR...
...A HEALER...
...A MAGE...

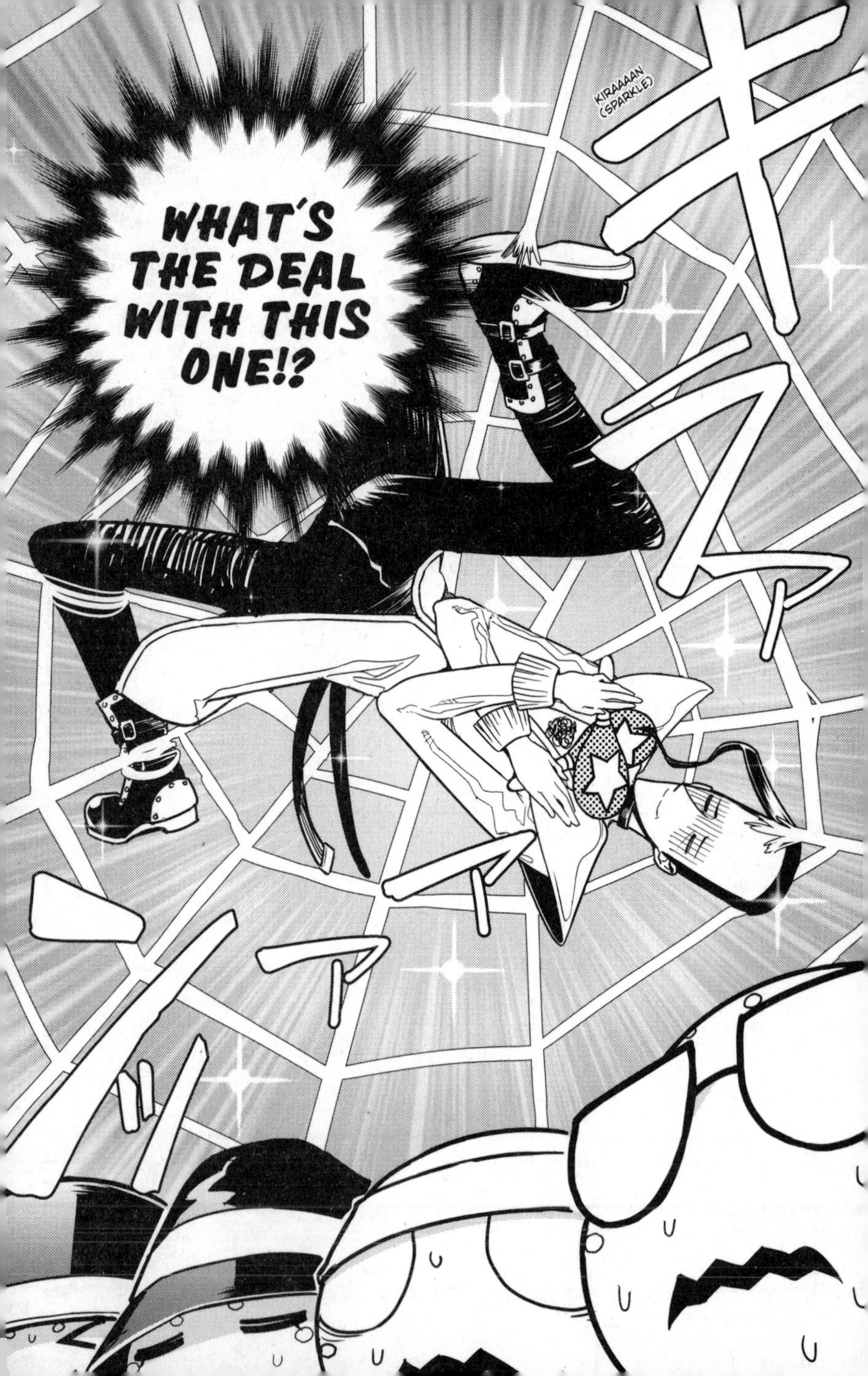
KIRAAAAN (SPARKLE)
WHAT'S THE DEAL WITH THIS ONE!?

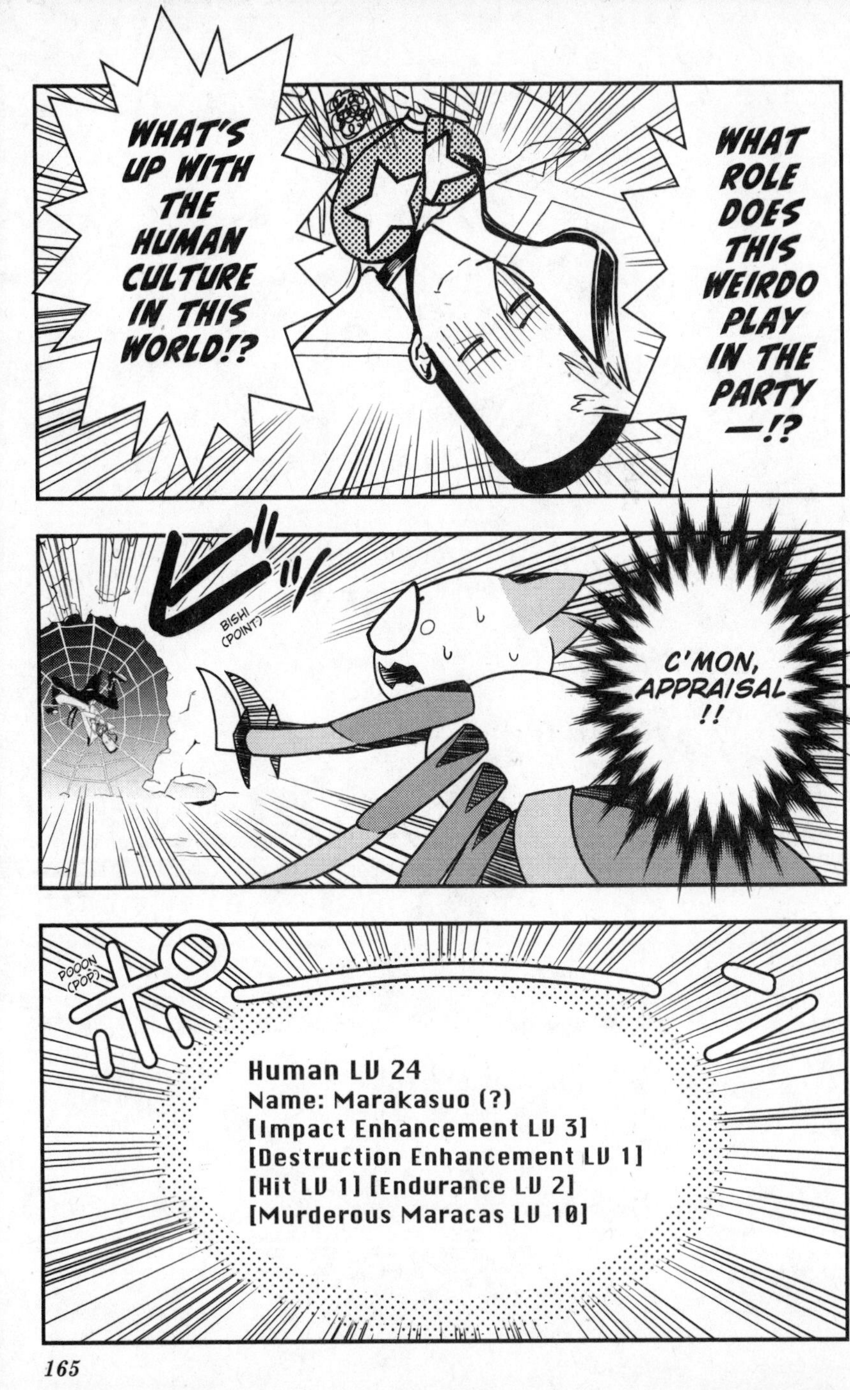
WHAT ROLE DOES THIS WEIRDO PLAY IN THE PARTY—!?
WHAT'S UP WITH THE HUMAN CULTURE IN THIS WORLD!?
C'MON, APPRAISAL!!
BISHI (POINT)
POOON (POP)
Human LV 24
Name: Marakasuo (?)
[Impact Enhancement LV 3]
[Destruction Enhancement LV 1]
[Hit LV 1] [Endurance LV 2]
[Murderous Maracas LV 10]

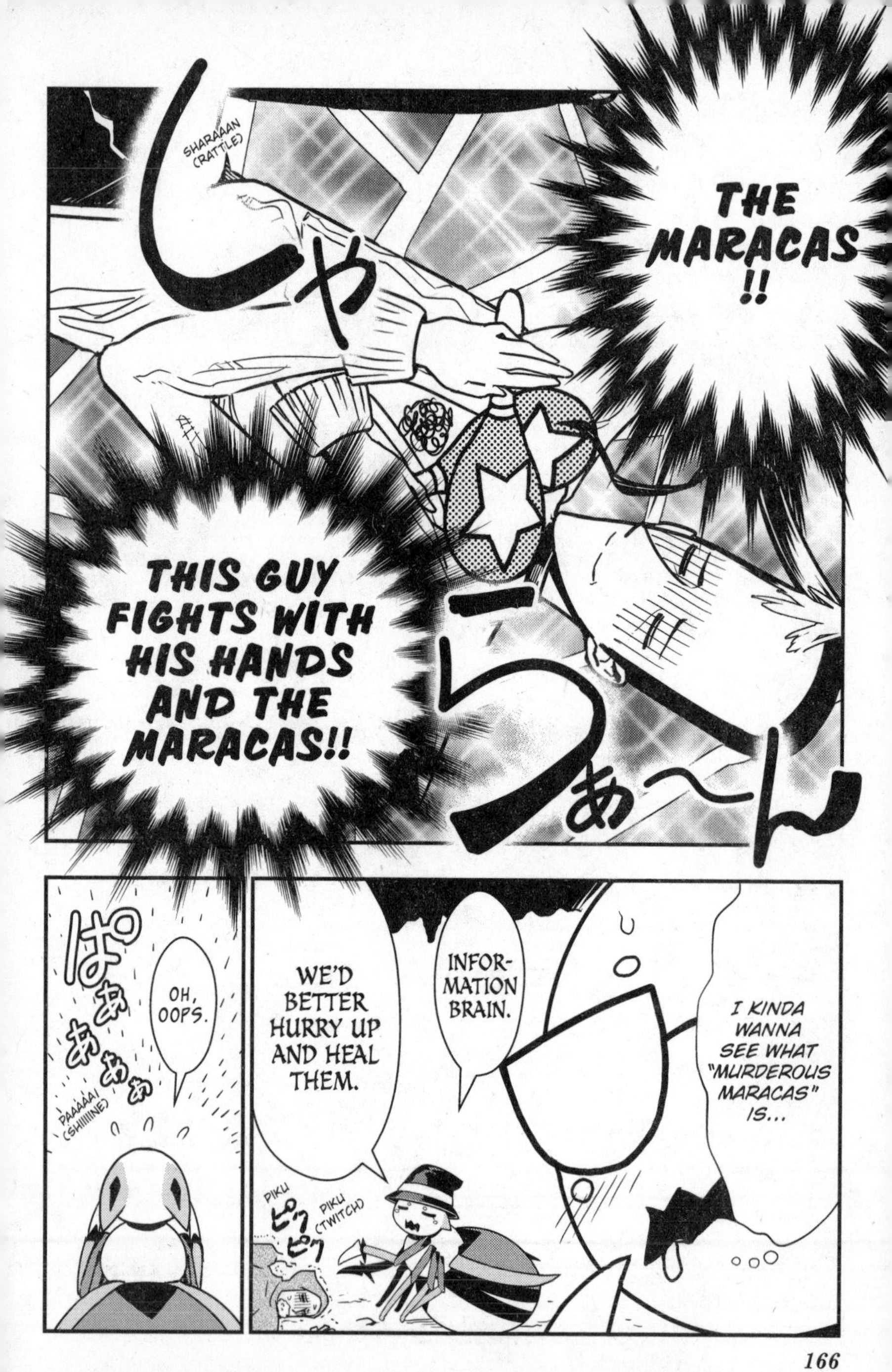
THE MARACAS!!
SHARAAAN (RATTLE)
THIS GUY FIGHTS WITH HIS HANDS AND THE MARACAS!!
I KINDA WANNA SEE WHAT "MURDEROUS MARACAS" IS...
INFOR-MATION BRAIN.
WE'D BETTER HURRY UP AND HEAL THEM.
PIKU PIKU (TWITCH)
OH, OOPS.
PAAAAA! (SHIIIIINE)

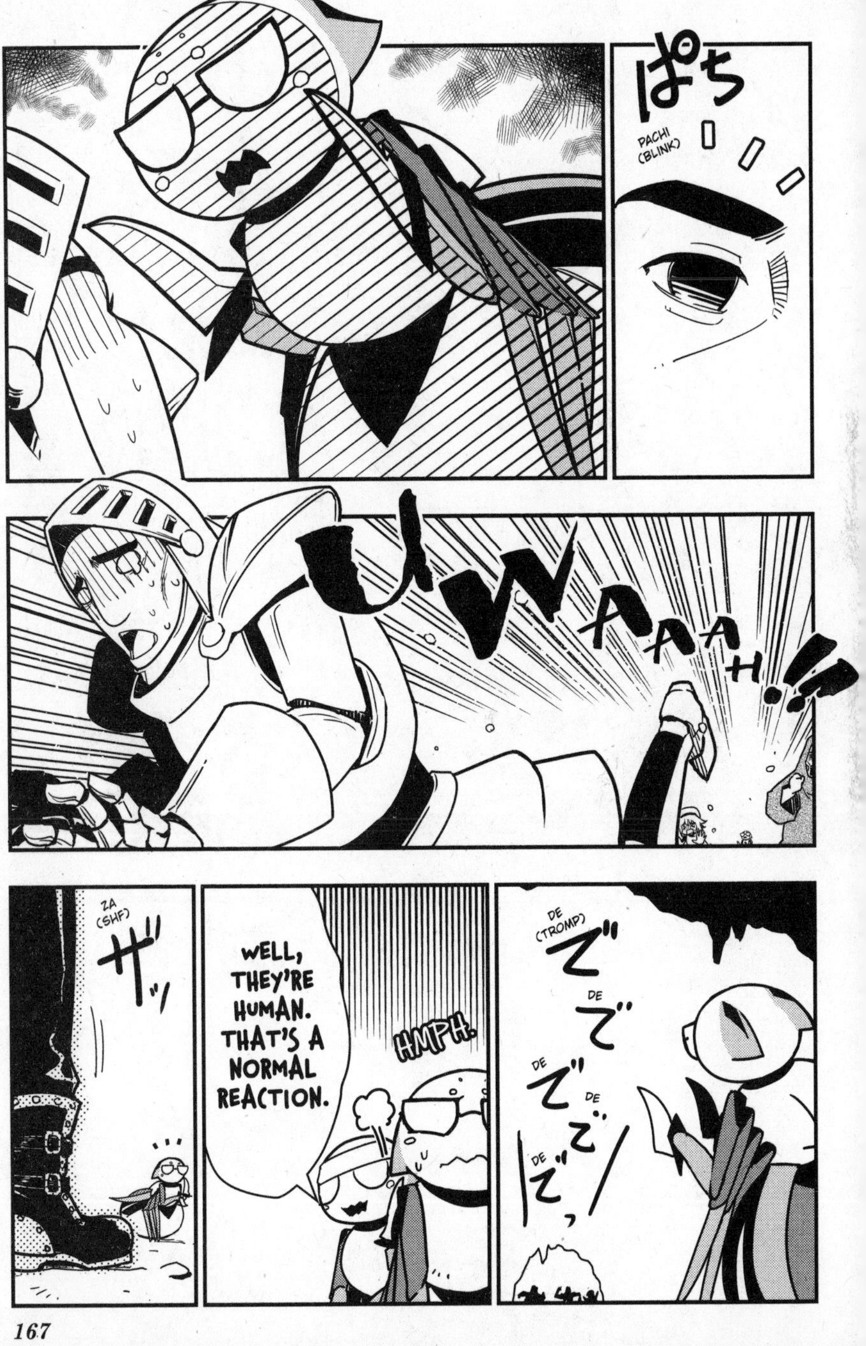
ぱち
PACHI (BLINK)
UWAAAH!!
DE (TROMP)
で
DE
で
DE
で
DE
で
DE
でっ
WELL, THEY'RE HUMAN. THAT'S A NORMAL REACTION.
HMPH.
ZA (SHF)
ザッ

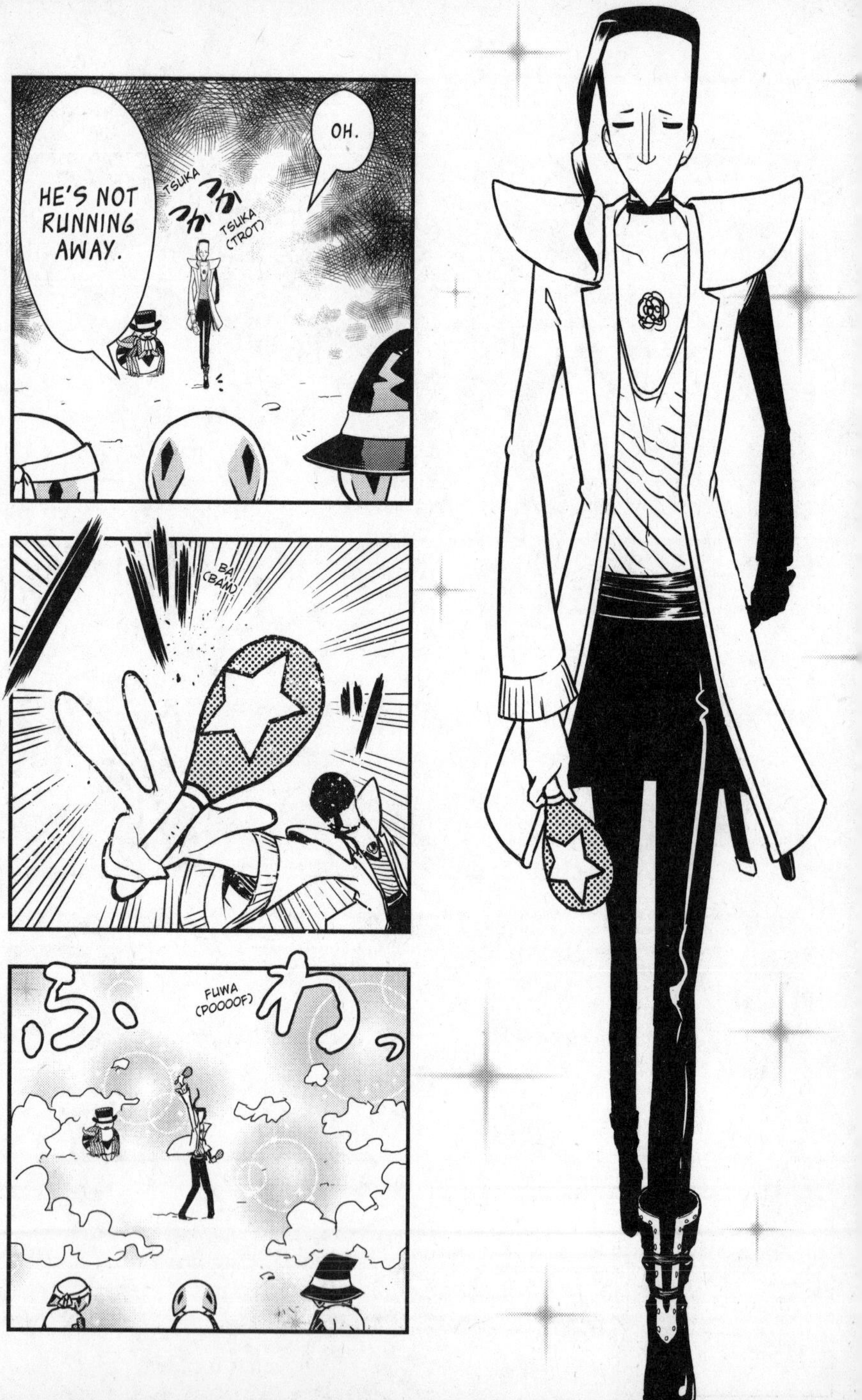
OH.
TSUKA TSUKA (TROT)
HE'S NOT RUNNING AWAY.
BA (BAM)
FUWA (POOOOF)

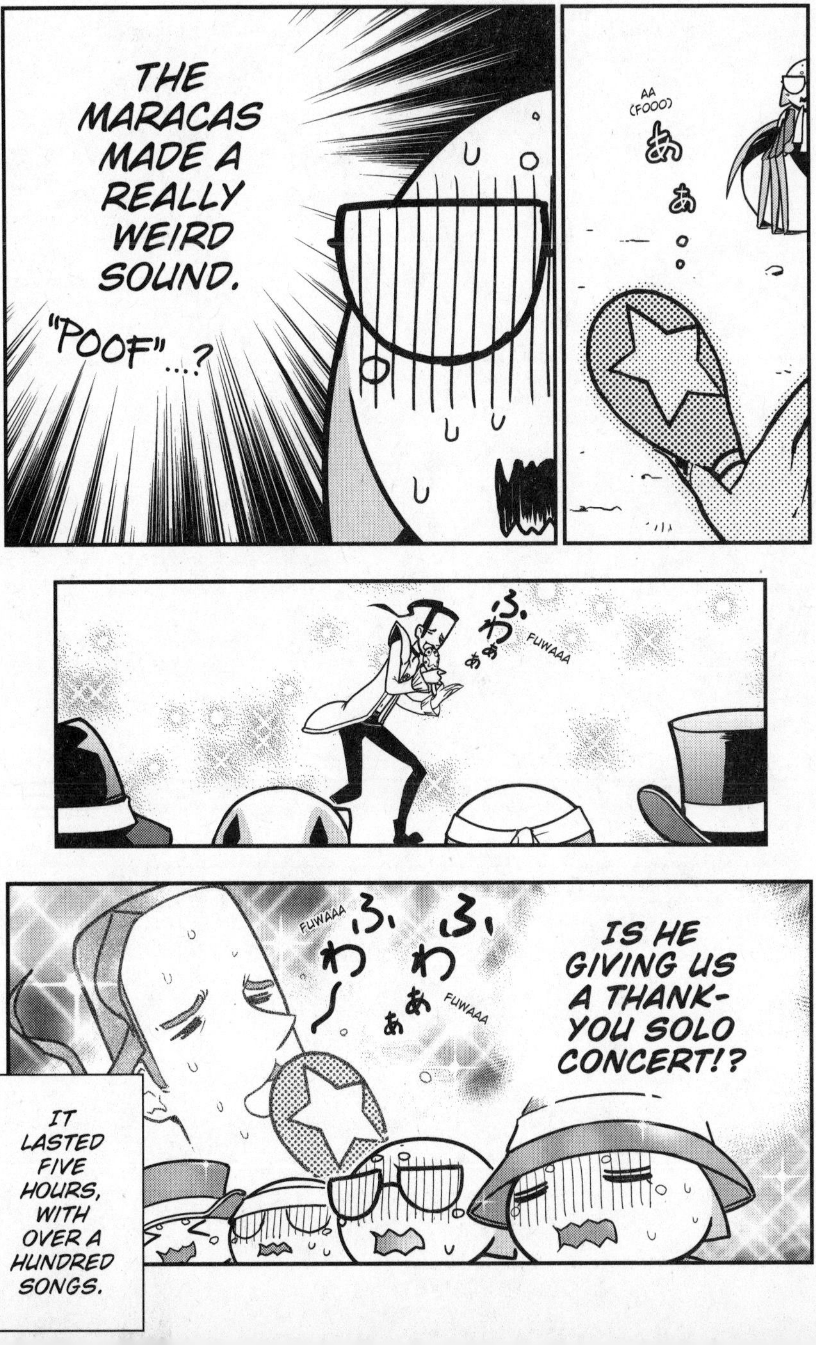

AA (FOOO)
ああ
THE MARACAS MADE A REALLY WEIRD SOUND.
"POOF"...?
ふわぁぁ
FUWAAA
IS HE GIVING US A THANK-YOU SOLO CONCERT!?
ふわぁぁ
FUWAAA
ふわ〜
FUWAAA
IT LASTED FIVE HOURS, WITH OVER A HUNDRED SONGS.

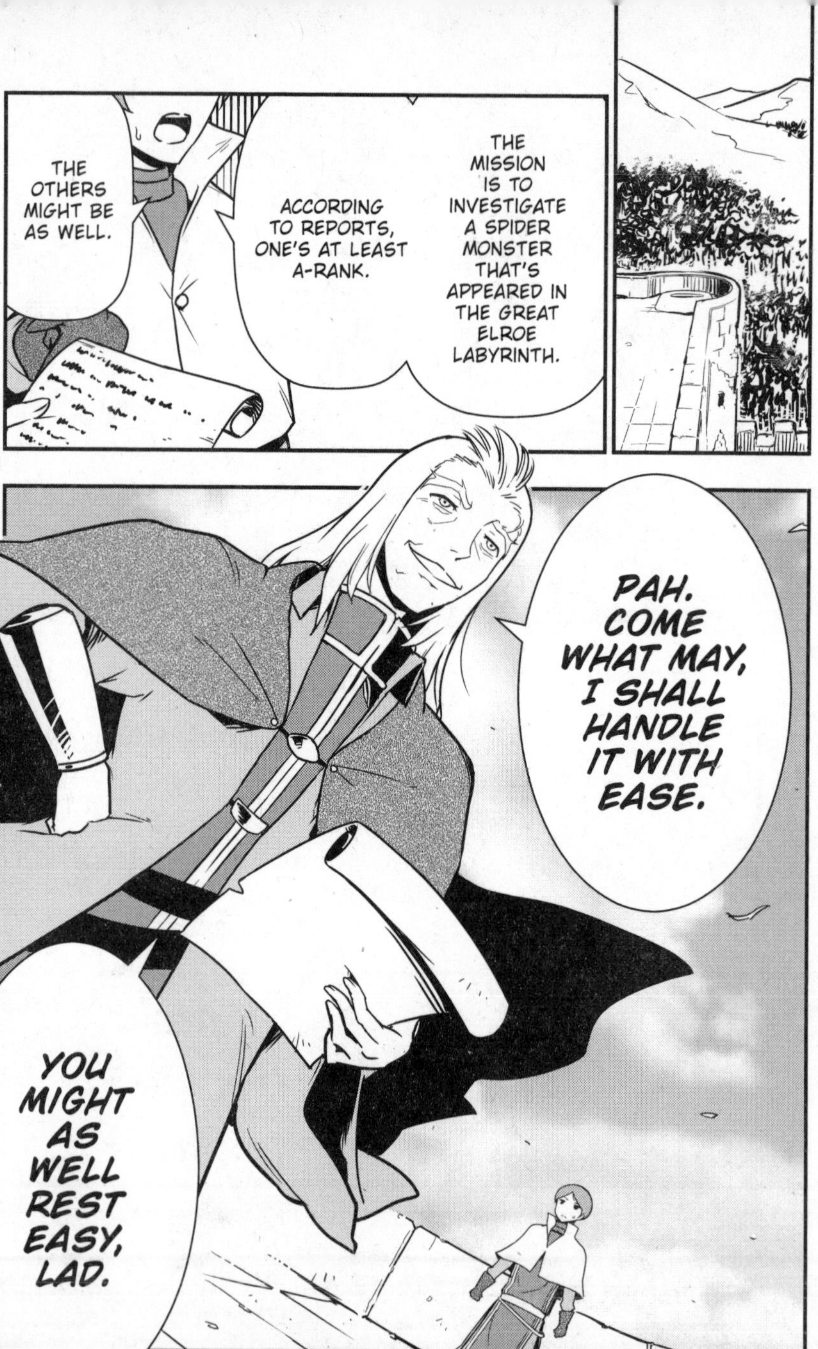
THE MISSION IS TO INVESTIGATE A SPIDER MONSTER THAT'S APPEARED IN THE GREAT ELROE LABYRINTH.
ACCORDING TO REPORTS, ONE'S AT LEAST A-RANK.
THE OTHERS MIGHT BE AS WELL.
PAH. COME WHAT MAY, I SHALL HANDLE IT WITH EASE.
YOU MIGHT AS WELL REST EASY, LAD.

So I'm a Spider, So What? The Daily Lives of the Kumoko Sisters ② End

AFTERWORD

Hello, everyone! My name is Gratinbird.

Hooray! It's Volume 2 at last!! Volume 2!!
Man, when I started Volume 1, I was trying to make a
nice, relaxed slice-of-life manga as a break from the tense,
thrilling battles of the main story…
But now it's a totally over-the-top comedy.

By the way, this manga is loosely set at the events that
occur about halfway through Volume 3 of the novels.
In terms of the manga adaptation, I picture it as being shortly
after Volume 6, chapter 30—right when Kumoko evolves
into an Ede Saine. From that point on, it probably
won't particularly connect to the main timeline, so I hope you'll
come along without worrying about it too much.

To the original author, Okina Baba-sensei;
the original illustrator, Tsukasa Kiryu-sensei;
the original manga adaptation creator, Asahiro Kakashi-sensei;
staff members Gou Yamamoto-san and Hatenan-san;
the editor; the designer;
and everyone else who has been involved
with *The Daily Lives of the Kumoko Sisters*:
Once again, thank you very much.

Things will get even crazier in Volume 3!
I hope you'll keep cheering for
the Kumoko sisters!

THE REAL
HEROINE →
(OR SO I'M TOLD)
RONANDT-
SAMA!

グラタン鳥
GRATINBIRD

AFTERWORD

ORIGINAL CREATOR: OKINA BABA

HELLO, I'M THE ORIGINAL AUTHOR, OKINA BABA.

THE GREAT ELROE LABYRINTH.

LIKE THE GALAPAGOS ISLANDS ON EARTH, IT'S A PLACE WHERE MANY UNIQUE CREATURES DWELL...EXCEPT IT'S IN A PARALLEL WORLD.

THE MONSTERS WHO LIVE THERE HAVE VERY UNUSUAL HABITS, UNBEKNOWNST TO THE OUTSIDE WORLD...

BUT THIS IS JUST RIDICULOUS, DAMMIT!

WHAT'S UP WITH THESE MONSTERS?

ISN'T THIS A BIT MUCH?

IN FACT, IS IT JUST ME, OR IS THE TECHNOLOGY IN THE LABYRINTH GETTING MORE ADVANCED THAN THE OUTSIDE WORLD?

IT TOTALLY IS ALREADY, ISN'T IT?

THAT TIME THE MONSTERS WERE MORE ADVANCED THAN THE HUMANS...

YOU COULD SAY THAT THE SPIDER SISTERS GET AWAY WITH IT BECAUSE OF THEIR KNOWLEDGE OF OUR WORLD.

BUT! HOW ARE THESE WILD MONSTERS COMPETING WITH OR EVEN GETTING AHEAD OF THEM, HUH!?

THE GREAT ELROE LABYRINTH IS AN ALARMING PLACE...

SO THIS IS THE BIGGEST LABYRINTH IN THE WORLD...

I HOPE YOU'LL KEEP COMING BACK TO GRATINBIRD-SENSEI'S VERSION OF THE GREAT ELROE LABYRINTH.

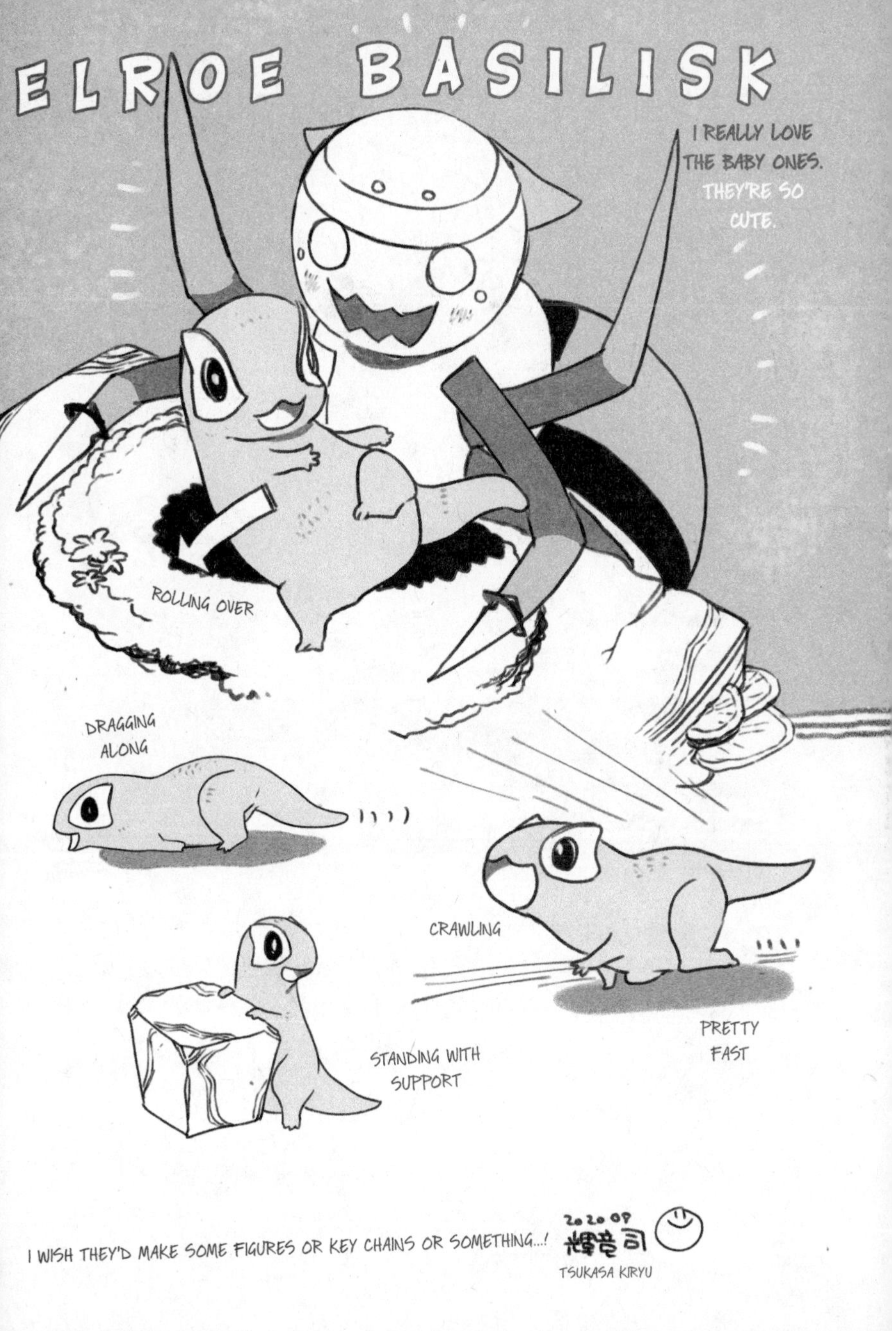
ELROE BASILISK
I REALLY LOVE THE BABY ONES. THEY'RE SO CUTE.
ROLLING OVER
DRAGGING ALONG
CRAWLING
PRETTY FAST
STANDING WITH SUPPORT
I WISH THEY'D MAKE SOME FIGURES OR KEY CHAINS OR SOMETHING...!
2020 09
輝竜司
TSUKASA KIRYU

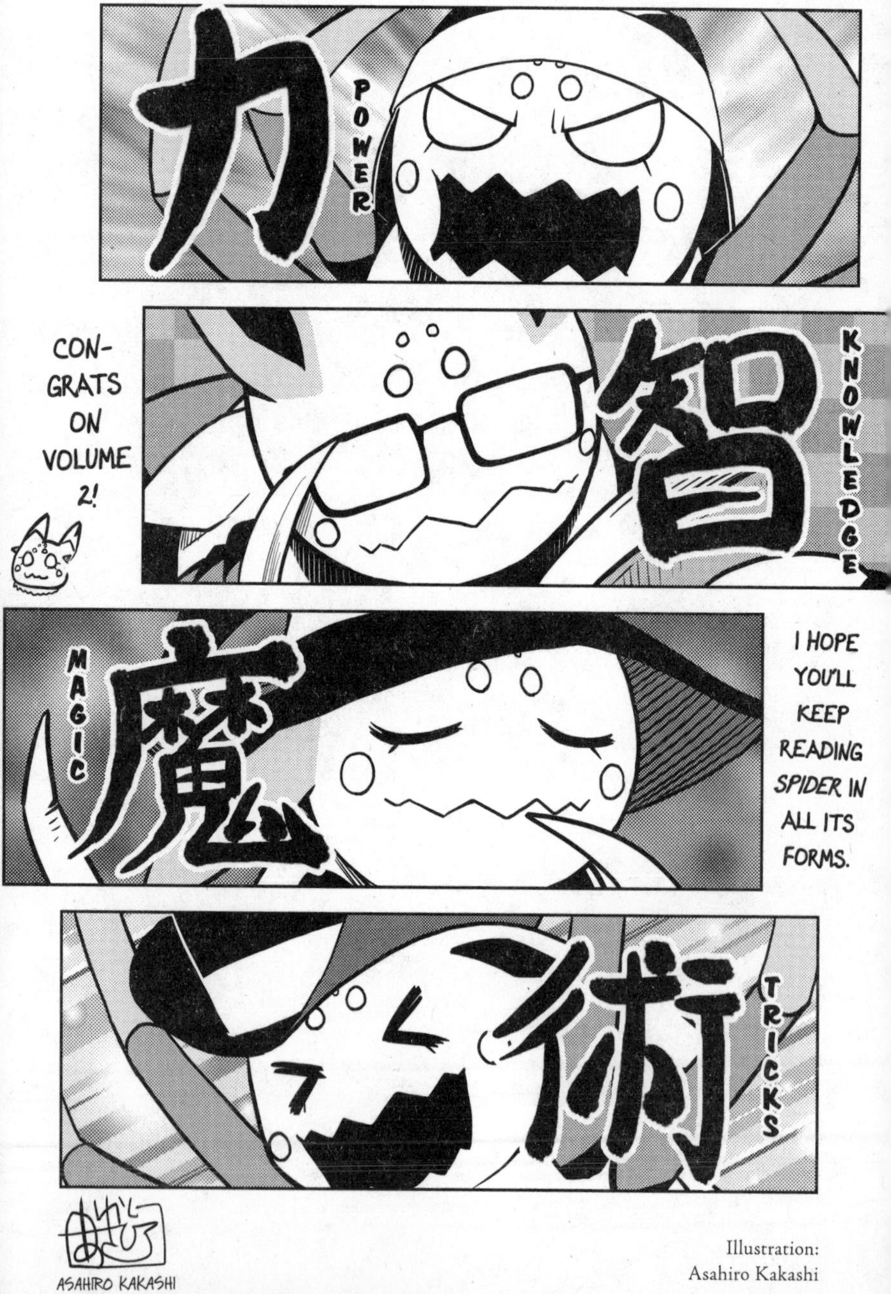
力
POWER
KNOWLEDGE
智
CON-GRATS ON VOLUME 2!
I HOPE YOU'LL KEEP READING *SPIDER* IN ALL ITS FORMS.
魔
MAGIC
術
TRICKS
ASAHIRO KAKASHI

Illustration:
Asahiro Kakashi

So I'm a Spider so What?
THE DAILY LIVES OF
THE KUMOKO SISTERS

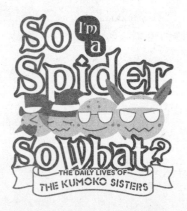

TRANSLATION NOTES

Common Honorifics

no honorific: Indicates familiarity or closeness; if used without permission or reason, addressing someone in this manner would constitute an insult.

-san: The Japanese equivalent of Mr./Mrs./Miss. If a situation calls for politeness, this is the fail-safe honorific.

-sama: Conveys great respect; may also indicate that the social status of the speaker is lower than that of the addressee.

-chan: An affectionate honorific indicating familiarity used mostly in reference to girls; also used in reference to cute persons or animals of either gender.

-tan: An even cuter version of -chan.

Page 4
The Hills Tribe refers to residents of Roppongi Hills, an area of Tokyo filled with high-rise towers and associated with luxurious lifestyles.

Page 35
The original Japanese text uses the word *uranai* to describe what #2 did. *Uranai* is commonly translated as "fortune-telling" in English. Fortune-telling could also be translated as "consulting with Lady Luck." And Lady Luck goes by many names—one of which is Fortuna. Fortuna is the Roman goddess of fortune, luck, and chance.

Page 108
"We are the wind!!" is a quote from the Japanese animated film *My Neighbor Totoro*, though in the movie they are most definitely not driving high-speed go-karts.

Page 116
Rocket Start is a technique in the Mario Kart video game series that allows for an extra boost of speed at the start of a race.

The Detective Is Already Dead

When the story begins without its hero

Kimihiko Kimizuka has always been a magnet for trouble and intrigue. For as long as he can remember, he's been stumbling across murder scenes or receiving mysterious attaché cases to transport. When he met Siesta, a brilliant detective fighting a secret war against an organization of pseudohumans, he couldn't resist the call to become her assistant and join her on an epic journey across the world.

...Until a year ago, that is. Now he's returned to a relatively normal and tepid life, knowing the adventure must be over. After all, the detective is already dead.

Volume 1 available wherever books are sold!

YEN ON
YenPress.com

TANTEI HA MO, SHINDEIRU. Vol. 1
ⓒnigozyu 2019
Illustration: Umibouzu
KADOKAWA CORPORATION

So I'm a Spider, So What?

THE DAILY LIVES OF THE KUMOKO SISTERS

2

Art: **GRATINBIRD**   Original Story: **OKINA BABA**

Character Design: **TSUKASA KIRYU, ASAHIRO KAKASHI**

Translation: **JENNY McKEON** Lettering: **BIANCA PISTILLO**

KUMO DESUGA, NANIKA? KUMOKO SISTERS NO NICHIJO Volume 2
© Gratinbird 2020
© Okina Baba, Tsukasa Kiryu, Asahiro Kakashi 2020
First published in Japan in 2020 by KADOKAWA CORPORATION, Tokyo.
English translation rights arranged with KADOKAWA CORPORATION, Tokyo, through TUTTLE-MORI AGENCY, INC.

English translation © 2022 by Yen Press, LLC

Yen Press
150 West 30th Street
19th Floor
New York, NY 10001

Visit us at yenpress.com
facebook.com/yenpress
twitter.com/yenpress
yenpress.tumblr.com
instagram.com/yenpress

First Yen Press Edition: February 2022

Yen Press is an imprint of Yen Press, LLC. The Yen Press name and logo are trademarks of Yen Press, LLC.

The publisher is not responsible for websites (or their content) that are not owned by the publisher.

Library of Congress Control Number: 2021943166

ISBNs: 978-1-9753-3673-8 (paperback)
978-1-9753-3674-5 (ebook)

10 9 8 7 6 5 4 3 2 1

WOR

Printed in the United States of America